T0330226

Evolutionary Economics and Human Nature

Frontispiece   Portrait of the Roman Emperor Marcus Aurelius on gold Aurius coin, c. AD 159–60, from a hoard of the same discovered by Museum of London archæologists in London in 2000. Marcus Aurelius' ideas on human nature were strongly endorsed by Charles Darwin—see Chapter 5. Courtesy of the Museum of London.

Evolutionary Economics and Human Nature

Edited by

John Laurent

Lecturer in the History of Science and Technology,
Griffith University, Brisbane, Australia

With a Preface by

Geoffrey M. Hodgson

Edward Elgar
Cheltenham, UK • Northampton, MA, USA

Published by
Edward Elgar Publishing Limited
Glensanda House
Montpellier Parade
Cheltenham
Glos GL50 1UA
UK

Edward Elgar Publishing, Inc.
136 West Street
Suite 202
Northampton
Massachusetts 01060
USA

A catalogue record for this book
is available from the British Library

ISBN 1 84064 923 2

Printed and bound in Great Britain by MPG Books Ltd, Bodmin, Cornwall

Contents

List of Contributors

Geoffrey Fishburn, School of Economics, University of New South Wales, Kensington, 2052, Australia.

Athol Fitzgibbons, School of Economics, Griffith University, Nathan, 4111, Australia.

Peter Groenewegen, Department of Economics, University of Sydney, Sydney, 2006, Australia.

Geoffrey M. Hodgson, Department of Economics, Social Sciences and Tourism, Business School, University of Hertfordshire, Hertford Campus, Mangrove Road, Hertford, Herts SG11 8QF, U.K.

Richard Joseph, Murdoch Business School, Murdoch University, Murdoch, 6150, Australia.

Rob Knowles, Department of History, University of Queensland, St Lucia, 4072, Australia.

Donald Lamberton, Graduate Program in Public Policy, Australian National University, Canberra, 0200, Australia.

John Laurent, School of Science, Griffith University, Nathan, 4111, Australia.

Erin McLaughlin-Jenkins, Division of Humanities, York University, Bethune 226, 4700 Keele Street, Toronto, Ontario, Canada M3J IP3.

Jason Potts, School of Economics, University of Queensland, St Lucia, 4072, Australia.

John Pullen, School of Economics, University of New England, Armidale, 2351, Australia.

Preface

Geoffrey M. Hodgson

For much of the twentieth century, mainstream economists treated human agents in their models and theories as if they were rational beings of unbounded computational capacity. These agents were presumed, through reason and deliberation, to be capable of appraising all options and choosing from among them the most advantageous. Perhaps no economist really believed that such infinitely powerful calculating machines actually existed, but it was upheld that such rational capacities were sufficiently representative of attentive humankind, especially at the cutting edge of business and trade.

This famous model of 'rational economic man' has existed in the thoughts of economists for a long time. But its triumph came after economics cut many of its surviving links with psychology and biology in the 1930s (Rabin, 1998; Hodgson, 1999, 2001). The rise of behaviourism in psychology made human beings as objects of stimulus and response, comparable with rats in a cage. Just as behaviourist psychology abandoned the investigation of the inner workings of the mind, economists became persuaded that they had little to learn from psychology. Moreover, the affair between the social sciences and biology ended by the 1920s, as many social scientists reacted against the use of eugenics and pseudo-biology in the service of racism and insurgent fascism (Degler, 1991).

By the late 1940s, both economics and sociology had been largely remodelled and placed within virtual impenetrable disciplinary boundaries. Economics was the universal science of 'rational choice' (Robbins, 1932) independent of considerations of cognitive disposition, historical time or geographical space. Sociology was the equally ahistorical 'science of action' (Parsons, 1937).

Mainstream economists became so besotted with their rational model of humanity that they came to believe in its capacity to explain almost every – if not every – aspect of human behaviour. Chicago led the way in inspiring rational choice models of behaviour, from suicide to church attendance (Azzi and Ehrenberg, 1975; Hammermesh and Soss, 1974). Most famously, Gary Becker (1981) won a Nobel Prize, partly for his intrusion of the utility-maximising rational actor into the familial household of love and parenting. The rational actor approach became so prestigious and popular that it was welcomed by James Coleman (1990) and others into the discipline of sociology, a subject weakened after the collapse of its former (Parsonian) core theory.

But these intrusions did not stop there. The imperial conquests of the rational actor model did not end with the capture of the human species. Experimental work with rats and other animals (Kagel et al., 1981, 1995) allegedly 'revealed' that animals have downward-sloping demand curves, supposedly just like humans. Accordingly, Becker (1991, p. 307) argued that: 'Economic analysis is a powerful tool not only in understanding human behavior but also in understanding the behavior of other species'. Gordon Tullock (1994) claimed that organisms – from bacteria to beavers – could be treated as if they have the same general type of preference function that is attributed to humans in the microeconomics textbooks. They were all regarded as utility-maximisers. Similarly, Janet Landa (1999, p. 95) argued that a rational actor model – with the addition of 'transaction costs' – could explain 'the high degree of cooperation and coordination of the activities of honeybees, ants and schooling fish'. Accordingly, core concepts were not only applied to all forms of human society since the origin of our species, but also to a large portion of the animal kingdom as well. Seemingly, we now have 'evidence' of the 'rationality' of everything in evolution from the amoeba onwards. However, this theoretical triumph suggests that such assumptions are telling us very little about specifically human societies, least of all about the unique complexities of modern human civilization. The specificities of human nature and human society are lost from view.

The problem with rational actor models is not that they provide an overly narrow view of self-interested 'rational economic man'. While self-interest is often assumed, it is also possible to build in versions of 'altruism' by making the rational actor sensitive to the utility of others (Collard, 1978). In principle, the maximising model can be twisted to fit any circumstance (Boland, 1981). Even the so-called anomalies revealed by experiments with human subjects can be explained away. If experiments show that some consumers appear to prefer a monetary reward that is less than the expected outcome, or appear to have intransitive preference orderings, then we can always get round these problems by introducing other variables. Crucially, the maximization of money is not the same as the maximization of utility, and the latter can be made to mean virtually anything.

The rational actor model is not weak because it is too narrow. It is weak because it is too broad and unspecific. Potentially, it can encompass all forms of behaviour, and not simply the behaviour of humans. Tune the utility function appropriately, and we get a closer approximation to the empirical data on real world behaviour. Utility theory is highly flexible. But this extensive flexibility raises questions about its explanatory depth.

A consequence is that utility theory can be used to make falsifiable predictions, but *only* when particular *auxiliary* assumptions are made. As Mark Blaug (1992, p. 232) observed: 'The rationality hypothesis by itself is rather weak. To make it yield interesting implications, we need to add auxiliary assumptions'. These add-on assumptions may concern the shape and arguments of the utility functions, the nature of the constraints, the existence of uniformities between agents, and so on. It is these *additional* assumptions that do the predictive work, not the assumptions of rationality or utility-maximisation *per se* (Shaper, 2000). By this argument, utility theory is not necessarily wrong. But it is manifestly inadequate. Utility theorists demonstrate these inadequacies themselves when they always have to bring in additional assumptions to make any meaningful empirical prediction.

Until James Coleman (1990) introduced the rational actor model into sociology, sociologists were fond of criticizing 'rational economic man' (Parsons, 1940). But the mistake of many sociologists during the twentieth century was to assume that human nature was infinitely malleable. It was argued that human nature was largely or wholly determined by cultural or institutional circumstances, with disregard of any psychological and biological constraints. While sociologists attacked economists for their allegedly 'narrow' view of economic man, both disciplines were dominated by an ahistorical and universal theory. While sociologists upheld the infinite plasticity of human nature, economists adapted their utility functions to encompass the behaviour of everybody and anything. In both cases the specificities of human nature were lost from view.

In stark contrast, one of the enduring defenders of a human economics in the dismal decades of universal rationality was Herbert Simon (1957). His notions of bounded rationality and satisficing behaviour, based respectively on limited computational capacity and specific aspiration levels, point to specific features of the human psyche and the human brain. Among others, Simon inspired Richard Nelson and Sidney Winter (1982) in their pioneering rehabilitation of evolutionary themes in economic analysis. After all, once we break from equilibrium analysis and consider the *process* of decision-making in an evolutionary context, then we are obliged to consider what agents can and cannot do in given circumstances. Agents become ongoing problem-solvers rather than bodies in equilibrium. As evolutionary concepts re-emerged in economics, Thorstein Veblen's (1898, p. 389) famous critique of the universal 'lightning calculator' of mainstream equilibrium economics was rehabilitated.

Following Simon, Nelson, Winter and others, it is necessary to bring back real human beings into social science. One of the first steps in this endeavour is to consider the realities of human nature, including its social, psychological and biological aspects. Of course, the familiar dangers of biological or psychological reductionism still exist. But a danger of error should not entirely preclude scientific enquiry in that domain. We have to understand human beings, not only as they have evolved over millions of years, but also as they have developed within and been moulded by specific institutions and cultures. As Ronald Coase (1984, p. 231) put it:

> Most economists make the assumption that man is a rational utility maximiser. This seems to me both unnecessary and misleading. I have said that in modern institutional economics we should start with real institutions. Let us also start with man as he is...modern institutional economics should study man as he is, acting within the constraints imposed by real institutions.

Both Simon and Coase were awarded the Nobel Prize in economics, but the majority of economists or sociologists has not yet heeded their strictures concerning the specificities of human nature. We have to examine the capacities and limitations of real human actors, and base our understanding of human decisions and actions upon these facts.

The essays collected here make some excellent first steps in this direction. They cover important aspects of human nature in the history of ideas and make some valuable suggestions for further enquiry. Although the history of ideas is now unfashionable, and research funding is directed to more obviously instrumental areas of enquiry, the preparation of future theoretical developments is often aided by a consideration of those in the past.

Revealed here is a much richer vision of human agents than that provided by the most complex of utility functions. We learn much here of the real views of human nature in the writings of Adam Smith, Thomas Robert Malthus, Alfred Marshall and several others. Many of the writings are placed in a Darwinian and evolutionary perspective, with the imperative that the study of human nature must be consistent with our understanding of human evolution, as well as understanding the way in which human beings are moulded by cultural and institutional circumstances. We are also informed of the rich view of human nature in the works of Charles Darwin himself, which undermines the mistaken notion that Darwinism promotes a view of human nature as greedy, uncooperative and self-seeking.

Furthermore, a theme that emerges in some of these essays is that an understanding of human nature and its evolution brings with it an appreciation is that much of human evolution and individual activity centres on the acquisition and deployment of knowledge. In contrast, if human beings were omniscient and infinitely capable calculating machines, then the difficulties in the acquisition and use of scarce knowledge would disappear from view. The evolutionary perspective found here begins to restore the question of knowledge to its proper place. No achievement could be more fitting, or even more instrumental, in the knowledge-intensive world of modern capitalism. It is by understanding humankind in its broad, evolutionary context that we can more fully appreciate some of the specificities of modern social structures.

REFERENCES

Azzi, C. and R. Ehrenberg (1975), 'Household Allocation of Time and Church Attendance', *Journal of Political Economy*, **38**(1), 27–56.

Becker, G.S. (1981), *A Treatise on the Family*, 1st edn, Cambridge, MA: Harvard University Press.

Becker, G.S. (1991), *A Treatise on the Family*, 2nd edn, Cambridge, MA: Harvard University Press.

Blaug, M. (1992), *The Methodology of Economics: Or How Economists Explain*, 2nd edn, Cambridge: Cambridge University Press.

Boland, L.A. (1981), 'On the Futility of Criticizing the Neoclassical Maximization Hypothesis', *American Economic Review*, **71**(5), 1031–6.

Coase, R.H. (1984), 'The New Institutional Economics', *Journal of Institutional and Theoretical Economics*, **140**, 229–31.

Coleman, J.S. (1990), *Foundations of Social Theory*, Cambridge, MA: Harvard University Press.

Collard, D. (1978), *Altruism and Economy: A Study in Non-Selfish Economics*, Oxford: Martin Robertson.

Degler, C.N. (1991), *In Search of Human Nature: The Decline and Revival of Darwinism in American Social Thought*, Oxford and New York: Oxford University Press.

Hammermesh, D.S. and N.M. Soss (1974), 'An Economic Theory of Suicide', *Journal of Political Economy*, **82**(1), 83–98.

Hodgson, G.M. (1999), *Evolution and Institutions: On Evolutionary Economics and the Evolution of Economics* Cheltenham: Edward Elgar.

Hodgson, G.M. (2001), *How Economics Forgot History: The Problem of Historical Specificity in Social Science* London and New York: Routledge.

Kagel, J.H., R.C. Battalio, H. Rachlin and L. Green (1981), 'Demand Curves for Animal Consumers', *Quarterly Journal of Economics*, **96**(1), 1–16.

Kagel, J.H., R.C. Battalio and L. Green (1995), *Economic Choice Theory: An Experimental Analysis of Animal Behaviour*, Cambridge and New York: Cambridge University Press.

Landa, J. (1999), 'Bioeconomics of Some Nonhuman and Human Societies: New Institutional Economics Approach', *Journal of Bioeconomics*, **1**(1), 95–113.

Nelson, R.R. and S.G. Winter (1982), *An Evolutionary Theory of Economic Change*, Cambridge, MA: Harvard University Press.

Parsons, T. (1937), *The Structure of Social Action*, 2 vols, New York: McGraw-Hill.

Parsons, T. (1940), 'The Motivation of Economic Activities', *Canadian Journal of Economics and Political Science*, **6**, 187–203.

Rabin, Matthew (1998), 'Psychology and Economics', *Journal of Economic Literature*, **36**(1), 11–46.

Robbins, L. (1932), *An Essay on the Nature and Significance of Economic Science*, 1st edn, London: Macmillan.

Shaper, C.F. (2000), 'Preferences, Choice and Explanation: "The Economic Approach"— A Case Study', Ph.D. Thesis, University of Cambridge.

Simon, H.A. (1957), *Models of Man: Social and Rational. Mathematical Essays on Rational Human Behavior in a Social Setting*, New York: Wiley.

Tullock, G. (1994), *The Economics of Non-Human Societies*, Tuscon, Arizona: Pallas Press.

Veblen, T.B. (1898), 'Why Is Economics Not an Evolutionary Science?', *Quarterly Journal of Economics*, **12**(3), 373-97. Reprinted in Thorstein B. Veblen (1919), *The Place of Science in Modern Civilization and Other Essays*, New York: Huebsch.

Introduction

John Laurent

In an Appendix to his somewhat idiosyncratic book of musings, *The Aristos*, the novelist John Fowles lists some fragments of teachings from the Greek Philosopher Heraclitus (*c.* 540–475 B.C.), including the observation: 'Men saw a log, one pushes, the other pulls. But in doing this they are doing the same thing...Such is the nature of men' (Fowles, 1968, p. 217). Fowles does not provide commentary, but presumably the aphorism is meant to illustrate Heraclitus' conception of the complementarity of forces in the cosmos, which are reproduced in microcosm in the co-operative actions of 'man' (humans). Be this as it may, Heraclitus' teaching (which is said to have influenced the young Plato—see Collingwood, 1945; Sambursky, 1956) is in stark contrast to the standard model of 'economic man', or *Homo œconomicus* in current mainstream economic theory. As summarised in a recent article by John Tomer (2001, pp. 281–2), economic man as usually conceived is 'self-interested, rational, unchanging, separate, and unreflective'; he has 'well-defined preferences for things' and is 'oriented to getting more of these to benefit the self'. According to a widely used microeconomics text, while such an individual's desire for particular goods is 'not infinite', in the aggregate, economic man's wants 'seem to be insatiable' (Mansfield, 1979, p. 8[1]).

But surely neither view – Heraclitus' complementarity, nor that commonly found in undergraduate textbooks (see also Schotter, 2001, pp. 17–24) – adequately encompasses the richness and complexity of 'the nature of man', which is the subject of this book. It may seem obvious enough that a starting point of training in economics might be a discussion of competing models of its main subject – human beings – but this would not appear to be normally the case (at least in Australia, where I write this). The economics degree course at the Queensland University of Technology in 2002, for example, contains subjects like 'International and Electronic Business', 'Business Information and Analysis and Communication', 'Firms, Markets and Resources', 'Business Cycles and Economic Growth', 'International Trade and Economic Competitiveness', and 'Financial and Monetary Economics', but nothing obviously identifiable as studies in human nature (unless, perhaps, one allows the subject on 'Economic Competitiveness'). However, this has not always been so. At Cambridge University in 1919 (when J.M. Keynes – who was deeply interested in human nature[2] – taught there), students were *obliged* to take related subjects such as 'Political Science' and 'History of Economic Theory', and to read books like Walter Bagehot's *English Constitution*, Adam Smith's *Wealth of Nations*, J.S. Mill's *On Liberty*, Henry Sidgwick's *Elements of Politics* and Graham Wallas's *Human Nature in Politics*. They could also include some classics, reading works like Plato's *Republic*, Aristotle's *Ethics* and *Politics*, and works by Cicero and Sallust. At the University of Sydney in 1940, economics students were required to take Psychology 1 or Philosophy 1, besides Political Theory, and to read Plato's *Phaedo* and *Dialogues*, Smith's *Wealth of Nations*, Keynes's *General Theory* and J.S. Mackenzie's *Manual of Ethics* (Anon., 1919, 1940). I fondly remember reading through Machiavelli's *The Prince* line-by-line with Dr Dick Staveley in the Economics Department at the University of Queensland in the 1970s, but this was nearing the end of an era.

Sadly, things are now very different. Not only do students not know anything about such matters, their teachers, often having themselves learnt little more than statistics and game theory, can't help them. Yet there are signs of a reaction against this situation, much of which has concentrated on what are seen as unreal assumptions concerning 'economic man'. In *The Death of Economics*, Paul Ormerod (1995) has contrasted the standard model of human nature, which many believe originated with Adam Smith, with more rounded accounts which, he pointedly notes, can also be shown to be derived in part from Smith, viz., *The Theory of Moral Sentiments*— which is the subject of Athol Fitzgibbons's chapter, below. Ormerod explains (ibid., p. 13) that a 'central theme of *Moral Sentiments* was…to show how there are propensities in human nature which incline us towards society, such as fellow feeling and the desire both to obtain the approval of others and to be worthy of that approval', and interestingly, Ormerod cites the research of Robert Axelrod in game theory – published in Axelrod's *The Evolution of Co-operation* (1984) – which shows that co-operative strategies, in which both players benefit, tend to dominate in Prisoner's Dilemma and similar games. Axelrod's conclusion is that co-operativeness, as well as competitiveness, may be deeply ingrained in human nature, and is equally a product of evolution. Recent research by Karl Sigmund and others reported in *Scientific American* (January 2002, pp. 81–5) tends to confirm Axelrod's findings, the authors concluding (citing two of Adam Smith's illustrious contemporaries): 'Centuries ago philosophers such as David Hume and Jean-Jacques Rousseau emphasized the crucial role of "human nature" in social interactions. Theoretical economists, in contrast, [have] long preferred to study their selfish *Homo economicus*…But we are no Robinson[Crusoe]s. Our ancestors' line has been social for some 30 million years and in social interactions, our preferences often turn out to be far from selfish'.

So game theory (which I have seen described as an 'underpinning of present-day economics'[3]) may not be altogether the arid exercise it sometimes appears to be to outsiders. Sigmund et al., in fact, nicely link game theory with Darwinian theory—that is, the theory of the 'Moral Sense' chapter in Darwin's *The Descent of Man*, which is examined in chapter 5 of the present volume. They go on to write: 'Ethical standards and moral systems differ from culture to culture, but we may presume that they are based on universal, biologically rooted capabilities...Hume and Rousseau would hardly be surprised. But today we have reached a stage at which we can formalize their ideas into game theory models that can be analyzed mathematically and tested experimentally' (ibid., p. 85).

Be this as it may, Sigmund et al.'s passing acknowledgement of the importance of *both* biology and culture in 'human nature' touches on an issue of central importance in any investigation of this broad subject, and one which will not be ignored here. As the title of this book indicates, the approach to this issue of biology and culture taken by the present writer and the other contributors is that of 'evolutionary economics'. But what does this mean? As will be seen, the varieties of opinion under this general rubric are such as to raise serious questions as to its usefulness; but given the increasing adoption of the phrase by economists working in a number of loosely related fields, it is deemed expedient here to accept it as a general paradigm for a certain *kind* of approach. This is not at all meant to impose an artificial uniformity on the various perspectives taken by the contributors and their subjects: there are important differences between them, some perhaps ultimately irreconcilable, and these will not be glossed over. But what it is hoped the reader will take away from this volume will be a sense of the importance of the subject of human nature for evolutionary economics, and some appreciation of its bearing on the thinking of significant writers in economics, philosophy and other fields of intellectual endeavour from the ancient Greeks to the present.

At the head of the Prologue to his book, *The Last Generation*, the zoologist Angus Martin (1975, p. 7) has a quote from fellow scientist George Gaylord Simpson which reads: 'All attempts to answer [the question: What is Man?] before 1859 are worthless and...we will be better off if we ignore them completely' (square brackets Martin's)—the date referring, of course, to the publication of Charles Darwin's *The Origin of Species*. Is this fair comment? No doubt some biologists would share this opinion (especially those with little or no training in the humanities, and with little interest in the same), and such an attitude has more than likely hardened, if anything, in more recent times with claims to 'know what it is to be human' being made by James Watson and others involved in mapping the human genome.[4] Yet Darwin himself, as chapter 5 of this book notes, was very well aware of the insights of earlier thinkers concerning the human condition, going back to Xenophon and the Roman Stoic Marcus Aurelius, and was more than happy to quote them, along with such other pre-1859 writers as David Hume ('There seems a necessity for confessing that the happiness and misery of others are not spectacles altogether indifferent to us'), Adam Smith, Thomas Malthus, Francis Bacon and Immanuel Kant. Among Darwin's books held at Christ's College, Cambridge, the Cambridge University Library and at Down House are Aristotle's *On the Parts of Animals*, Virgil's *Opera* (works) and Euripides' *Hecuba*.[5]

Some of these authors will be looked at in the following chapters, beginning with Geoff Fishburn's study of 'the nature of man' in Greek thought. As will be seen, just as Darwin felt no need to ignore the ideas of the Greeks and others, so needn't we. This is not necessarily to take a 'Whiggish' view of history (to use Herbert Butterfield's term for histories like Lord Macaulay's, which viewed British history from the vantage point of the emergence of the Whig political party at the end of the seventeenth century[6]), as Geoff Fishburn makes clear. Much of what the ancients wrote, it is true, we would now regard as plainly wrong (as with Aristotle's description of the brain as an organ for cooling the blood[7]), and as quaint reflections of the thought-forms of a bygone era (one wonders how some of *our* ideas may appear centuries hence). Nevertheless, we are still frequently struck with the perspicacity of some of these ancients' observations: in any case, for better or worse, their ideas are woven into our intellectual heritage, and are part and parcel of our thinking.

That is to say, our *assumptions* about human nature have been partly shaped by history. Much has been written about the similarities and differences between biological and cultural evolution, and whether the second of these kinds of 'evolution' can be regarded as a continuation of the first. As I mention in my chapter on Darwin, Sir Alister Hardy's opinion that 'evolution is still proceeding, only now we call it history' would probably not be supported by many fellow biologists, at least in terms of their understanding of evolution, i.e., natural selection of (relatively rare) survival-enhancing genetic mutations. Such an understanding, when applied to humans, brings into focus the generally accepted view (see Gould, 1992) that, *physically* anyway, humans have not changed at all in the last 30,000 years or more (many anthropologists would say at least 50,000 years[8]). Certainly no significant biological evolution has occurred in *historical* time. As John Marsden, Executive Secretary of the Linnean Society of London, well expressed it in a letter to me, it is a 'serious misapprehension' on the part of those who try to put Darwinism in a modern context to 'believe that Darwin ever expected his idea [of natural selection] to be applied to such short timescales as a few decades or less' (as some 'evolutionary' economists attempt to do).[9]

Yet clearly *some* kind of 'evolution' of the human species has occurred in the last few thousand years, anyway. Sociobiologists may want to posit changes in the human genome to account for this, but this view has been strongly challenged by, among others, Friedrich Hayek, who, as Geoff Hodgson (1994, pp. 161–2) explains, strongly rebutted the view that 'language, morals, law, and such like' are transmitted by biological processes rather than being 'the products of selective evolution transmitted by imitative learning'. A certain kind of selection is going on in human history, but it is at the cultural rather than genetic level. Whether this is a 'Lamarckian' process at work (inheritance of acquired characteristics, after the French biologist Jean-Baptiste de Lamarck, 1774–1829) is a moot point. Geoff Hodgson (2001a) thinks not; perhaps it is something between Darwinian selection and cultural transmission of learned behaviours, etc., as with the Baldwin effect (see chapter 5), whereby survival-enhancing behaviours operate in tandem with genetic change by allowing time for favourable mutations to be selected.

But these are still large questions. 'Cultural transmission' is a convenient but rather vague sobriquet for what is no doubt a multiplicity of mechanisms. Perhaps the most well-known explanation currently on offer in this area is Richard Dawkins's 'meme' concept, first outlined in his *The Selfish Gene* (Dawkins, 1976), and later elaborated upon in *The Blind Watchmaker* (Dawkins, 1986). Essentially the idea is that, as with genes, 'information' can be 'replicated' (in this case, in the brain) and passed on to later generations as a written or spoken 'phenotype'. As might be expected, Dawkins's notion has been the target of severe criticism for its naïveté and simplistic reduction of human culture to collections of 'bits' or 'atoms' of information (Maynard Smith, 1993; Midgley, 2001), one reviewer going so far as to declare that ' "mimetics" has…proved a sterile metaphor, of little value in understanding history or society' (Coyne, 2001). Perhaps Dawkins is really not saying much more than Darwin did when – as I cite him in chapter 5 – he referred to the importance of language in the acquisition of technical skills and the passing on of this knowledge to offspring and later generations. Precisely *how* this happens may be open to debate (and the future investigations of neurophysiologists, linguists and others), and is outside the scope of this book.

Darwin, it is true, did not dwell on this subject of language and cultural evolution in any great detail, but another nineteenth-century writer who did was Henry Drummond (1851–97), author of the best-selling *The Ascent of Man* (1894). In this book Drummond shows a thorough grasp of the differences between biological and cultural evolution, and the role of language in the latter, as in the following lines:

> No serious thinker, on whichever side of the controversy, has succeeded in lessening to his own mind the infinite distance between the Mind of Man and everything else in Nature…[And] when it is asked, what brought about this sudden rise of intelligence in the case of Man? There is a wonderful unanimity…as to the answer. It came about…in connection with the acquisition by Man of the power to express his mind,

that is to *speak*. Evolution, up to this time, had only one way of banking the gains it won—heredity. To hand on any improvement physically was a slow and precarious work. But with…language there arose a new method of passing on a step in progress…When [a man] did anything he would now *say* it; when he learned anything he could pass it on; when he became wise wisdom did not die with him (Drummond, 1894, pp. 157–8, 191–2).

So, for Drummond, in what is really the essence of the Dawkins theory, we now have a *parallel* mechanism for the transmission of survival-enhancing behaviours to future generations. Humans are no longer limited in their responses to environmental contingencies by their genetic 'programming', as in other species. Of course, Drummond's sharp distinction here between 'Man' and other species is not quite the true picture—as Drummond recognizes elsewhere in his book. And interestingly, in a chapter on 'The Evolution of Language', Drummond links the origin of speech to what he sees as the necessity for communication between members of social groups in various species, including our pre-human ancestors. Drummond writes:

> The success of the co-operative principle…depends upon one condition: the members of the herd [troop of monkeys, etc.] must be able to communicate with one another…Without that power, the sociality of the herd [etc.] is stultified…
>
> Now what interests us with regard to these [vocalizations, etc.] is that they are *language*. The evolution we have been tracing is nothing less than the first stage in the evolution of Speech. Any means by which information is conveyed from one mind to another is Language. And language existed on the earth from the day animals began to live together (Drummond, 1894, pp. 199–200).

A striking example of communication of specific information in social groups has been described in African vervet monkeys. As James Trefil (1997) explains, it had long been known that vervets have a warning system whereby members of a troop will scream at the sight of danger, which is usually in the form of a snake, leopard, or eagle (the monkeys' main predators). What has been discovered and confirmed in more recent years, however, is that vervets have three distinct warning cries – a different one for each predator – to which the troop will respond in different ways: At the sound of a 'snake cry', the other monkeys in the troop will stand up and look around at the ground; the 'leopard cry' sends them out to the smallest branches of the trees; and the 'eagle cry' makes them rush into the bushes or thick foliage. As Alverdes (1932, p. 133) many years ago argued, following Darwin (see chapter 5, below), in 'the higher animals, the comradeship between members [of a troop, etc.] finds its expression in their very strong affective reaction to the specific cry of fear or warning'; and here we have a concrete instance of this phenomenon among our primate cousins. And chances are, we share something of this behavioural tendency, given our ancestry of '30 million years of social interactions' noted by Sigmund et al.[10]

'Human Nature', then, probably involves a substantial element of co-operativeness as well as selfishness. Indeed, from an evolutionary point of view, it is this element which probably lies at the basis of our legal and ethical systems, those institutions which most clearly demarcate us (besides our intelligence, which very likely grew partly in response to the demands of social interaction[11]) from the rest of the animal kingdom. As Drummond (a devout Christian—see Moore, 1986) recorded in his notebooks, now housed in Edinburgh University library, our 'mental and moral nature is merely a development of the natural'.[12]

A major theme of *The Ascent of Man* is the emergence of what Drummond calls 'love' (after the zoologists Patrick Geddes and Arthur Thompson, authors of *The Evolution of Sex*, which Drummond cites extensively), or altruism, as against 'hunger', or egoism (again using Geddes's and Thompson's terminology). Thus was Drummond able to find meaning in the evolutionary story that he felt could be accommodated within his Christian beliefs. Of course, he was still faced with a duality, though perhaps 'hunger' was not quite the same thing as evil. While a permanent, and equal, duality or polarity of the forces of light and darkness is not a tenet of Christian belief, it was of the ancient Persian religion of Zoroastrianism, which evolved into the Manichæism of which Augustine was for some years a votary before his conversion to Christianity (see chapter 2). Empedocles' (c. 495–435 B.C.) 'two great dynamic powers…Amity and Strife…[which] acted upon the universe'(see Geoff Fishburn's chapter) is a Greek version of this ancient cosmology.[13]

And Zoroastrianism has always had some appeal to people seeking an explanation for the presence of evil in the world, among these being the nineteenth-century writer Samuel Laing. In *A Modern Zoroastrian*, Laing (1904) acknowledges Drummond's contributions, but says he parts company with what he sees as Drummond's 'confounding analogy with identity' (p. 12). Nevertheless, Laing essentially reproduces Drummond's model, adding another element: the identification of altruistic idealism with socialist economics. As Laing (1904, p. 117) expresses it: 'The contrast between labour and capital or free trade and protection is only a particular case of [the] larger polarity, between what is called in scientific language egoism and altruism, or, in more popular phraseology, individualism and socialism'.

Laing's formulation encapsulates the essence of the ancient debate over whether human beings are primarily self-centred or social. Plato and Aristotle may have believed, as Geoff Fishburn shows, that man was 'by nature a "political" animal' (*Zoon politikon*—some translations read 'social': see Aristotle, 1979, p. 74), but not all philosophers agreed. Epicurus (342–270 B.C.), as Geoff Fishburn also notes, regarded the *polis* (city-state) as an 'artificial arrangement originating in a "social contract" for mutual protection', and the Epicurean Lactantius apparently thought 'There is no such thing as human society', and that 'each individual looks out for himself; there is no-one who feels affection for another, except for his own benefit'. The original text of Thomas Hobbes's (1588–1679) well-known pessimistic view of man, as articulated in his chapter, 'Of the Natural Condition of Mankind, as concerning their Felicity and Misery' in *Leviathan*, reads as follows:

> Hereby it is manifest, that during the time men live without a common Power to keep them all in awe, they are in that condition which is called Warre, and such a warre, is of every man against every man. For Warre consisteth not in Battel only, or in the act of fighting; but in a tract of time, wherein the Will to contend by Battel is sufficiently known...So the nature of Warre consisteth not in actual fighting only; but in the known disposition thereto, during all the time there is no assurance to the contrary...And the life of man [is] solitary, poore, nasty, brutish, and short (Hobbes, 1651, p. 62).

While not many economists today, surely, would want to concur with Hobbes's bleak picture,[14] some, in the apparent belief that they are merely acknowledging Darwin's affirmation of the 'struggle for existence' in human affairs as in the rest of nature, would still want to stress the inevitability of relentless competition. Jack Hirshleifer, for example, has argued that '[c]ompetition is the all-pervasive law of natural-economy interactions', and that 'the evolutionary approach suggests that self-interest is ultimately the prime motivator of human as of all life' (quoted Hodgson, 1994, pp. 28–9). Theodore Bergstrom (2001) is aware of Richard Dawkins's contention, '[i]f you look at the way natural selection works, it seems to follow that anything that has evolved by natural selection should be selfish', and agrees that, prima facie anyway, 'individual selection theory suggests a world populated by resolutely selfish *[H]omo œconomicus* and his zoological (and botanical) counterparts' (pp. 1, 5). The philosopher Ayn Rand, author of books like *Capitalism: The Unknown Ideal*, would agree that such is the way the world is: 'This country [the U.S.] was not based on selfless service, sacrifice, renunciation or any precept of altruism. It was based on a man's right to the pursuit of happiness. His own happiness. Not anyone else's' (Rand, n.d., pp. 83–4). As Gordon Gekko would have it, 'Greed is good. Greed works...Greed clarifies, cuts through and captures the essence of the evolutionary spirit' (Lipper, 1988, p. 175).

I said a few paragraphs back that a major theme of Drummond's *Ascent of Man*, by contrast, is the emergence of 'love', or altruism, through the evolutionary process. This idea has been taken up with enthusiasm by the Left, for example the Marxist biochemist and historian of Chinese science, Joseph Needham (1900–1995). Needham elevates the concept of *emergence* to the status of a general principle, traceable in all evolutionary development. In a commemorative review of Drummond's works, originally written in the 1930s, Needham (1986) draws attention to the various levels of organization – atomic, molecular, cellular, organismic, social – with which Drummond deals, and the different laws that, according to Needham, operate at these levels. Thus, as Needham quotes Drummond, 'when we pass from the inorganic we come to a new set of laws', and similarly, with regard to the emergence of *consciousness* in man:

> To say that self-consciousness has arisen from sensation, and sensation from the function of nutrition, let us say, in the *Mimosa pudica* or Sensitive Plant, may be right or wrong; but the error can only be serious when it is held that that accounts...for the transition...Man, in the last resort, has self-consciousness, *Mimosa* sensation; and the difference is qualitative as well as quantitative (Drummond, 1894, pp. 161–2, cited Needham, 1986).

'Qualitative', for Drummond and Needham, is meant to convey a difference in *kind*, rather than just degree. This was also one of the points Drummond was making when he wrote about the 'infinite distance between the Mind of Man and everything else in Nature' made possible, in part, by the evolution of speech. It is true that a case can be made for the 'cultural' transmission of information between generations in some non-human species, however, this is at a very limited level. Examples often adduced include bird-song (Manning, 1979, pp. 54–8), 'tool' use in chimpanzees (termite fishing and nut cracking—van Lawick-Goodall, 1971; Leakey, 1995) and the washing of sweet potatoes by Japanese macaque monkeys (Bernstein, 2000). But as Glen McBride has cogently argued in terms of the relationship between communication and 'culture' in non-human animals, animals have *primary* interactions: the communication is 'between you and me, here and now'; and while some animals can do a little more than this, it is 'not much' more (McBride, 2000, p. 198).

So for all intents and purposes there *are* qualitative differences between humans and other species, notwithstanding much common biology (humans and chimpanzees, for example, share 98.76 percent of their DNA [Hacia, 2001] and the proteins this codes for). And this is particularly the case in the social sphere—one of the levels that arise as a result of evolutionary processes in Drummond's and Needham's scheme. Another writer on the Left who attached much importance to qualitative change as a product of evolution was Thomas Alfred Jackson, who is the subject of Erin McLaughlin-Jenkins's chapter in this volume. Interestingly, Jackson also introduced another element into the discussion—the effect of 'holism' (a term coined by Jan Christiaan Smuts in the 1920s[15]), or the *interactions* of the parts of a whole which, in Jackson's view, can substantially affect evolutionary outcomes. As a convinced Marxist, Jackson saw this whole process as a dialectical one:

> One can have *all* the parts of a watch or a machine, and yet not have the watch or the machine *as a whole*. The whole is created not by the simple aggregation...of the parts, but by their specific interrelations, in which case the whole is *qualitatively*

'greater' than all the parts in separation. In social life this fact plays a big part, as Marx shows in his *Capital*...

[I]t is this law, vital to dialectics (the law of the transformation of quantity into quality)...which gives capitalist production its superiority over small production, and the bigger Capital its superiority over the smaller (Jackson, 1936, p. 587, italics and parenthesis in original).

In Jackson's view then, simplistic, reductionist accounts of human nature are inadequate for an understanding of social phenomena. As Erin McLaughlin-Jenkins explains, notwithstanding Jackson's early enthusiasm for Darwin (and indeed, Marx himself asserted that *The Origin of Species* 'contains the natural-history foundation for our view point'[16]), he soon became disenchanted with Darwin's (and Herbert Spencer's) 'reduction of humans to mere quantitative superiority, insisting that humans were qualitatively distinct from animals'. Jackson was thus forced to seek common ground between Marx and evolution (the truth of which, as a Secularist, he unreservedly accepted), eventually settling on drawing upon Darwin for demonstrations of biological change, and Marx for social change. Thus in *Dialectics: The Logic of Marxism and Its Critics*, Jackson insisted that once humans began creating their own subsistence, they entered a dialectical relationship with nature which consisted of *both* a continuity and a radical break. As he writes:

History develops from...Nature, yet is the reverse of a simple *continuation* of Nature...History...involves a continuous and development-producing interaction between Mankind (in its collective-relation) and Nature as a result of which both Mankind (collectively) and Nature are *altered*. History is the becoming process of human Society. It is the *unity* – the synthetic result of – the interaction between the opposites Mankind – as biological species – and the rest of Nature. History therefore can no more be understood apart from Mankind (Jackson, 1936, p. 188, italics in original).

Jackson's emphasis on 'Mankind' in its 'collective relation' is of course indicative of the Left, and is in fact a leitmotif of *Dialectics*. Earlier in the book Jackson writes that 'in the very act of subduing Nature mankind has created a new thing, *human society* – the totality of the interactions between men – begotten by mankind's collective production-activity, its collective imposition of will upon Nature'; and contrasts this with the ' "atomic" sociology which sees in society nothing but individuals in simple juxtapostion' (ibid., pp. 110–11). At the same time, Jackson is suspicious of 'essentialist' accounts of human nature (as is the Left still), which creates something of a difficulty for him in his acceptance of Darwinism—especially the Darwin of the 'moral sense' chapter in *Descent of Man*. Such accounts, in Jackson's estimation, amount to an 'alternative form of the atomic view—the notion that something "mysterious" and "ultimate" in the *nature* [Jackson's emphasis] of man as an individual makes him constantly seek association with his fellows' (ibid., p. 125).

Jackson's position is thus complex, but it is a subtle one—much more so than the simplistic sociobiological 'selfish gene' dogmatism of E.O. Wilson, Richard Dawkins and others, which would reduce human sociality to pre-programmed ant-like behaviour. There is no doubt that, as McLaughlin-Jenkins shows, Jackson fully accepted the importance of 'orthodox' Darwinism's findings for an understanding of the human condition—that '[h]umanity is part of nature', and that the biological differences between species and varieties – as between man and ape – were 'formal and superficial only'. But there was more to it than that. For Jackson, just as '[t]he living organism cannot be understood solely from a study of electronic particles, or of atoms, or of any of the succeeding stages', and each 'stage' in the evolution of life represents 'a qualitative transformation of Nature considered in its totality', so 'the appearance of Mankind as a biological species constitutes in one aspect a quantitative continuation, and in another a revolutionary transformation of Nature' (ibid., p. 278). And how was this transformation to occur? This is the crux of Jackson's argument, and 'yet another sense in which Darwin's work was revolutionary': it was the demonstrable fact that '*Men change themselves in the operation of changing Nature*'. 'Man', to be fully understood, 'must be studied in mankind's historical movement' (ibid., pp. 240, 298, italics Jackson's). History, then, is the key to understanding the human condition generally (and as Joan Robinson, 1987, among others, would argue, the economy specifically—see also Hodgson, 2001b, c).

It is ironic, given the world-view of the next theorist discussed in this volume, Kenneth Boulding (a Christian who, according to Robert Solo [1984, p. 470], held a 'peculiar animus...towards Marx and all his works') that Jackson's vision of man, emphasizing, as it did, human *agency,* was remarkably close to Boulding's. Just as Jackson (1936, p. 191) argues that, for Marx, 'human agents are included in the sum total of productive or economic forces', so too does Boulding want to emphasize that, in the total evolutionary scheme of things, man alone has the capacity to form mental images of the kind of society he wants, and the capability of bringing this about. Borrowing a term from the Jesuit philosopher, Teilhard de Chardin (1965) – one of the major influences on Boulding's thought (see Silk, 1976) – Boulding, in his numerous publications, wanted to stress that it is man who uniquely enlarges his niche in the biosphere, and creates the systems of the sociosphere, through emergence of the *noosphere*—the domain of interacting human minds. So that, as Solo (1984, p. 470) explains, all 'social production, productivity, development and evolution' are now in man's hands. Like Drummond, Needham and Jackson, Boulding is convinced of the validity of the emergence idea: with the evolution of the brain of *Homo sapiens*, and the generation of human knowledge, everything changed. In a kind of Lamarckian process, according to Boulding, human social and economic life now operate through a 'noogenetic' structure, involving the neurology of the human brain and communications technologies. Knowledge generated and disseminated by these means now dominates life to such an extent that the 'biogenetic structure cannot account for the variety of human artifacts' (Boulding, 1984, pp. 122–3).

At the same time, as Richard Joseph shows, Boulding's conception of 'artifacts' is a broad, and some would argue, flawed one in a number of respects. One of Boulding's strongest critics in this connection is Elias Khalil. In Khalil's (1996, p. 83) view, rather than offering an 'evolutionary' economics (as in his 1981 book with that title[17]), Boulding is really arguing for an 'ecological account of the transformation of artifacts'. Khalil cites various usages of the term 'artifacts' by Boulding, including not only material creations such as buildings, machines, and cars, but also organizations, corporations, political parties—even biological entities like trees, horses and grass. Khalil regards this usage as illegitimate, or at least manifestly unhelpful; and indeed it is difficult to see how such usage can be accommodated within evolutionary accounts of biological and social phenomena as usually understood. Moreover, as Khalil points out, Boulding is very liberal with his use of the term 'species', and can employ this for entities that he elsewhere describes as artifacts. Thus, together with notions like noogenetic 'mutations', by which he apparently means changes in technology, Boulding can argue things like '[t]he automobile is now as much a species in the world ecosystem as is a horse' (Boulding, 1992, p. 173). Khalil protests at what he sees as inordinate use of *analogy* (as, presumably, would Samuel Laing—see above), insisting that Boulding's claims have nothing to do with biological categories, just as his conception of a continuity between biological and cultural evolution falls down with his failure to differentiate between units of evolution (be these genes, organisms, or human artefacts) and the environment in which these 'evolve'.

Boulding makes no apology for the latter. As Richard Joseph notes, Boulding 'is not particularly bound by the accepted tenets of Darwinian…evolution', and sees the universe as a total system of interacting parts from which the 'environment' cannot be separated. Joseph quotes Boulding as arguing: 'There is no such thing as an "environment", if by this we mean a surrounding system that is independent of what goes on inside it. Particularly, there is no sense at this stage of evolution on earth in talking about "the environment" as if it were nature without the human race'.

Boulding is not, of course, the first major economist to attempt to integrate his subject within broader evolutionary theory. Veblen, as is well known, tried to do it (Hodgson et al., 1998), as did Alfred Marshall (Thomas, 1991; Nightingale, 1993; Hodgson, 1994; Laurent, 2000a). And as with Boulding, much of Marshall's writing in this area relies heavily on imaginative comparisons and pure analogy—as where Marshall talks about 'the development of the organism, whether social or physical [which] involves an increasing subdivision of functions between its separate parts on the one hand, and on the other a more intimate connection between them' (Marshall, 1920, p. 24). Marshall is here using the ancient organic metaphor for society, which goes back at least to Plato,[18] St Paul and St Augustine (see chapter 2), and which reached its most formal elaboration, somewhat incongruously, in the hands of Herbert Spencer (1910, ch. XVI; see also Hodgson, 1994, pp. 80–98), who strongly influenced Marshall (Laurent, 2000a). But, as Peter Groenewegen shows in chapter 6 of this volume, Marshall was also deeply concerned with questions of human nature *per se*, and the bearing of this on the workings of the social or 'economic organism' (a phrase Marshall also uses, e.g., Marshall, 1920, p. 769).

Early in *Principles of Economics*, Marshall (1920, p. 14) cautions that 'economics cannot be compared with the exact physical sciences: for it deals with the ever-changing and subtle forces of human nature'; and while he is prepared to qualify this view in a footnote to the effect that people in the *aggregate* tend to behave in a tolerably predictable manner, he nevertheless makes it clear that he is very sensible of the limitations of this predictability. To this extent, Marshall has little time for the 'abstract and bloodless' economic man of J.S. Mill and others, as he explains in his 1902 letter to John Neville Keynes cited by Groenewegen. In the *Principles* Marshall returns to this position a number of times, as in the following passages:

> [E]thical forces are among those of which the economist has to take account. Attempts have indeed been made to construct an abstract science with regard to the actions of an 'economic man', who is under no ethical influences and who pursues pecuniary gain warily and energetically, but mechanically and selfishly. But they have not been successful, nor even thoroughly carried out (Marshall, 1920, p. vi).

> [Economists] deal with man as he is: not with an abstract or 'economic' man; but a man of flesh and blood. They deal with a man who is largely influenced by egoistic motives in his business life to a great extent with reference to them; but who is [not] below delight in doing his work well for its own sake, or in sacrificing himself for the good of his family, his neighbours, or his country (ibid., p. 27).

There are in other words, for Marshall, at least two sides to human nature: the egoistic and the altruistic, a conviction that, as Peter Groenewegen shows in his extract from Marshall's inaugural lecture at Cambridge, was held by Marshall from an early date. Did this greatly affect Marshall's economics in any specific sense? Arguably, yes, in terms of his confidence in the viability and economic soundness of the co-operative movement. It would appear that Marshall had Darwin's *Descent of Man* (a copy of which he possessed[19]) in mind when he wrote the above lines, that is, at least chapter IV of that work, on 'The Moral Sense'. That this was surely the case is attested to in further passages in *Principles of Economics*, as where Marshall directly cites Darwin's argument for the natural selection, at the group level, of altruistic propensities: 'Thus the struggle for existence causes in the long run those races to survive in which the individual is most willing to sacrifice himself for the benefit of those around him; and which are consequently the best fitted collectively to make use of their environment' (Marshall, 1920, p. 243). Marshall also shows that he read Darwin's *Origin of Species* when he summarizes Darwin's argument for the evolution of such behaviour in other species: 'And going beyond the narrower interests of the family to those of the race, we find that in many so-called social animals such as bees and ants, those races survive in which the individual is most energetic in performing varied services for the society without the prompting of direct gain to himself' (ibid.; cf. Darwin, 1901, p. 162).[20]

So Marshall is aware of the 'collective' side of human as well as other life, and this is an element in his economics. Some authors have in fact referred to Marshall's 'small s' socialism (see, e.g., Henry, 1995), and while this is perhaps taking things a little far, there is no doubt some sympathy for socialistic idealism in his writing, especially in his earlier writing. At the very least, Marshall is willing to recognize the possibility of an 'evolution' of human nature, in historical terms, in line with changing economic conditions, which he saw as encompassing collectivist tendencies:

> The growing earnestness of the age, the growing intelligence of the mass of the people, and the growing power of the telegraph, the press, and other means of communication are ever widening the scope of collective action for the public good; and these changes, together with the spread of the co-operative movement, and other kinds of voluntary association are growing up under the influence of various motives besides that of pecuniary gain (Marshall, 1920, p. 25).

Whatever the case, Marshall's sympathies with and enthusiasm for co-operation are beyond question, as is illustrated in his Presidential Address to the twenty-first Co-operative Congress at Ipswich in 1889, in which, while he conceded that 'the direct effect of the struggle for survival in the animal kingdom is to cause those animals to flourish which are fittest to derive benefits from the environment', he was nevertheless confident that 'human nature' made possible the satisfying of this law through co-operation (Marshall, 1889, p. 9). Marshall became friendly with well-known labour leaders such as Tom Mann and Ben Tillett at around this time, and this strengthened his interest in co-operation and collectivism generally. In 1892 Marshall and Mann were both appointed to a Royal Commission on Labour, and questioned each other in this capacity, at one point Marshall asking Mann: 'Is not the way to make co-operation effective to apply it in production as well as in trade?' (to which Mann answered in the affirmative) (Groenewegen, 1996, p.171).

This subject of the practicability of co-operation is obviously related to the issue of egoism versus altruism, and was clearly close to Marshall's heart. His interest in the subject evidently withstood his disappointment with socialism in his later years (Groenewegen, 1995, ch. 16), as can be seen in numerous paragraphs in the last edition of *Principles of Economics*, such as this one:

> Co-operation might seem likely to flourish in agriculture and to combine the economics of production on a large scale with many of the joys and the social gains of small properties. It requires habits of mutual trust and confidence; and unfortunately the bravest and the boldest, and therefore the most trustful, of the countrymen have always moved to the towns, and agriculturists are a suspicious race. But Denmark, Italy, Germany and lately Ireland have led the way in a movement which seems full of promise for organized co-operation in the handling of dairy produce, in the making of butter and cheese; in buying farmers' requisites and in selling farmers' produce: and Britain is following in their wake (Marshall, 1920, p. 655).

Arguably, in this sphere of business anyway, Marshall's faith appears to have been well placed. Dairy co-operatives today are hugely successful world wide (the recently created Fontera co-op. in New Zealand controls 22 percent of the country's exports and accounts for 7 percent of GDP[21]); and as co-operation so clearly bears on the broader question of human nature generally, perhaps something more about this subject can be said here.

When Marshall asked Tom Mann whether co-operation could be made to work more effectively in production as well as in trade (distribution), dairying and other agricultural co-operatives were in their relative infancy in Britain (in 1911 there were still only 29 registered co-operative dairies in the country[22]), whereas co-operative wholesale societies had been flourishing for nearly half a century. In the 1860s Marx had in fact asked whether the 'co-operative factories' being established at the time might not represent 'within the old form [of society] the beginnings of the new', where 'the antagonism between capital and labour is overcome' (Marx, 1909, p. 521). By 1944, as T.A. Jackson (1945) noted, the movement which had begun with the Rochdale Pioneers a century before (i.e. in England—they had begun a little earlier in France, see Furlough, 1991) claimed nine million members in over a thousand societies in Britain, joined in federating bodies like the Co-operative Union and the Co-operative Wholesale Society (CWS). And by this time also, *productive* activities such as food canning, dairy processing and soft-drink and furniture making had taken up a large part of the work of the societies: in 1938 the CWS had 182 factories with nearly 50,000 employees (Tilley, 1995).

The first co-operative store in Australia was opened in Brisbane, Queensland, in 1859, and by 1999 there were 195 consumer and producer co-operatives registered in this State, the largest being the Mackay Sugar Co-operative and the Queensco-Unity Dairy Foods Co-operative, trading as Dairy Farmers.[23] Producer societies quickly became the more common type in Australia, with its predominantly rural-based economy, a pattern which was assisted by government legislation. In the case of dairying, the Queensland government, through a Meat and Dairy Produce Encouragement Act of 1893, provided loans for the setting up of co-operative cheese and butter factories, these quickly becoming established in towns like Gympie (which was reputed, for a time, to have the largest butter factory in the world), Toowoomba, Crow's Nest, Oakey, Esk, Kingaroy, Nanango, Beaudesert and Kingston.[24] North-Eastern New South Wales also became an important dairying district from the 1890s onwards, with co-operative processing factories established at Lismore, Byron Bay, Ballina, Casino, Uki and Bellingen, among other centres (Connery, n.d., 1980; Ryan, 1995). Again, government support greatly helped: as with the building of a new jetty at Byron Bay making use of coastal transport provided by the North Coast Steam Navigation Company (from 1891). By 1909 the New South Wales north coast is said to have far exceeded the rest of the state in butter production and other dairy produce, the Byron Bay factory alone producing around 5,000 tons of butter a year (*Brisbane Courier*, 15 June 1907; Ashton, 1951; O'Dwyer, 1983).

The spirit of co-operation is captured in the minutes and reports of meetings of the Southern Queensland Co-operative Dairy Company in Kingston, Queensland (see Figure 0.1). The decision to form a co-operative was made at a public meeting at Beenleigh (south of Brisbane) in April 1906, a representative of dairy farmers in the district declaring that they were in favour of 'joining hands' to start a factory. Statistics 'in favour of Co-operation' were presented, and at a further meeting a prospectus was drawn up based on capitalization of £8,000 divided into £1 shares, shareholders having voting powers to a maximum of three votes depending on the number of shares held. A penalty of £10 for supplying cream to another factory was also agreed upon.[25] The factory's opening ceremony in June 1907 was attended by about 300 people, the majority arriving 'in their own traps with their wives and families with them, bent on celebrating the occasion by making a holiday of it'. In his opening address, James Stodart, MLA reminded those present that the factory 'was purely a co-operative one, and by making it a success they would all gain the advantage' (*Brisbane Courier*, 10 June 1907). And a success it proved to be. Within four years the factory had been paid for, the number of suppliers (beginning with 130) had increased, extending to the Logan and Albert Valleys further south, and the Samford Valley north-west of Brisbane;[26] and according to the co-operative's Chairman of Directors, William Stephens, MLA, 'no other factory...had made such progress as the Kingston'. Stephens went on to say that he thought 'it was a great compliment when certain proprietary factories told their suppliers that they would pay Kingston prices' (*Minutes*, 25 March 1911).

The Kingston butter factory went on to reach its peak year of production in 1934, with an output of 3,367 tons, but by the 1950s the number of dairy farmers supplying cream had significantly declined due to increased urbanization in the district, and the co-operative finally sold its factory to a private concern in 1958.[27] By that date, however, a number of other co-operatives were flourishing, some totally dominating the economic life of the towns in which they were

Figure 0.1 The Southern Queensland Co-operative Dairy Company's butter factory at Kingston, South-East Queensland, c. 1915. Courtesy of the John Oxley Library, Brisbane. Negative number 31213.

situated—as with Esk, for example, which also ran its own department store (*Gatton Star*, 15 May 1959), and Moe, in Victoria.[28]

The sugar industry in Queensland and northern New South Wales – which, like dairying, depends on central processing on a scale beyond the capacities of individual producers – has also been largely organized on a co-operative basis. In Queensland, the industry was given a major boost with enabling legislation similar to that put in place for the dairying industry, viz., a Sugar Works Guarantees Act of 1893, under which canegrowers could combine to form a co-operative and obtain capital to erect and equip a central mill by mortgaging their land to the government.[29] This was later supplemented with other assistance, such as loans for building cane tramways to connect with Queensland government railways.[30] Perhaps inevitably, a number of mills soon found themselves unable to meet their obligations and were thus taken over by the Queensland Treasury, which continued to operate them as government enterprises (five mills – Nerang, Moreton, Mount Bauple, Gin Gin and Proserpine – finding themselves in this position by 1906[31]); but by the early 1960s, of the thirty-two mills then operating, fifteen were run by the canegrowers as co-operatives.[32] Due to amalgamations and some rationalization in the industry (partly in response to recent abolition of tariff protection), there are currently twenty-eight sugar mills operating in Queensland and northern New South Wales, of which six in Queensland and (all) three in New South Wales are run as co-operatives, with a further four (Mossman, Mulgrave, Tully and Isis) run as 'co-operative companies' (with limited shareholding by non-growers).[33] Another privately-owned mill, Moreton (at Nambour, north of Brisbane), under threat of closure, is presently looking at options for continuing production, including as a co-operative *(Nambour and District Chronicle*, 13–19 February 2002).

Co-operation, then, *can* work in some industries. (In Victoria in 2001, 35 percent of farmers surveyed were in agricultural co-operatives of one sort or another, and currently the Dairy Farmers co-op has an annual turnover of $A 1.4 billion.[34]) So a tacit recognition of the co-operative side of human nature daily operates in significant sectors of the economy. At a minimum, as has often been pointed out, business of *any* kind could hardly be conducted without some basis of trust. Co-operation does not have to rely upon idealistic and unrealistic assumptions; indeed there is frequently remarkable consensus among people in even diametrically opposed economic philosophies on this subject. T.A. Jackson, the communist, as Erin McLaughlin-Jenkins documents, was on the management and education committees of the Crawley and Ifield Co-operative Society (which had its own dairy and bakery).[35] Similarly, the Queensland branch of the Australian Communist Party, *c.* 1951, was urging that 'legislation be enacted to enable [sugar cane] suppliers to proprietary mills, by majority vote, to acquire such mills and operate them as co-operative concerns', and remarkably, was citing former Liberal Queensland Premier, Samuel Griffith, under whose administration the 1893 Acts helping establish co-operatives in the dairying and sugar industries were first proposed, in support.[36]

Griffith (1845–1921), as it happens, besides being an astute politician (with an eye on votes), had a lifelong interest in questions of human nature, beginning with his studies of works like Horace's *Epistles* and Aristotle's *Ethics* at Sydney University in the 1860s.[37] Convinced of the truth of Aristotle's axiom that 'man is by nature a political animal',[38] Griffith early accepted the proposition that 'there is little difference between right as social law and right as individual law',[39] and by the 1880s was writing articles like 'Wealth and Want' for the socialist newspaper *The Boomerang* (in which he averred that unrestricted competition led to the 'complete domination of the weak by the strong'), and was being described by fellow jurist Alfred Stephen as having 'a smack of communism'.[40] But Griffith was no communist, nor was his contemporary, Alfred Marshall. Both were merely endeavouring to restore some balance to assumptions about human nature, which at their time were no doubt often coloured by the social Darwinist arguments of Herbert Spencer and others (see chapter 5[41]) and which were certainly a misrepresentation of the totality of Darwin's view. Another contemporary of Marshall, Peter Kropotkin (1842–1921), saw this clearly, as Rob Knowles shows in his chapter. Drawing on authorities as diverse as Cicero, Jeremy Bentham and Adam Smith, as well as Darwin, Kropotkin – a geographer, who had studied nature closely in the wilds of Siberia – became convinced of the pervasiveness of 'collectivity' in the living world, and that this was as much a feature of nature as competition. Especially was this so, in Kropotkin's view, of *human* nature: 'We all know that…without sympathy and mutual aid, human kind must perish', Kropotkin (1927, p. 10) argued in his anarchist manifesto, *The Conquest of Bread*, and elaborated upon at length in *Mutual Aid: A Factor of Evolution*:

> As soon as we study animals – not in laboratories and museums only, but in the forest and the prairie, in the steppe and the mountains – we at once perceive that though there is an immense amount of warfare and extermination going on amidst various species, and especially amidst various classes of animals, there is, at the same time, as much, or perhaps even more, of mutual support, mutual aid, and mutual defence amidst animals belonging to the same species or, at least, to the same society. Sociability is as much a law of nature as mutual struggle (Kropotkin, 1972 [1902], p. 18).

With regard to humans, Kropotkin quoted Darwin's *Descent of Man* in support: 'The small strength and speed of man, his want of natural weapons, etc., are more than counterbalanced, firstly, by his intellectual faculties; and secondly by his *social qualities*, which led him to give and receive aid from his fellow men' (Darwin, 1875, p. 64, quoted ibid., p. 109, emphasis Kropotkin's). Chief among these 'social qualities' in Kropotkin's view was the natural propensity for *sympathy*, which impels humans as well as other species to care for their fellows, whether immediate relatives or not (as in food-sharing, which is a common feature of hunter-gatherer societies—see Irvine, 1933; Robson, 2001) and which is a key plank in Darwin's theory of the origin of the 'moral sense' in humans (see chapter 5).[42] And both Darwin (1875, p. 106) and Kropotkin found a 'precursor' for their recognition of the importance of sympathy as the social cement that binds the members of societies together in Adam Smith. In his pamphlet *Anarchist Morality*, Kropotkin (1892, pp. 16–17) noted that 'in *The Theory of Moral Sentiment* [sic]...Adam Smith has laid his finger on the true origin of the moral sentiment', and that he 'does not seek it in mystic religious feelings; he finds it simply in the feeling of sympathy'. While expressing disappointment that Smith had not 'understood that this same feeling of sympathy, in its habitual stage, exists amongst animals as well as amongst men', Kropotkin nevertheless praises Smith for having sought 'the explanation of morality in a physical fact of human nature'.

An anarchist and hero of the Left (see, e.g., Kropotkin's [1913] Preface to Emile Pataud's and Emile Pouget's *Syndicalism and the Co-operative Commonwealth*, which also has a Foreword by Tom Mann[43]) finding a soul-mate in Adam Smith – the apostle of free-market economics for many – would nodoubt have surprised some of Kropotkin's readers. But as Athol Fitzgibbons argues in his chapter, there are two sides to Smith's economics: the competitive ('greed is good') side, and the side which emphasizes the importance of social cohesion. Smith's economics were '*not*', Fitzgibbons maintains, 'exclusively concerned with self-love'; nor is one confronted with a 'schizophrenic' Smith, a market economist on the one hand, and a 'more obscure' philosopher on the other (as in Cropsey, 2001 [1957]). Fitzgibbons does not take up the evolutionary argument, probably wisely; but it is tempting to draw comparisons with the two dimensions of Darwin—competition and co-operation (or Geddes's and Thompon's 'Hunger and Love', or Empedocles' 'Strife and Amity'), as I discuss above and in chapter 5. Smith had no particular notion of evolution, let alone natural selection; nevertheless, he comes remarkably close to Darwin (who notes Smith's 'striking' first chapter of *The Theory of Moral Sentiments)* when he writes things like 'Man, who can only subsist in society, was fitted by nature to that situation for which he was made'(cited Denis, 1999, p. 75). Smith's 'Maker' was not natural selection, but God, who, as Fitzgibbons explains, was very real for Smith, even if not in terms of mainstream Protestant Christian theology of his time. Nearer to Smith's understanding, Fitzgibbons explains, was the world-view of Cicero and the other Stoics, who saw the 'cardinal virtues' as the moral force binding society together. As Cicero himself wrote in *On Duty (De Officiis)*: 'Men themselves are here for the sake of their fellow men, that they may mutually assist one another. We ought then to follow Nature here and contribute to the common good by exchanging deeds of helpfulness, both giving and receiving, and by our skill, our labour, and our talents bind more closely together the association of men with men' (Cicero, 1948, pp. 328–9).

But as Smith knew, competition is also part of human nature. And nowhere among the classical economists, perhaps, is this fact brought into sharper focus than in the writings of the next major figure discussed in the volume, Thomas Malthus. Indeed, as readers will know, it was largely Malthus who introduced *Darwin* to the idea of the all-pervasiveness of competition and the 'struggle for existence' in human society—though Adam Smith may have helped Darwin here also (see Robson, 2001), at the same time offering some balance to the picture. However this may be, it is certain that Darwin's copy of the sixth edition of Malthus's *An Essay on the Principles of Population* (Malthus, 1826) has marked passages which reveal much about Darwin's debt to the economist, for example the following, where Malthus is writing about the Australian Aborigines of the Hawksbury River district:

> In a country, the inhabitants of which are driven to such resources ['witchety' grubs, ants, etc.] for subsistence, where the supply of animal and vegetable food is so extremely scanty, and the labour necessary to produce it is so severe, it is evident, that the population must be very thinly scattered in proportion to the territory (Malthus, 1826, Vol.1, p. 29).

The point Malthus is making of course is that in such circumstances competion for these scarce food resources will be particularly severe, and only those with the necessary enterprise and energy will survive and have offspring (from which Darwin deduced that those so favourably endowed, and their heredity, would be *naturally selected*—see F. Darwin, 1995). Elsewhere in his copy of *Principles of Population*, Darwin has marked a passage which reads, 'It appears clearly from the very valuable tables of mortality, which Sussmilch has collected, and which include periods of fifty or sixty years, that all the countries of Europe are subject to periodical sickly seasons, which check their increase' (ibid., p. 499), and has written against this: '& animals'—showing he has extended Malthus's observations concerning human society to the rest of the animal kingdom. It is true, as John Pullen notes in his chapter, that in the last two chapters of the original (1798) *Essay* Malthus comes close to Darwin's eventual formulation – at least on a 'spiritual' plane ('let us not querulously complain that climates are not equally genial...that all God's creatures do not possess the same advantages' [Malthus, 1926, p. 379—see also Hodgson, 2001c, p. 333]) – but there is no evidence that Darwin read this original version.

More important for Darwin, arguably, was Malthus's stress on enterprise. And the corollary of this, as John Pullen highlights, was Malthus's preoccupation with *indolence*, and the 'influence of so general and important a principle in human nature'. Laziness, torpor, idleness, sloth—whatever terms one chose, were a constant danger and a canker in the human constitution, in Malthus's view, and needed to be rooted out or at least risen above. Failure to do so inevitably had destructive results, Malthus believed, such as a fall in effective demand, since the desire to consume was 'practically limited by the countervailing luxury of indolence' (a view contrasting with that of Adam Smith – as Pullen shows – and also with such modern writers as Edwin Mansfield, as indicated above). But in so arguing, Malthus revealed a more generous and human side of his thinking. If sloth, indolence etc., can be overcome, human beings are not necessarily condemned to the consequences of their 'nature'—a term which, it is clear, did not imply something immutable in Malthus's understanding. In Malthus's pre-Mendelian world, there was not the sharp nature/nurture divide that we draw today (however uncertainly).[44] Thus indolence – that 'important principle in human nature' – could just as easily be an acquired as an innate trait, as Pullen shows in his discussion of Malthus's views on the Irish peasantry: 'In defence...of the Irish peasant', Malthus wrote, 'it may be truly said, that in the state of society in which he has been placed, he has not had a fair trial; he has not been subjected to the ordinary stimulants which produce industrious habits.'

It remains true, however, that Malthus's view of the human condition remained a sober and pragmatic one—'taking man as he is', and unsympathetic with the utopianism of contemporaries like the Marquis de Condorcet, and also William Godwin (1756–1836), a cordial protagonist burdened with 'false ideas of the perfectibility of human nature' (Smyth, 1842, p. 73). Malthus, remarkably like modern evolutionary writers such as Stephen Jay Gould (see above and chapter 5), doubted whether 'since the world began, any organic improvement whatever of the human frame can be clearly ascertained'.

Fritz Machlup, I suspect, would have agreed, given his deep understanding of the decisive role of *language* in the *cultural*, rather than physical, evolution of human beings since the emergence of *Homo sapiens*, as Don Lamberton shows in his chapter. Machlup (1902–83) was a complex character, often described as a neo-classical economist, who trained under that towering figure in free-market economics, Ludwig von Mises, but who developed his own cast of economic theorizing, focusing on knowledge production and dissemination. And this was within a thoroughgoing evolutionary framework, as with his friend and longtime colleague, Kenneth Boulding. To the extent that biological evolution hinges on the process of 'information' transfer from one generation to the next, Don Lamberton is surely right in suggesting that Machlup would have found the Human Genome Project fascinating (as no doubt would have Boulding); but in any event, the subject of information (or better, knowledge) generation and transfer generally was of great interest to Machlup, and became central to a whole new way of looking at the economy. Before Machlup, knowledge was largely a black box in economic theory, something which somehow accounted for the economic growth that the traditional 'factors of production', land, labour and capital, and possibly entrepreneurship, failed to account for. As Don Lamberton shows, Machlup changed all that. Beginning with his work on patents in the 1930s (see Machlup, 1958), Machlup was eventually able to demonstrate the contribution to GNP not only of education *per se*, but of whole areas of economic activity previously neglected—science and technology, information services, and later information machines (computers). By the early 1970s, the torch lit by Machlup had been taken up by others, notably Don Lamberton himself, who further refined and added to Machlup's insights.

But as indicated, Machlup's interests ranged widely, as Lamberton shows, taking in the whole question of the role of accumulated knowledge in human 'evolution' (in the sense originally proposed by Henry Drummond), made possible by the emergence of language. Don Lamberton quotes the anthropologist Ian Tattersall (2000) on this subject (though I have difficulty with Tattersall's reference, in the article concerned, to the 'invention' of language, as if its appearance was itself a cultural event), and Machlup would surely have agreed with the general thrust of Tattersall's argument—especially the view that 'it is the ability to form mental symbols that is the fount of our creativity'. Machlup has in fact – in an essay on Friedrich Hayek's contributions to economics (Machlup, 1977, pp. 13–59) – referred to a discussion by Hayek on the 'primacy of the abstract', in which the Nobel laureate draws attention to the 'well established fact' that 'most animals [including humans] recognize…abstract features long before thay can identify particulars' (ibid., p. 50). Kenneth Boulding would have wholeheartedly agreed (see above, and Richard Joseph's chapter), as would, surely, any number of writers interested in the seemingly almost miraculous workings of the human imagination (e.g. Samuel, 1949).

Jason Potts's argument that human mental evolution can be seen in the evolution of language in conjunction with visual imaging of the environment takes this theme of the role of the imagination in human creativity further, and in constructing some original applications of some of the latest claims of evolutionary psychology, provides a fitting concluding chapter to this volume. In his discussion on Ian Tattersall's (2000) thoughts on language, Don Lamberton alluded to Tattersall's caution that we have *no idea* (Tattersall's actual terminology) at present 'how the modern human brain converts a mass of electrical and chemical discharges into what we experience as consciousness'. This is essentially an accurate assessment of the situation, notwithstanding some of the arguments of 'cognitive science', which wants to explain consciousness – which presumably evolved for its enormous advantages in dealing with the physical environment – by explaining it away—dismissing consciousness, in effect, as an illusion (see, e.g., Dennett, 1991), and defining the brain as a computer (thought = computation).

Jason Potts is aware of the inadequacy of such models, which he interestingly ties in with what he sees as models of human nature in economic theory.

He suggests that economics, over the past couple of centuries, has been charac-terized by at least three false conceptions of man, those of automaton, demon, and cyborg. The 'demon' model of man as economic agent most closely ap-proximates the *Homo œconomicus* beloved of much economic theorizing (especially in econometrics with neo-classical assumptions), and is totally ra-tional, in that its behaviour is completely in accordance with physical reality, has full information, and has no computational limitations: it is a Turing ma-chine and 'does not actually have a mind'. Another assumption of the 'demon' model of *Homo œconomicus* is that its central processing apparatus is a *tabula rasa* – a blank sheet – upon which anything and everything can be written, an ancient idea probably most familiarly associated with the British philosopher John Locke (Wynne, 1731).[45] In the 'cyborg' model (see p. 197, Figure 11.1), which Jason Potts cites from Philip Mirowski (2002) and which grew out of the beginnings of widespread use of the computer from the mid-twentieth century onwards, the economic agent is computationally constrained (like a computer), and is subject to *bounded* rationality, programmed responses, etc. The approxi-mation with the human condition was improving, but still fell short. Some replacement, nevertheless, of the demon model with the cyborg paralleled the great advancement of computational techniques throughout the second half of the twentieth century and, as seen, among other things came to dominate think-ing about the workings of the human mind.

To replace these two models, Jason Potts proposes a third, the *nomad*. This model is intended to overcome some of the limitations of the demon and cyborg models by taking account of current evolutionary thinking, especially as for-mulated in the arguments of evolutionary psychology. The central claim of evolutionary psychology, or EP, as it is commonly designated, is that the cogni-tive and behavioural responses of modern humans are very much influenced by our ancestral environment—that in which we evolved. Specifically, the human mind is is not a *tabula rasa*, but rather, a number of *modules* – the 'massive modularity hypothesis' (see, e.g., Buss, 1999; but cf. Rose and Rose, 2001) – which evolved to deal with particular recurrent problems in our forbears' envi-ronment, such as accurately determining one's position vis-à-vis dangerous predators (perception of distance, three dimensional imaging, etc.) and coping with the intricacies of social life (e.g. face recognition, and possibly monitoring of reciprocal exchanges—see also chapter 5). Concomitant with this theory is the idea that some *other* environmental exigencies are *not* well coped with by our mental equipment, i.e., certain modern problems not encountered by our primordial ancestors (such as extracting patterns from data arrays). Thus, ac-cording to EP, we have inherited powerful cognitive devices to deal with some of life's problems, but not others.

Jason Potts's suggestion, then, is that the human economic agent must learn to utilize the equipment that he does have by consciously adapting it to changed circumstances. Fortunately, the mind is remarkably adaptable and creative, and has certain special abilities, such as visualization, or imaging, which is part of consciousness and of which no computer is capable, search processes, and, perhaps most importantly, language. Jason Potts characterizes this new model as the 'nomad' since early *Homo sapiens* and his ancestors lived a nomadic life for many millennia, and it is likely that even language – which, as seen (cf. Drummond, above), makes possible new levels of evolution – has evolved in tandem with these other abilities to enable us to form mental maps of the landscape, among other things. For modern man, these evolved adaptations to search in complex environments form a strong basis for conceptualizing the economic agent as one who, primarily, has a mind and constructs knowledge: the nomadic instinct can be used as a theory of the origin of creativity in terms of the creation and organization of knowledge. Human beings are not the prisoners of their heredity; it provides the mainspring for a vibrant economy.

ACKNOWLEDGMENTS

I wish to thank my contributing authors for their support for, and commitment to this project, not only in writing their papers, but in putting up with my unreasonable requests and idiosyncrasies. The support and help of the publishing and editorial staff at Edward Elgar Publishing, especially Edward Elgar and Alexandra Minton, is gratefully acknowledged, as is Peter Pegg's expertise and efficiency in formatting the manuscript (and in providing much editorial assistance besides). Jill Bowie and Robin Neill read much of the manuscript and offered valued suggestions.

I acknowledge, also, the generous assistance of the staff of numerous libraries and archival repositories, including the staff of Griffith University Library; the Fryer Library, University of Queensland (especially Maira Turaids and Bill Dealy); the John Oxley Memorial Library, Brisbane, Queensland; Megan Lyneham, University of Queensland Archivist; Adam Perkins and Godfrey Waller of the Department of Manuscripts and University Archives, Cambridge University Library; Rosalind Moad, King's College, Cambridge Archivist; Gillian Lonergan, Archivist, Co-operative College, Loughborough, U.K.; Alison Pearn and Nick Gill of the Darwin Correspondence Project; Sheila Noble, User Services Librarian, Special Collections, Edinburgh University Library; Vivien Taylor, Head, Special Collections, Queen's University Libraries, Kingston, Ontario; Tori Reeve, Curator, Down House; Jenny Hall, Roman Curator, Museum of London; and Erne Perrett, President, Kingston (Queensland) and District Historical Society.

Thanks, also, to the following people for all their help in various ways: David Burch, Roslyn Cox, Ian Eddington, Wayne Hudson, Peter Jones, Alison Kay,

Ted Kolsen, Mike Kirk, Rob Laurent, Ian Lowe, Laurie Neill, Roy MacLeod, Phillip McDonald, John Marsden, Jim Moore, John Morgan, Sue Newton, John Nightingale, Hilary Perrott, George and Yvonne Simmons, Max Standage, and David and Isabella Thorpe.

I am grateful to the Syndics of Cambridge University Library; the Modern Archives Centre, King's College, Cambridge; the W.D. Jordan Special Collections and Music Library, Queen's University Libraries and University Archives, Kingston, Ontario; and Edinburgh University Library, Special Collections for permission to quote from the Charles Darwin Collections, the J.M. Keynes papers, the V.C. Wynne-Edwards papers and Henry Drummond's notebook (cat. no. DK. 3.33) respectively. An earlier version of my chapter on Augustine has been accepted for publication by *History of Economics Review*, and I wish to express gratitude to the editor of that journal, John King, for permission to re-publish much of that article in the present volume. Financial assistance towards the cost of preparing the manuscript was provided by my employer, Griffith University, and is gratefully acknowledged.

I wish to extend a special word of thanks to Geoff Hodgson for finding the time in a busy schedule to write the Preface.

NOTES

1. This is in a section on 'Human Wants'. The latest edition of this work (Mansfield, 1997) does not even have such a section, and for 'humans' substitutes 'individual units' and 'economic aggregates'.
2. See Laurent (2001).
3. This was in a review of the film, *A Beautiful Mind* (about the Nobel Prize-winning economist John Forbes Nash Jnr), in *Time Off* magazine, 6 March 2002.
4. See, for example, H. Rose and S. Rose (2001), p. 18.
5. On the back soft-cover of his copy of Friedrich Walther's *Der Hund* (Giessen: C.F. Heker, n.d.) Darwin has written: 'March 29 1857. Find out what classics translated. Athenaeum London Library. Aristotle; Pliny; Xenophon; Varro; Columella; Oppianus; Treviranus'.
6. See Butterfield (1931).
7. Aristotle (1952), Book II, 7. 25–30.
8. Elizabeth Kolbert, 'The Ice Age Cometh', *The Age* (Melbourne), 16 March 2002.
9. John Marsden, Executive Secretary, Linnean Society of London, to the author, 6 January 2002.
10. For 'family trees' showing the primate ancestry of humans dating back to about 30 million years, see McBride and Berrill (1973), p. 361; and Leakey (1995), p. 9. See also M. Leakey et al. (2002).
11. James Randerson, 'Early Learning', *New Scientist*, 16 March 2002, p. 11.
12. Henry Drummond, notebook (April, 1880), p. 70 (Edinburgh University Library, special collections, cat. no. DK. 3.33). Drummond's further reading recorded in this notebook included Plato's *Republic*, Augustine's *Confessions* and Bagehot's *Physics and Politics* (see chapter 5, below).
13. For an informative discussion on the origins and philosophy of Zoroastrianism, see Bouquet (1956), pp. 97–102.
14. It should be said though, that Hobbes does soften his position somewhat in *Human Nature and De Corpore Politics* (Hobbes, 1999), chapter IX, pp. 16–17 ('Of Love', and 'Charity').

15. See J.C. Smuts (1926).
16. Marx to Engels, 19 December 1860, in Marx (1978), p. 359.
17. K. Boulding (1981).
18. As in Book VIII of *The Republic*, where Socrates tells Glaucon that 'just as a sickly body requires but a small additional impulse from without to bring on an attack of illness, and sometimes even without any external provocation is divided against itself, so in the same way, does not this city, whose condition is identical with that of a diseased body, require only slight excuse of an external alliance introduced by the one party from an oligarchical city, or by the other from a democratical, to bring on an acute disease and an inward battle?' (Plato, 1997, p. 273; cf. A.R. Wallace, as cited in chapter 2, below).
19. It is held in Cambridge University Library—I am grateful to Peter Groenewegen for this information.
20. It is tempting to see something of Plato here too, as where Socrates tells Cebes, in *Phaedo*, that in the transmigration of souls, 'those who have practised popular and social goodness' are 'likely to go back into the race of…social creatures similar to their kind, bees perhaps, or wasps or ants; and to return to the human race again, and be born from those kinds of decent men' (Plato, 1993, p. 34).
21. *Australian Financial Review*, 8 February 2002.
22. J. Clayton (1911), p. 64.
23. Co-operatives Act 1997, List of Co-operatives by Name and Balance Sheet List (Queensland Office of Fair Trading, typescript, August 1999); Laurent (2000b).
24. Gillespie (2001); Anon. (1923); T. Barker and J. Byford (1988); M.J. Fox (1919–1923), Vol. I, pp. 607–10; M. Neill (1997); N. Teese (2001); *Brisbane Courier*, 20, 28 August 1906, 7 June 1907.
25. Southern Queensland Co-operative Dairy Company, *Minutes*, 12 April, 25 May, 17 August 1906.
26. N. Teese, *supra*; Pat Fischer, 'They Came to Stay', *Sweet Sea News* (Jacob's Well, Qld), August 1999; 'Pimpama Township' (typescript, John Oxley Memorial Library, Brisbane); Draper et al. (1984).
27. 'History of the Kingston Butter Factory' (Logan City Historical Museum Inc., brochure, n.d.).
28. *Moe Advocate*, Golden Anniversary of the Moe Co-operative Dairying Co. Ltd Supplement, 1955; information supplied by John Morgan, former shareholder.
29. Anon. (n.d. *c.* 1913), pp. 77–8; *Votes and Proceedings of the Queensland Legislative Assembly*, 1893 (3 vols), Vol. I, p. 238. At around the same time, the Queensland government also drafted legislation amending the Crown Lands Acts to 'promote settlement by Co-operative Communities'(ibid., p. 110). A number of these 'communities', or communes, were established in the Gayndah district of Queensland, such as at Gooroolba ('Resolute'), and were successful for a short time. (Information supplied by Rob Laurent. See also Metcalf, 1998).
30. *Debates of the Queensland Legislative Council and the Legislative Assembly during the Third Session of the Twentieth Parliament*, Vol. CXXVII, 9 July–6 December 1917, pp. 1408–9.
31. 'Report upon the Government Central Sugar Mills', in *Queensland Parliamentary Papers printed during the Fourth Session of the Fifteenth Parliament* (2 vols), Vol. II, 1906, p. 279.
32. W. Kidston (*c.* 1963).
33. Anon., 'Rocky Point Mill' (typescript brochure produced by the mill at Woongoolba, Queensland); information provided by Pat Taylor, Queensland Office of Fair Trading; J. Kerr (1996); Fox (1919–1923), Vol. II, pp. 823–4.
34. *Weekly Times* (Melbourne), 11 July 2001; *The Courier-Mail* (Brisbane), 9 March 2002.
35. W.J. Denman and T.A. Jackson (1938) p. 9.
36. See note 29; Australian Communist Party, 'Program for the Sugar Industry' (4-page brochure, n.d. *c.* 1951); 'Break CSR's Grip!' (typescript address, *c.* 1951, by James Henderson, Queensland State Secretary, ACP. Jackson's [1945] *Socialism: What? Why? How?* is amongst Henderson's books and pamphlets held by the Fryer Library, University of Queensland). The Communist Party gained some of its strongest support in the sugar growing districts of North Queensland at this time—see Menghetti (1981); Riedlinger (1991).
37. S.W. Griffith, personal papers, John Oxley Memorial Library, Brisbane (notebooks, 1862, cat. nos. OM64/10/3/14, 18); R.B. Joyce (1984), p. 9.

38. Colin Sheehan (1998).
39. *Supra*, note 37 (notebook—Aristotle's *Ethics*).
40. *Boomerang* (Brisbane), 22 December 1888 (Griffith's article was reprinted as 'The Distribution of Wealth' in the Sydney *Centennial Magazine*, July 1889, pp. 833–42); Joyce, *supra*, n. 37, p. 150. Joyce says that Griffith's diary shows that just before writing the article he had been reading *Das Kapital*, W.M. Dawson's *German Socialism* and Edward Bellamy's *Looking Backwards*.
41. Spencer has been quoted as writing: '[T]he poverty of the incapable, the distresses that come upon the imprudent, the starvation of the idle and the shouldering aside of the weak by the strong...are the decrees of a large far seeing benevolence'. (R. Scott, 1984, p. 154). In his withering parody of such views, *The Individualist* (a copy of which I found amongst some remaining books from the library of the Southern Queensland Co-operative Dairy Company), Philip Gibbs (1908) writes of the 'noble individualism' and 'the struggle for existence which is the divine law of life' (p. 237).
42. The major group-selection theorist V.C. Wynne-Edwards (see chapter 5) agrees with both Kropotkin (Wynne-Edwards, 1962, p. 127) and Darwin here. In some notes laid in his copy of *The Descent of Man* (now housed in Special Collections in the library of Queen's University, Kingston, Ontario), Wynne-Edwards has written, for example, referring to some lines by Darwin in the 'Moral Sense' chapter in this book, 'Sympathy an essential part of indeed the foundation of the social instinct'.
43. E. Pataud and E. Pouget, *Syndicalism and the Co-operative Commonwealth* (Oxford: New International Publishing Co., 1913), pp. v–vi (Mann), vii–xiii (Kropotkin). Mann asks readers to 'notice how many times the authors refer to the great value of the Co-operative Societies. In industry and in Agriculture, artisan and peasant alike find the change [to the 'Co-operative Commonwealth'] made easy where Co-operation is known, the lesson to us is, that *all* workers should, without delay be identified with the Co-operative movement, Distributive and Productive'. In his Preface, Kropotkin concurs, and interestingly (cf. Marshall), in *Fields, Factories and Workshops*, Kropotkin (1912, p. 118) cites the dairying industry as an illustration of co-operation in practice:

     Everyone knows that it is now Danish butter which rules the prices in the London market, and that this butter is of a high quality, which can only be attained in co-operative creameries with cold storage and certain uniform methods in producing butter.

44. The expression, however, goes back at least to Shakespeare, as in *The Tempest*, IV. i., where Prospero says of Caliban: 'A devil, a born devil, upon whose nature Nurture will never stick'.
45. Locke (as quoted in Wynne, 1731, p.19) wrote: 'Let us...suppose the mind to be, as we say, *white Paper*, void of all Characters, without any *Ideas*: How came it to be furnished? Whence has it all the Materials of Reason and Knowledge? To this I answer, in a Word, from *Experience*, and Observation. This, when employ'd about External Sensible Objects, we may call *Sensation*: By this we have the Ideas of *Bitter*, *Sweet*, *Yellow*, *Hard*, etc. which are commonly called *Sensible Qualities*, because convey'd into the Mind by the *Senses*. The same *Experience*, when employed about the Internal Operations of the Mind, perceiv'd and reflected on by us, we may call *Reflection*: Hence we have the *Ideas* of *Perception*, *Thinking*, *Doubting*, *Willing*, *Reasoning*, etc.'.

REFERENCES

Alverdes, F. (1932), *The Psychology of Animals, in Relation to Human Psychology*, London: Keegan Paul, Trench, Trübner & Co. Ltd.

Anon. n.d. (*c.* 1913), *Sugar*, London: A. and C. Black.

Anon. (1919), *The Student's Handbook to the University and Colleges of Cambridge*, Cambridge, U.K.: Cambridge University Press.

Anon. (1923), *History of Queensland Dairying*, Brisbane: Queensland Council of Agriculture.

Anon. (1940), *Calendar of the University of Sydney for the Year 1940*, Sydney: Thomas Henry Tennant, Government Printer.

Aristotle (1952), 'On the Parts of Animals', in R.M. Hutchins (ed.), *Great Books of the Western World*, Vol. 9 (Aristotle: II), Chicago: Encyclopaedia Britannica Inc.

Aristotle (1979), *Ethics*, Harmondsworth, Middlesex: Penguin.

Ashton, L.G. (ed.) (1951), *Dairy Farming in Australia*, Canberra: Commonwealth Department of Commerce and Agriculture.

Axelrod, R. (n.d. *c.* 1984), *The Evolution of Co-operation*, New York: Basic Books.

Barker, T. and I. Byford (1988), *Harvests and Heartaches: Images and Stories of Queensland's Agricultural Past*, Brisbane: Queensland Department of Primary Industries.

Bergstrom, T.C. (2001), *Evolution of Social Behaviour: Individual and Group Selection Models*, University of California Santa Barbara Economics Department Working Paper Archive, 14-01 (http://www.econ.ucsb.edu/working_papers.html#2001).

Bernstein, I.S. (2000), 'Cognitive Capacities of Old World Monkeys based on Studies of Social Behaviour', in P.F. Whitehead and C.J. Jolly (eds), *Old World Monkeys*, Cambridge, U.K.: Cambridge University Press.

Boulding, K. (1981), *Evolutionary Economics*, Beverly Hills, California: Sage.

Boulding, K. (1984), 'Foreword: A Note on Information, Knowledge and Production', in M. Jussawalla and H. Ebenfield (eds), *Communication and Information Economics: New Perspectives*, Amsterdam: North-Holland, pp. vii–ix.

Boulding, K. (1992), 'Punctuationism in Societal Evolution', in A. Somit and S.A. Peterson (eds), *The Dynamics of Evolution*, Ithaca, N.Y. and London: Cornell University Press, pp. 171–86.

Bouquet, A.C. (1956), *Comparative Religion*, Harmondswork, Middlesex: Penguin.

Buss, D.M. (1999), *Evolutionary Psychology: The New Science of the Mind*, Needham Heights, MA: Allyn & Bacon.

Butterfield, H. (1931), *The Whig Interpretation of History*, London: G. Bell.

Cicero, M. (1948), *Selected Works*, Roslyn, N.Y.: Walter J. Black.

Clayton, J. (n.d. *c.* 1911), *Co-operation*, London: T.C. and E.C. Black.

Collingwood, R.G. (1945), *The Idea of Nature*, Oxford: The Clarendon Press.

Connery, M.L. (n.d.), *The Way It Was*, Uki, N.S.W.: Uki and South Arm Historical Society.

Coyne, J.A. (2001), 'The Case of the Missing *Carpaccio*', review of S.R. Palumbi, *The Evolution Explosion: How Humans Cause Rapid Evolutionary Change* (New York: W.W. Norton, 2001), *Nature*, **412**, 586–7.

Cropsey, J. (2001) [1957], *Polity and Economy, with Further Thoughts on the Principles of Adam Smith*, South Bend, Indiana: St Augustine's Press.

Darwin, C. (1875), *The Descent of Man and Selection in Relation to Sex*, London: John Murray.

Darwin, C. (1901) [1859], *On the Origin of Species by means of Natural Selection*, London: Ward, Lock & Co. Ltd.

Darwin, F. (1995), *The Life of Charles Darwin*, London: Senate.

Dawkins, R. (1976), *The Selfish Gene*, Oxford: Oxford University Press.

Dawkins, R. (1986), *The Blind Watchmaker*, Harlow, U.K.: Longman.

Dawson, Wm.D. (1888), *German Socialism and Ferdinand Lasselle: A Biographical History of German Socialistic Movements this Century*, London: Swan Sonnenschein.

Denis, A. (1999), 'Was Adam Smith an Individualist?', *History of the Human Sciences*, **12**(3), 71–86.

Denman, W.J. and T.A. Jackson (1938), *Fifty Years: Being the Story of the Crawley and Ifield Co-operative Society Ltd*, Reading, U.K.: C.W.S. Printing Works.

Dennett, D.C. (1991), *Consciousness Explained*, Boston, MA: Little Brown & Co.

Draper, B.A., W. Draper and E. Kemp (1984), 'Changing Times in the Bunya District', in various authors, *Samford Reminiscences*, Samford, Qld: Samford and Districts Historical Museum Committee, pp. 23–5.

Drummond, H. (1894), *The Ascent of Man*, London: Hodder and Stoughton.

Fowles, J. (1968), *The Aristos*, London: Pan Books Ltd.

Fox, M.J. (1919–1923), *The History of Queensland: Its People and Industries* (3 vols), Brisbane: States Publishing Co.

Furlough, E. (1991), *Consumer Co-operation in France: The Politics of Consumption, 1834–1930*, Ithaca, N.Y. and London: Cornell University Press.

Gibbs, P. (1924) [1908], *The Individualist*, London: Grant Richards.

Gillespie, A. (2001), *Pomona: The Historical Centre of Noosa Shire—Historical Series Issue No. 5—Using the Land*, Pomona, Qld: Cooroora Historical Society Inc.

Gould, S.J. (1992), *Life's Grandeur: The Spread of Excellence from Plato to Darwin*, London: Vintage.

Groenewegen, P. (1995), *A Soaring Eagle: Alfred Marshall 1842–1924*, Aldershot, Hants., U.K.: Edward Elgar.

Groenewegen, P. (ed.) (1996), *Official Papers of Alfred Marshall: A Supplement*, Cambridge, U.K.: Cambridge University Press.

Hacia, J.G. (2001), 'Genome of the Apes', *Trends in Genetics*, **17**(11), 637–45.

Henry, J.F. (1995), 'Professor Stigler's report on Alfred Marshall's *Lectures on Progress and Poverty*, an addendum', *Marshall Studies Bulletin*, **V**, 39–40.

Hobbes, T. (1651), *Leviathan, or The Matter, Forme and Power of a Commonwealth Ecclesiastical and Civil*, London: Printed for Andrew Crooke.

Hobbes, T. (1999), *Human Nature and De Corpore Politico* (ed. J.C.A. Gaskin), Oxford: Oxford University Press.

Hodgson, G.M. (1994), *Economics and Evolution: Bringing Life Back into Economics*, Cambridge, U.K.: Polity Press.

Hodgson, G.M. (2001a), 'Is Social Evolution Lamarckian or Darwinian?', in J. Laurent and J. Nightingale (eds), *Darwinism and Evolutionary Economics*, Cheltenham, U.K. and Northampton, MA, U.S.A.: Edward Elgar, pp. 87–120.

Hodgson, G.M. (2001b), 'The Evolution of Capitalism from the Perspective of Institutional and Evolutionary Economics', in *idem*, Makoto Itoh and Nobuharu Yokokawa (eds), *Capitalism in Evolution*, Cheltenham, U.K. and Northampton, MA, U.S.A.: Edward Elgar, pp. 63–82.

Hodgson, G.M. (2001c), *How Economists Forgot History: The Problem of Historical Specificity in Social Science*, London: Routledge.

Hodgson, G.M. et al. (1998), Special issue of *Cambridge Journal of Economics* on Veblenian Evolutionary Economics, **22**(4), 397–495.

Irvine, R.F. (1933), *The Midas Delusion*, Adelaide: Hassell Press.

Jackson, T.A. (1936), *Dialectics: The Logic of Marxism, and Its Critics – An Essay in Exploration*, London: Lawrence and Wishart Ltd.

Jackson, T.A. (1945), *Socialism: What? Why? How?*, London: Communist Party.

Joyce, R.B. (1984), *Samuel Walker Griffith*, St Lucia, Qld: University of Queensland Press.

Kerr, J. (1996), *Only Room for One: A History of Sugar in the Isis District*, Childers, Qld: Isis Central Sugar Mill Company Ltd.

Khalil, E.L. (1996), 'Kenneth Boulding: Ecodynamicist or Evolutionary Economist?', *Journal of Post-Keynesian Economics*, **19**(1), 83–100.

Kidston, W. (n.d. *c*. 1963) (compiler), *Co-operative Study Manual*, Brisbane: Co-operative Federation of Queensland.

Kropotkin, P. (1892), *Anarchist Morality*, London: Freedom Pamphlets.

Kropotkin, P. (1972) [1902], *Mutual Aid: A Factor of Evolution*, London: Allen Lane.

Kropotkin, P. (1912), *Fields, Factories and Workshops*, London: Thomas Nelson and Sons Ltd.

Kropotkin, P. (1913), Preface, in E. Pataud and E. Pouget, *Syndicalism and the Co-operative Commonwealth*, Oxford: New International Publishing Co.

Kropotkin, P. (1992) [1922], *Ethics: Origin and Development*, Montreal/New York: Black Rose Books.

Kropotkin, P. (1927), *The Conquest of Bread*, New York: Vanguard Press.

Laing, S. (1904), *A Modern Zoroastrian*, London: Watts & Co.

Laurent, J. (2000a), 'Alfred Marshall's Annotations on Herbert Spencer's, *Principles of Biology*', *Marshall Studies Bulletin*, **VII**, 1–6 (http://www.cce.unifi.it/dse/marshall/laure7.htm).

Laurent, J. (2000b), 'Co-operation: The Missing Element in Economics Text Books', *Journal of Economic and Social Policy*, **5**, 57–70.

Laurent, J. (2001), 'Keynes and Darwinism', in J. Laurent and J. Nightingale (eds), *Darwinism and Evolutionary Economics*, Cheltenham, U.K. and Northampton, MA, U.S.A.: Edward Elgar, pp. 63–84.

Leakey, M., A. Hill, J.D. Kingston and S. Ward (2002), 'New Cercopithecoids and a Hominoid from 12.5 Ma in the Tugen Hills succession, Kenya', *Journal of Human Evolution*, **42**(1/2), 75–94.

Leakey, R. (1995), *The Origin of Humankind*, London: Phoenix.

Lipper, K. (1988), *Wall Street*, New York: Berkley Books.

Machlup, F. (1958), *An Economic Review of the Patent System*, Study 15 of the Senate Subcommittee on Patents, Trademarks, and Copyrights, Washington D.C.: Government Printing Office.

Machlup, F. (1977), 'Hayek's Contribution to Economics', in *idem*, *Essays on Hayek*, London: Routledge and Kegan Paul, pp. 13–59.

Malthus, T.R. (1826), *An Essay on the Principle of Population* (2 vols), 6th edn, London: John Murray.

Malthus, T.R. (1926), *First Essay on Population 1798*, London: Macmillan and Royal Economic Society.

Manning, A. (1979), *An Introduction to Animal Behaviour* (3rd edn), London: Edward Arnold.

Mansfield, E. (1979), *Microeconomics: Theory and Applications* (3rd edn), New York: W.W. Norton and Company.

Mansfield, E. (1997), *Applied Microeconomics*, New York: W.W. Norton and Company.

Marshall, A. (1889), *Presidential Address to the Twenty-First Annual Co-operative Congress*, Manchester: Co-operative Union Ltd.

Marshall, A. (1920), *Principles of Economics* (8th edn), London: Macmillan.

Martin, A. (1975), *The Last Generation—The End of Survival?* Glasgow: Fontana/Collins.

Marx, K. (1909), *Capital: A Critique of Political Economy* (3 vols), Vol. III, Chicago: Charles H. Kerr & Company.

Marx, K. (1978), *The Essential Marx* (ed. S.K. Padover), New York: Mentor Books.

Maynard Smith, J. (1993), *Did Darwin Get it Right? Essays on Games, Sex and Evolution*, London: Penguin Books.

McBride, G. (2000), *The Genesis Chronicles: The Evolution of Human Kind*, St Leonards, N.S.W.: Allen & Unwin.

McBride, G. and J.J. Berill (1973), *Animal Families*, Surry Hills, N.S.W.: Reader's Digest Association Pty Ltd.

Menghetti, D. (ed.) (1981), *The Red North: The Popular Front in North Queensland*, Townsville, Qld: History Dept, James Cook University of North Queensland (Studies in North Queensland History No. 3).

Metcalf, Bill (1998), *The Gayndah Communes*, Rockhampton, Qld: Central Queensland University Press.

Midgley, M. (2001), 'Why Memes?', in H. Rose and S. Rose (eds), *Alas Poor Darwin: Arguments Against Evolutionary Psychology*, London: Vintage, pp. 67–84.

Mirowski, P. ((2002), *Machine Dreams: Economics Becomes a Cyborg Science*, New York: Cambridge University Press.

Moore, J. (1986), 'Evangelicals and Evolution: Henry Drummond, Herbert Spencer and the Naturalisation of the Spiritual World', *Scottish Journal of Theology*, **38**, 383–417.

Needham, J. (1986) [1943], 'The Naturalness of the Spiritual World: A Re-appraisement of Henry Drummond', in *idem*, *Time: The Refreshing River*, Nottingham: Spokesman.

Neill, M. (1997), *Pictures from Arcadia*, Brisbane: The Author and Copy Right Publishing Co. Pty Ltd.

Nightingale, J. (1993), 'Solving Marshall's Problem with the Biological Analogy: Jack Downie's *Competitive Process*', *History of Economics Review*, No. 20, 74–95.

O'Dwyer, M.R. (1983), *St Angela's by the Sea: History of the Ursulines in Tweed Heads*, Fairfield, N.S.W.: W.R. Bright & Sons.

Ormerod, P. (1995), *The Death of Economics*, London: Faber and Faber.

Plato (1993), *Phaedo*, Oxford: Oxford University Press.

Rand, A. (n.d. *c.* 1961), *For the New Intellectual*, New York: Signet.

Riedlinger, P. (1991), 'The Red North Recalled: Radical Perspectives on Working Class Life in North Queensland', *Oral History Association of Australia Journal*, No. 13, 114–119.

Robinson, J. (1987), 'The Disintegration of Economics', in R. Albelda, C. Gunn and W. Walker (eds). *Alternatives to Economic Orthodoxy: A Reader in Political Economy*, Armonk, N.Y.: M.E. Sharp Inc., pp. 60–67.

Robson, A.J. (2001), 'The Biological Basis of Economic Behaviour', *Journal of Economic Literature*, **XXXIX**, 11–33.

Rose, H and S. Rose (eds) (2001), *Alas Poor Darwin: Arguments Against Evolutionary Psychology*, London: Vintage.

Ryan, M. (1980), *Casino: From Crossing Place to Municipality*, Casino, N.S.W.: Municipality of Casino.

Ryan, M. (1995), *Norco 100: A Centenary History of Norco, 1895–1995*, Lismore, N.S.W.: Norco Co-operative Ltd.

Sambursky, S. (1956), *The Physical World of the Greeks*, London: Routledge and Kegan Paul.

Samuel, Rt Hon. Viscount (1949), *Creative Man and Other Addresses*, London: The Cresset Press.

Schotter, A. (2001), *Microeconomics: A Modern Approach*, Boston: Addison Wesley.

Scott, R. (1984), 'The Dark Abyss of Pysh: The Language of Economic Rationalism', in C. Pybus (ed.), *Columbus'* [sic] *Blindness and Other Essays*, St Lucia, Qld: University of Queensland Press, pp. 146–56.

Sheehan, C. (1998), ' "Man is by Nature a Political Animal"; Sir Samuel Griffith as seen by *Queensland Figaro*', in J. Macrossan et al., *Griffith, the Law and the Australian Constitution*, Brisbane: Royal Historical Society of Queensland, pp. 51–67.

Silk, L. (1974), *The Economists*, New York: Basic Books Inc.

Smuts, J.C. (1926), *Holism and Evolution*, London: Macmillan.

Smyth, W. (1842), 'Godwin', in *idem*, *Lectures on History: Second and Concluding Series on the French Revolution* (3 vols), Vol III, Cambridge and London: J. and J. Deighton and William Pickering, pp. 48–73.

Solo, R. (1984), 'Solo on Boulding', in H.W. Spiegel and W.J. Samuels (eds), *Contemporary Economists in Perspective*, Greenwich, Connecticut and London: JAI Press Inc., pp. 461–71.

Spencer, H. (1910), *First Principles*, London: Williams and Norgate.

Suissa, J. (2001), 'Anarchism, Utopias and Philosophy of Education', *Journal of Philosophy of Education,* **35** (4), 627–46.

Tattersall, J. and J.H. Matternes (2000), 'Once We Were Not Alone', *Scientific American*, **282**(1), 38–44.

Teese, N. (2001), *Hurricane Lamps and Handmilking: A History of Dairy Farming along the Logan and Albert River Valleys*, Veresdale Scrub, Qld: The Author.

Teilhard de Chardin, P. (1965), *The Phenomenon of Man*, London: Collins/Fontana.

Thomas, B. (1991), 'Alfred Marshall on Economic Biology', *Review of Political Economy*, **3**(1), 1–14.

Tilley, J. (1995), *Churchill's Favourite Socialist: A Life of A.V. Alexander*, Manchester: Co-operative Union Ltd.

Tomer, J.F. (2001), 'Economic Man vs Heterodox Man: The Concepts of Human Nature in Schools of Economic Thought', *Journal of Socio-Economics*, **30**, 281–93.

Trefil, J. (1997), *Are We Unique?* New York: John Wiley & Sons Inc.

van Lawick-Goodall, J. (1971), *In the Shadow of Man*, London: Collins.

Venable, V. (1975), *Human Nature: The Marxian View*, Gloucester, Mass: Peter Smith.

Wynne, J. (1731), *An Abridgement of Mr Locke's Essay Concerning Human Understanding* (4th edn), London: Printed for J.J. Knapton, A. Bettesworth, J. Pemberton and T. Astley.

Wynne-Edwards, V.C. (1962), *Animal Dispersion in Relation to Social Behaviour*, Edinburgh and London: Oliver and Boyd.

1. Evolution and the Nature of Man in Greek Thought

Geoffrey Fishburn

Gnôthi sauton – 'know thyself' – was inscribed over the temple at Delphi, but what was this 'self' which was to be known, and from where was its existence derived?

A truly comprehensive answer to this question – and an explication of the injunction, no less relevant today than when first inscribed – would necessarily take us across many fields: from creation myths to religious practices; from Herodotus (who wondered at, and documented, the varieties of human experience which he encountered) to Xenophon; from Pericles to Lysias to Aristophanes (who each, directly or indirectly, had something to say about 'being human'); from the poets to the proto-scientists. But from all of these, save perhaps for the last, we obtain only possible illustrations, not direct evidences.

Our inquiry is more modest (if no less difficult for all that). The Greeks had, from earliest times, an understanding that 'man' was neither god nor beast, but where exactly, and on what grounds, he should be located between the two was not always clear. We can, nevertheless and in the best post-Darwinian spirit, take as a possible point of entry into this question such thoughts as the Greeks had on the subject of what, for the moment, we shall call 'a theory of evolution'.

For the very good reason that we do not judge the child by the adult who has yet to become, we cannot judge Greek thought in the light of theories which were to be much later developed, within a different intellectual framework, after centuries of speculation and argument and accumulated observation. Any thoroughgoing 'precursors of Darwin' project would, accordingly, be of its very nature intellectually vacuous (although this is not to say that it has not been elsewhere attempted).

Yet all is not lost in rejecting such an approach, for there is still much to be learnt from what the early Greek thinkers had to say, not least because their speculations were part of the legacy inherited by later generations who came to work in the same fields.

At a minimum, and in order to mark it out from both non-scientific as well as other scientific areas of thought, 'evolutionary thought' should embrace at least some of the following:

1. That not all present biological forms have always existed;
2. That some (or all) biological forms owe their existence to pre-existing forms;
3. That different forms succeeded one another in time; and
4. That in some sense there was 'development' of successive forms.

We know, certainly, that Darwinian evolutionary thought contains all of these elements (and more besides); the principal question to be addressed here is the extent to which some or all of these elements can be found in Greek thought. As a secondary, but important, question we shall explore the manner in which, for the Greeks, any such 'evolutionary thinking' was to have a bearing on their conception of the nature and role of Man.

THE IONIAN SCHOOL

It is with the sixth century (all dates quoted in this chapter are B.C.) that we first see the beginnings of what we can now recognize as 'scientific' thinking, albeit still carrying the load of earlier (and of course, popular) myth and legend:

> First of all, they (Thales, Anaximander, Anaximines and their successors throughout the Greek world) conceived the universe as a self-contained mechanism, without design or purpose, ruled by necessity from within, not by a Divinity or other agency from without. So doing, they broke boldly from the past, initiating a profoundly significant revolution in human thought. They conceived also the universality of change, and a fundamental substance infinite in extent, out of which the multiform world of their experience had differentiated, out of which indeed countless worlds had arisen and decayed through infinite time, in cycles that carried throughout the universe the conception of recurrent change so familiar to their mundane experience. Thus, in sweeping speculations, they sketched a developing universe, made mechanically intelligible by the partition of the basic substance into ultimate particles, which varied in size and shape but which were eternal and indestructible as the stuff of which they were composed. They were also inherently active, capable of moving in all directions in a structureless void. It was from the movement of these atoms, governed by necessity but without purpose or plan, that aggregates, infinite in number and variety, shaped themselves into earth and sun and moon and stars and all other objects whatsoever, great and small (Torrey and Felin, 1937, pp. 6–7).

Two members of the Ionian School (or 'Milesians') will be taken here for quotation and discussion, as being particularly relevant to our inquiry; of these, it is the name of Anaximander (*c.* 611–546) which first deserves our present attention. There survives, unfortunately, only a small fragment which can be

directly attributed to him, but later doxographers have been taken as presenting
reliably his views:

> The first animals were generated in moisture and enclosed in thorny barks; as they
> grew older, they came out onto the drier [land] and, once their bark was split and
> shed, they lived in a different way for a short time.
>
> In the beginning, man was similar to a different animal, namely, a fish.
>
> In the beginning, man was generated from living things of another kind, since the
> others are quickly able to look for their own food while only man requires prolonged
> nursing. Therefore if he had been so in the beginning he would not have survived
> (Kahn, 1960, pp. 109–10).

Sketchy and speculative though this is, it was a remarkable start; but scientific thought had to wait another two-and-a-half millennia before (on the basis
of much greater empirical evidence than could ever have been available to the
Milesians) Charles Lyell, in what is noted (*Oxford English Dictionary* [Second
Edition, 1989]) as the first use of the word 'evolution' in its modern biological
context, was to write:

> It appears from geological observations, that plants and animals of more simple or-
> ganization existed on the globe before the appearance of those of more compound
> structure, and the latter were successively formed at later periods: each new one
> being more fully developed than the most perfect of the preceding era.
>   Of the truth of the last-mentioned geological theory, Lamarck seems to have been
> fully persuaded; and he also shews that he was deeply impressed with a belief preva-
> lent amongst the older naturalists, that the primeval ocean invested the whole planet
> long after it became the habitation of living beings, and thus he was inclined to assert
> the priority of the types of marine animals to those of the terrestrial, and to fancy, for
> example, that the testacea of the ocean existed first, until some of them, by gradual
> evolution, were improved into those inhabiting the land (Lyell, 1991 [1832], p. 11).

We should, nevertheless, see Anaximander's contribution for what it was, no
more and no less, for:

> In spite of the claims sometimes made that Anaximander anticipated Darwin, it is
> clear that the underlying belief here is not evolutionary, but the concept of the species
> man, differing from other species in a physical characteristic—its early helplessness:
> 'other creatures are soon self-supporting, but man alone needs prolonged nursing'.
> Crude and fantastic though the theory is, it constitutes a first step away from tradi-
> tional legend and prejudice in the direction of the biological study of mankind (Baldry,
> 1965, pp. 25–6).

One of the 'later Ionians', Empedocles (*c.* 495–435), merits special attention
here. Our knowledge of his teachings is not helped either by the fragmentary
writings now extant, his poetic mode of expression, or the later accounts of

what he was supposed to have thought (as has been argued in, for example, O'Brien, 1969, pp. 200ff.), but on two matters at least there is agreement (since these can be read relatively unambiguously from what we know of his writings): firstly, that all matter is composed of the four elements earth, air, fire, and water; and secondly, that two great dynamic powers acted upon the universe, which are variously referred to (or translated as) 'Love and Hate', 'Lovingness and Strife', 'Aphrodite and Wrath', or 'Amity and Strife' ('For even as Love and Hate were strong of yore/ They shall have their hereafter; nor I think/ Shall endless Age be emptied of these Twain' [fragment 16, tr Leonard, 1908]):

> Modern commentators have seen parts of the biological theory of Empedocles as a primitive anticipation of Darwin's theory of evolution. For Empedocles, as for Darwin, life is contingent. Nature is a spendthrift, creating many unfit creatures, until some succeed in surviving in sufficient numbers and procuring descendants also adapted to their surroundings. The contingency is accounted for by Empedocles through the ever-continuing contest between Strife and Amity, for Amity is not entirely free to fashion the creatures she wants, but has to work with the material – the elements and their combinations – which she *happens* at each time to have at her disposal. She plays the role of the final cause, but only so far as fortuitous circumstances allow (Lambridis, 1976, p. 101, italics in original).

Nor should we under-estimate the shift in the groundwork of Greek thought on the 'nature of man' which was accomplished in the sixth and fifth centuries, firstly, by the Ionians; and secondly, by the accounts of Herodotus (*c.* 485–423).

Earlier mythological accounts, unlike the proto-scientific speculations of the Ionians dealing with the origin of human life in general, had placed the arrival of the first humans at particular places:

> Many lands claimed the honour of Earth's first human progeny…The Boeotians boasted: 'The Titan Prometheus took our clay, which Ge provided, breathed into the form and it came alive. Look here at Panopea, here are the clay stands left over from that first man.' But other Boeotians disagreed: 'Everyone knows that our ancestor Alalcomeneus was the first man. He came out of the water, rising like a seal from Lake Copais…It was not enough for Mother Earth (the Athenians said) that animals and mere vegetables should possess the world. She made man out of her earthy body so that she could see intelligence at work, and feel the devotion of such beings. Of course, she chose to begin in Attica. Our Attic earth was pure and fertile ground for the generation of such a being, who would surpass all others in reason and give due worship to the gods. Cecrops was the first being of this kind, mortal but not yet wholly human, a man above but a serpent below the waist'. But that claim got black looks from the people of Argos. Phoroneus was their first man, who had come to land out of conjunction of the river and the sea. When Prometheus stole fire from the gods, Phoroneus taught the Argives how to use this gift. Armed with holy fire, they claimed to be the first people to emerge from the savage world of beasts (Foss, 1994, pp. 102–3).

And human nature being what it is, as the anthropologists have taught us, such local creation-myths would have served as much to reinforce local pride as to foster the projection of what was held as being locally estimable to humanity as a whole. The claims of the Athenians, just noted, are of particular relevance here. Nor was it only the speculations of the Ionian philosophers which encouraged the Greeks to think of 'man' in general, rather than specific or local, terms: the accounts of Herodotus – many of which today are seen as no less speculative than those of the philosophers, although given great credence at the time and for long afterwards – had at least the effect of awakening Greek thought to a diversity of creation-myths and ways of being in the world, in short, of reinforcing the idea that, the diversity of surface appearances notwithstanding, some common 'humanity' must necessarily exist:

> The ferment of ideas towards the close of the fifth century B.C. brought to the fore a number of conceptions...further developed and elaborated in later generations: the notion of a single universal and permanent 'human nature'; the belief that certain physical attributes are common to all men; the concept of a human unity made up of diverse elements; the rejection of traditional divisions between men as artificial and relative, not natural or absolute; the picture of 'civilised man' as the human norm (Baldry, 1965, p. 52).

Aristotle, with whom we shall principally deal in the next section, was to give an account of his predecessors, or at least of what he believed them to have held—an account which, we should note, was to be taken as definitive until the much later recovery and interpretation of such fragmented writings as are still extant:

> Thales, the founder of this (the Ionian] school of philosophy, says the permanent entity is water (which is why he also propounded that the earth floats on water). Presumably he derived this assumption from seeing that the nutrition of everything is moist, and that heat itself is generated from moisture and depends upon it for its existence (and that from which a thing is generated is always its first principle)... Anaximenes and Diogenes held that air is prior to water, and is of all corporeal elements most truly the first principle. Hippasus of Metapontum and Heraclitus of Ephesus held this of fire; and Empedocles – adding earth as a fourth to those already mentioned – takes all four. These, he says, always persist, and are only generated in respect of multitude and paucity, according as they are combined into unity or differentiated out of unity. Anaxagoras of Clazomenæ – prior to Empedocles in point of age, but posterior in his activities – says that the first principles are infinite in number. For he says that as a general rule all things which are, like fire and water, homoeomerous, are generated and destroyed in this sense only, by combination and differentiation; otherwise they are neither generated nor destroyed, but persist eternally (*Metaphysics* I. iii: 5, 8–9; tr Tredennick, 1936).

PLATO, ARISTOTLE, AND THE *SCALA NATURÆ* ('LADDER OF NATURE')

The Ionians, then, had advanced ideas of fluidity of matter and movement through time which, however speculative and, as we now know, erroneous, might have in many fields yielded eventually, through reason and experiment, scientific accounts as we now understand them, not least being that of evolutionary biology. (We recall, in this respect and more recently, the rise and then disproof of ideas such as 'phlogiston,' 'ether,' and élan vital.) But the Greeks, masters of Reason, were little inclined towards Experiment – 'With very few exceptions, the Ancient Greeks throughout a period of eight hundred years made no attempt at systematic experimentation' (Sambursky, 1956, p. 2) – and in any event, this promising start in the direction of scientific truth was to come to a halt with the doctrines of Plato (428–348) and Aristotle (384–322), which by the sheer weight of their ancient authority were to underpin science (and later, inform theology) far beyond fourth-century Greece.

Aristotle's own views had developed partly as an extension of, and partly in reaction to, the fundamental agenda which Plato had set:

> The first is an answer to the question: *Why* is there any World of Becoming, in addition to the eternal World of Ideas, or, indeed, to the one supreme Idea? The second is an answer to the question: What principle determines the number of kinds of being that make up the sensible and temporal world? And the answer to the second question is for Plato—or at all events for the philosopher who holds forth in the dialogue [*Timaeus*] implicit in the answer to the first (Lovejoy, 1961, p. 46).

The 'principle of plenitude,' an expression which Arthur Lovejoy claims as his own, involved:

> …us[ing] the term to cover a wider range of inferences from premises identical with Plato's than he himself draws; i.e., not only the thesis that the universe is a *plenum formarum* in which the range of diversity of *kinds* of living things is exhaustively exemplified, but also any other deductions from the assumption that no genuine potentiality of being can remain unfulfilled, that the extent and abundance of the creation must be as great as the possibility of existence and commensurate with the productive capacity of a 'perfect' and inexhaustible Source, and that the world is the better, the more things it contains' (Lovejoy, 1961, p. 52, italics in original).

And, for Plato, we know that this was not as a matter of observation or experiment, but arose from logical necessity:

> The Idea of the Good is a necessary reality; it cannot be other than what its essence implies; and it therefore must, by virtue of its own nature, necessarily engender finite existents. And the number of kinds of these is equally predetermined logically; the Absolute would not be what it is if it gave rise to anything less than a complete world

Figure 1.1   Portrait of Plato (c. 427–347 BC), thought to be a first-century Roman copy of an original by the Greek sculptor Silanion. Courtesy of the Fitzwilliam Museum, Cambridge.

in which the 'model,' i.e., the totality of ideal Forms, is translated into concrete realities. It follows that every sensible thing that is, is because it – or at all events, its sort – cannot but be, and be precisely what it is' (Lovejoy, 1961, p. 54).

The Platonic world, then, admitted of diversity – for to suppose otherwise would be to allow for a deficiency in the imagination of the Absolute, and therefore be self-contradictory – but not of any essential change, for this too would suppose that an imperfect world had once been brought into being by the Absolute. In such a world there is no room for 'evolution', in any sense.

But Plato's teachings were to have greater influence in the fields of government and ethics (and much later, religion, in the form of Neoplatonism) than in the field of biology. His pupil, Aristotle, was to have the more enduring influence here:

Aristotle's physical doctrine was accepted as dogma for sixty generations. No other personality in the history of science, and very few in the whole course of human culture, had so deep and long-lasting an influence on subsequent thought. Already in the Ancient World Aristotle's views, or the views propounded in his name, bore the stamp of a supreme authority which only a few bold spirits dared to reject...His influence on physical science and the general picture of the cosmos was on the whole more negative than positive. For this there were two main reasons: Aristotle's approach to natural phenomena sprang from a conception which held no key to the physical world, although it did have something to offer for the biological sciences, in which Aristotle's achievements were greatest. Moreover, Aristotle tended to fit all his findings into fixed patterns and then to construct on them a general theory which he declared absolute (Sambursky, 1956, pp. 80–81).

It is not Aristotle-the-observer with whom we could have much quarrel; his observations of the nature and development of plants and animals in *De Partibus Animalium* ('Parts of Animals'), *De Generatione Animalium* ('Generation of Animals'), *De Anima* ('Soul'), and elsewhere, were to be long unrivalled as, for example, in the following:

But there is one other remarkable feature that he knew before it was rediscovered, almost in our own time. In certain male cuttle-fishes, in the breeding season, one of the arms develops in a curious fashion into a long coiled whip-lash, and in the act of breeding may then be transferred to the mantle-cavity of the female. Cuvier himself knew nothing of the nature or the function of this separated arm. And indeed, it was he who mistook it for a parasitic worm. But Aristotle tells us of its use and its temporary development, and of its structure in detail, and his description tallies clearly with the accounts of the most recent writers (Thompson, 1921, p. 146).

And along much the same lines:

For men of science, the *Generation of Animals* has a special interest, in that it is the first systematic treatise on animal reproduction and embryology, containing records of observations, marking out schemes of classification, and suggesting methods of dealing with problems, much of which has proved of permanent value; indeed, Aristotle's work was not resumed until after the lapse of nearly two thousand years, and some of his observations were not repeated until comparatively recent times (Peck, 1963, p. vi).

Aristotle was, however, to leave behind more than just a model of how the inquiring naturalist should proceed; he was to leave a powerful idea:

> There are in the Platonic dialogues occasional intimations that the Ideas, and therefore their sensible counterparts, are not all of equal metaphysical rank or excellence; but this conception not only of existences but also of essences as hierarchically ordered remains in Plato only a vague tendency, not a definitely formulated doctrine. In spite of Aristotle's recognition of the multiplicity of possible patterns of classification, it was he who chiefly suggested to naturalists and philosophers of later times the idea of arranging (at least) all animals in a single gradual *scala naturæ* according to their degree of 'perfection'. For the criterion of rank in this scale he sometimes took the degree of development reached by the offspring at birth; there resulted, he conceived, eleven general grades, with man at the top and zoophytes at the bottom (Lovejoy, 1961, p. 58).

> The result was the conception of the plan and structure of the world which, through the Middle Ages and down to the late eighteenth century, many philosophers, most men of science, and, indeed, most educated men were to accept without question— the conception of the universe as a 'Great Chain of Being,' composed of an immense, or – by the strict but seldom rigorously applied logic of the principle of continuity – of an infinite, number of links ranging in hierarchical order from the meagerest kind of existence, which barely escape non-existence, through 'every possible' grade up to the *ens perfectissimum* – or, in a somewhat more orthodox version, to the highest possible kind of creature, between which and the Absolute Being the disparity was assumed to be infinite – every one of them differing from that immediately above and immediately below it by the 'least possible' degree of difference (Lovejoy, 1961, p. 59).

Yet, we still ask, what is the problem here?—Charles Darwin made frequent use of the words 'higher' and 'lower' in his *Origin of Species*, and was particularly insistent upon the truth and relevance of 'that old canon in natural history,' *Natura non facit saltum* ('Nature does not make a leap'). Perhaps we should follow D'Arcy Thompson in ascribing to Aristotle a greater flexibility and less rigidity than Lovejoy would appear to allow:

> Many commentators have sought for Aristotle's 'classification of animals'; for my part I have never found it, and, in our sense of the word, I am certain that it is not there. An unbending, unchanging classification of animals would have been something foreign to all his logic; it is all very well, it becomes practically necessary, when we have to arrange our animals on the shelves of a museum or in the arid pages of a 'systematic' catalogue; and it takes a new complexion when, or if, we can attain to a real or historical classification, following lines of actual descent and based on proven facts of historical evolution. But Aristotle (as it seems to me) neither was

bound to a museum catalogue nor indulged in visions either of a complete *scala naturæ* or of an hypothetical phylogeny. He classified animals as he found them and, as a logician, he had a dichotomy for every difference which presented itself to his mind (Thompson, 1921, p. 158).

Yet it seems to me that Thompson has, in the enthusiasm for his subject, largely missed the point: we may grant Aristotle's skill and flexibility as a taxonomist, but changing taxonomic labels does not imply that the creatures to which such labels have been attached have themselves changed through time, or in short, that 'evolution' in any sense has occurred. In fact, it can be argued that, for Aristotle at least, creatures were what they were and where they were *of necessity*, and hence of unchanging essential form and function – the complete antithesis of any notion of 'evolution', but an idea which was nevertheless 'accepted as dogma for sixty generations', not least of which were those of the Greeks who were his more immediate successors.

Given however the wealth of observation and attempts at functional classification (as noted above) there is always the temptation to suppose that Aristotle had in the background of his thought, or at least was edging towards, some notion of 'evolution', in much the way as the next great taxonomist, Linnaeus, was to do two millennia later. But there is no good reason to suppose that this was in fact the case, and every reason, from an appreciation of the intellectual framework which he had inherited from Plato, that this could never have been the case.

Aristotle did not simply add observation to Plato's philosophical framework:

From the Platonic principle of plenitude the principle of continuity could be directly deduced. If there is between two given natural species a theoretically possible intermediate type, that type must be realized – and so on *ad indefinitum*; otherwise, there would be gaps in the universe, the creation would not be as 'full' as it might be, and this would imply the inadmissible consequence that its Source or Author was not 'good', in the sense which that adjective has in the *Timaeus* (Lovejoy, 1961, p. 58).

Observation and continuity – how agreeably 'evolutionary', even 'Darwinian', we might yet be tempted to conclude. But we should be wrong to so do, for Aristotle's own logic precludes an ingredient essential to any 'evolutionary' account, that of change through time. For if a species were to exist now which had not previously existed it would imply a gap diachronically no less contradictory to the 'good' than a corresponding gap synchronically. Yet there are sufficient passages in Aristotle, particularly those which bear upon development of the individual organism, for it to have been argued that, from our contemporary perspective and however he might have seen himself, Aristotle yet deserves the title of 'evolutionist'.

This is the possibility ('Was Aristotle an Evolutionist?') once addressed directly and at length by Harry Torrey and Frances Felin. Their negative finding, after examination of the texts and previous argument in favour of the proposition, is worth quoting at length, not least because of what it has to say concerning the role of preconceptions in science, from Aristotle to the precursors of modern evolutionary theory (and, dare we suggest, still today):

> There were no facts available to the Harvard botanist [Asa] Gray that were not equally accessible to the Harvard zoologist [Louis] Agassiz. What separated them were not facts but preconceptions. Gray was ready to accept the idea of specific mutability, Agassiz, on the other hand, continued vigorously to reaffirm his old conviction that species were categories of the Creator's thought, divine and immutable.
>
> Similarly, Aristotle had adopted early and retained throughout his life the conception of immutable specific types. Yet the evidence in favor of the fixity of specific types is surely no weightier than the evidence for their mutability. Neither Aristotle nor Agassiz could demonstrate their convictions. Nevertheless, they held them, and looked without enthusiasm on all suggestions to the contrary.
>
> It is idle to inquire whether, had Aristotle held Agassiz's professorship at Harvard, he would have approved *The Origin of Species*. To do so, he would have been obliged to revolutionize his conception of species, accelerating the process by revolutionizing his conception of adaptation as well. For adaptations to Aristotle were manifestations of eternal ends. The significance of vestigial organs appears to have eluded him entirely...Discovery, in fact, was but the recognition of such ends in terms of final causes. They were not causes at all in the modern scientific sense. On the contrary, they turned his eyes away from causal mechanisms and postponed for many long sterile centuries the prime discovery of the working hypothesis (Torrey and Felin, 1937, p. 16).

Teleology can have no place in any true evolutionary theory, but chance must. Aristotle was a teleologist *par excellence* and, consequently, would admit of no great role for chance. To take but one source (*De Partibus Animalium*) for illustration of this, beginning with the question of 'cause':

> ...we see that there are more causes than one concerned in the formation of natural things: there is the Cause for *the sake of which* the thing is formed, and the Cause for which the *beginning of the motion* is due. Therefore another point for us to decide is which of these two Causes stands first, and which comes second. Clearly the first is that which we call the 'Final' cause – that for the sake of which the thing is formed – since that is the *logos* of the thing – its rational ground, and the *logos* is always the beginning for products of Nature as well as for those of Art (*De Part. An.*, I. i [639b15], tr Peck, 1968, italics in original).

Thus Aristotle, after then dismissing the role of chance as he believes it to have been taken by Empedocles ('So Empedocles was wrong when he said that many of the characteristics which animals have are due to some accident in the process of their formation' [640a20]), comes, in a perhaps question-begging way, to fit 'man' into the picture:

Art is the *logos* of the article without the matter. And similarly with the products of chance: they are formed by the same processes that art would employ. So the best way of putting the matter would be to say that *because* the essence of man is what it is, *therefore* a man has such and such parts, since there cannot be a man without them. If we may not say this, then the nearest to it must do, viz., that there cannot be a man at all otherwise than with them, or, that it is well that a man should have them. And upon this these considerations follow: Because man is such and such, therefore the process of his formation must of necessity be such and such and take place in such a manner; which is why first this part is formed, then that. And this similarly with all the things that are constructed by Nature (*De Part. An.*, I. i [640a30, 640b], tr Peck, 1968, italics in original).

BEYOND ARISTOTLE

Aristotle's legacy was two-fold: on the positive side (as we would see it) he had replaced speculation with fact; on the negative side (as we must now also see it), he had advanced a fundamentally 'un-evolutionary' scheme of nature. Given his magisterial authority it is little wonder that with his passing (in 322) the impulse towards original thought in biology generally, let alone in any 'evolutionary' direction, should have largely come to an end amongst the Greeks. A younger contemporary of Aristotle, Theophrastus (*c.* 371–287), wrote extensively on biological matters, notably regarding plants, but how much of what we now know of his writings was original with him, and how much is derived from Aristotelian texts which are no longer extant, is uncertain. In any event:

With the death of Theophrastus about 287 B.C. pure biological science substantially disappears from the Greek world, and we get the same type of deterioration that is later encountered in other scientific departments. Science ceases to have the motive of the desire to know, and becomes an applied study, subservient to the practical arts (Singer, 1921, p. 183).

Theophrastus has, nevertheless, been regarded as more than just a relatively minor post-Aristotelian biologist. There is, first, his teaching (as claimed by Porphyry) of a practical explanation for common humanity:

So in my opinion there are two grounds for saying that there is kinship or a common relationship between Greek and Greek, and between barbarian and barbarian, and indeed between all men; either because they spring from the same ancestors, or because they share the same upbringing and ways and the same stock. Hence we regard all men as akin and related to each other; and indeed for all animals the beginnings from which their bodies have developed are the same (quoted Baldry, 1965, p. 143).

And second, he had raised the problem of the notions of, and the distinction between, the 'wise' and the 'unwise' man, a matter of concern to Socrates (469–

399) and Plato after him, but of 'comparatively little importance' (Baldry, 1965, p. 145) to Aristotle. (The 'wise man' in *Metaphysics* I. ii, 2 ff. 'knows all things…', but this is wisdom-as-knowledge, rather than wisdom-in-judgement, which is the question at issue here.)

Greeks, Athenians especially, of the fourth century had every reason for considering these – the 'unity of mankind' and the nature of the 'wise' and 'unwise' – to be questions of importance. The Delian League (478), of the Greeks united against the Persians, was but a distant memory, of a time of amity before the outbreak of the first Peloponnesian War (461) between Athens and Sparta – in which, as Thucydides recorded, the war began with 'the rest of the Greek nation…inclining towards one side or the other, some at once, others having only the intention,' in which 'the Other' was no longer non-Greek but a fellow Greek (with all the usual consequent demonising in time of war) – which finally ended (404) almost as the fifth century itself did, with the defeat and destruction of Athens. Insofar as the 'nature of man' had been taken as a projection of 'being Greek,' it would surely have been now seen as being something less than admirable, even, perhaps, not greatly different from that of the 'lower' beasts. And there had been more than sufficient folly on all sides for the idea to form – or to the extent that it had been overlooked, rediscovered – that a man was 'wise' by virtue of other things than aristocratic birth or demagogic skill.

Aristotle may well have, as we have seen, put the lid on progress in biology (and obviously, 'evolutionary biology') for the (long) time being. But there was one area left open for speculation, an area which raised directly the question of Man as a species-being, and which was to preoccupy his contemporaries and immediate successors in the Greek world, their later Roman followers, and through (or in reaction to) them, Christian writers to the present day.

We return to the *scala naturæ*, and with it that 'highest possible kind of creature, between which and the Absolute Being the disparity was assumed to be infinite' (Lovejoy, *supra*). Aristotle, whilst employing various schemes of classification, was bound, logically, to find them all in agreement when it came to this 'highest creature' (however they might give different rankings further down the scale). Soul (*psychê*) was one such criterion which, moreover, gave a unique position to Man:

> In the *De Anima* another [in addition to the strictly physical] hierarchical arrangement of all organisms is suggested, which was destined to a greater influence upon subsequent philosophy and natural history. It is based on the 'powers of soul' possessed by them, from the nutritive, to which plants are limited, to the rational, characteristic of man 'and possibly another kind superior to his', each higher order possessing all the powers of those below it in the scale, and an additional differentiating one of its own. Either scheme, as carried out by Aristotle himself, provided a series composed of only a small number of large classes, the sub-species of which were not necessarily capable of a similar ranking (Lovejoy, 1961, p. 58–9).

More explicitly, we are told:

The different 'parts' or 'faculties' of Soul can be arranged in a series in a definite order, so that the possession of any one of them implies the possession of all those which precede it in the list:

(1) nutritive Soul   in all plants
(2) sentient Soul   in all animals
(3) appetitive Soul   in some animals
(4) locomotive Soul   in some animals
(5) rational Soul   in man only
(Peck, 1968, pp. 84–5).

Much could be (and indeed, has been) written on the matter of 'soul', or more exactly, on the proper rendering and connotations of the Greek *psychê*; but we must be content here with dealing not directly with this matter, but with the views of just two schools of thought for whom the characterization of the 'wise' man – and by implication, of what it was that 'man' had it in his nature to be, or not to be – was an application of the faculty of 'rational Soul,' defining a fundamental polarity in Greek thought at that time: the Epicureans and the Stoics.

We are at a disadvantage in dealing with these 'philosophers of self-consciousness' (Marx) in that so little of their original writings is now known to us, and so much of what was said concerning what they held has come down to us through a variety of later late-Hellenistic and Roman writers – Plutarch, Seneca, Epictetus, Cicero, Marcus Aurelius, to name but some of the more notable – each of whom had his own interpretation to give, and his own philosophical barrow to push. We can, however, at least accept a modern synoptic account to start with:

The Stoa believed that man was not an isolated creature but a member of a community; while the Epicureans said that the wise man would not take part in public affairs, unless obliged to, the Stoics said that he would unless prevented. Its less human side came from the single-minded insistence that only virtue is good, such things as health, position, pleasure, being 'indifferent', and that all emotions were bad (emotion is defined as 'irrational and unnatural movement of the soul'). The wise man is as far from feeling pity as he is from feeling envy; and 'just as you drown as surely when one inch under the water as on the bottom', so every act which fails even by a little to be perfect is bad, every man who fails to be perfectly wise is a fool. Wise men are very rare; therefore virtually all men are bad, incapable of a truly good action (Dover, 1980, p. 151).

We can gain some leverage on the question of the 'nature of man' as it had by then developed in Greek thought by explaining, however briefly, how these contrasting positions were arrived at.

The Epicureans, one cannot help but feel, might as well have come out of the late twentieth century (A.D.) as of the early fourth century (B.C.): they were the supreme individualists. 'Whereas Plato and Aristotle saw the city-state as a natural institution founded on natural justice, man being by nature a "political" animal and living in society "for the sake of the good life", Epicurus regarded the *polis* as an artificial arrangement originating in a "social contract" for mutual protection' (Baldry, 1965, pp. 147–8. italics in original); and lest it be thought that the claim just made to modernity of the Epicureans be exaggerated: 'There is no such thing as human society; each individual looks out for himself; there is no-one who feels affection for another, except for his own benefit' (Lactantius, quoted Baldry, 1965, p. 146, with the caution that this might be from a 'hostile source').

If the Epicureans should appear to us today to have an almost 'survival of the fittest,' 'biological,' approach to the formation of community – was 'Epicurean man' a forebear of *Homo œconomicus*? – Stoic belief derived from quite the opposite – not just from the application, as with the Epicureans also, of rationality as the defining characteristic of 'man', but of action as an expression of 'the doctrine that the entire cosmos is permeated and governed by a *Logos*, a divine principle of rationality, which is implanted in the form of reason in every human soul' (Baldry, 1965, p. 151, italics in original).

CONCLUSION

There was no word in Greek which properly translates into our word 'evolution,' in anything like our modern sense. That the idea as such should not have formed in the Greek mind is scarcely surprising given that, as we have seen, what could have been a promising start in this direction – a start which at least had within it the seeds of fulfilment of a 'theory of evolution' as initially suggested here – was to be effectively brought to an end by Aristotle.

So far as the 'nature of man' goes, we could well ask whether we should not see it as indicative of the long journey of Greek thought across nearly six centuries that the maxim 'know thyself' should find expression, in a way, in the title of a comedy by the Roman Hellenist, P. Terentius Afer ('Terence', *c.* 190–159), *Heautontimorumenos*, which translates as 'The Self-Tormenter'. Still, and for all that that might signify, there is yet a sensibility which was to be passed from the Greek world to the Roman, and beyond, to the present:

MENEDEMUS: Chreme, tantumne est ab re tua oti tibi
Aliena ut cures, eaque nihil quae ad te attinent?

CHREMES: Homo sum: humani nihil a me alienum puto.
Vel me monere hoc, vel percontari puta.
Rectum est? ego ut faciam: non est? te ut deterream.
(*Heautontimorumenos*, I.i,23).

MENEDEMUS: Have you so much leisure, Chremes, from your own affairs, that you can attend to those of others-those which don't concern you?

CHREMES: I am a man, and nothing that concerns a man do I deem a matter of indifference to me. Suppose that I wish either to advise you in this matter, or to be informed myself: if what you do is right, that I may do the same; if it is not, then that I may dissuade you (tr Riley, 1874).

REFERENCES

Baldry, H.C. (1965), *The Unity of Mankind in Greek Thought*, Cambridge, U.K.: Cambridge University Press.

Dover, K.J. (ed.) (1980), *Ancient Greek Literature*, Oxford and New York: Oxford University Press.

Foss, M. (1994), *Gods and Heroes. The story of Greek mythology*, London: Michael O'Mara Books Limited.

Kahn, Charles H. (1960), *Anaximander and the Origins of Greek Cosmology*, New York: Columbia University Press.

Lambridis, H. (1976), *Empedocles (with an introductory essay Empedocles and T.S. Eliot by Marshall McLuhan)*, Studies in the humanities No. 15, Alabama: The University of Alabama Press.

Leonard, W.E. (1908), *The Fragments of Empedocles* (Open Court paperback edition, 1973), La Salle, U.S.: Open Court Publishing Company.

Lovejoy, A.O. (1961), *The Great Chain of Being. A Study in the History of an Idea*, Cambridge, MA: Harvard University Press.

Lyell, C. (1832), *Principles of Geology* (Volume II) (University of Chicago Press reprint, 1991) London: John Murray..

O'Brien, D. (1969), *Empedocles' Cosmic Cycle. A reconstruction from the fragments and secondary sources*, Cambridge, U.K.: Cambridge University Press.

Peck, A.L. (tr) (1963), *Aristotle—Generation of Animals*, London: William Heinemann and Cambridge, MA.: Harvard University Press.

Peck, A.L. (tr) (1968), *Aristotle in twenty-three volumes*, Vol. XII, 'Parts of Animals', London: William Heinemann and Cambridge, MA: Harvard University Press.

Riley, H.T. (1874), *The Comedies of Terence*, New York: Harper and Brothers.

Sambursky, S. (1956), *The Physical World of the Greeks*, London: Routledge and Kegan Paul.

Singer, C. (1921), 'Biology', in R.W. Livingstone (ed.), *The Legacy of Greece*, Oxford: Clarendon Press.

Thompson, D.W. (1921), 'Natural Science', in R.W. Livingstone (ed.), *The Legacy of Greece*, Oxford: Clarendon Press.

Torrey, H.B. and F. Felin (1937), 'Was Aristotle an Evolutionist?', *Quarterly Review of Biology*, **12** (1), 1–18.

Tredennick, H. (tr and ed.) (1936), *Aristotle. The Metaphysics, Books I–IX*, London: William Heinemann and Cambridge MA: Harvard University Press.

2. Augustine on Economic Man

John Laurent

In a couple of previously published articles (Laurent, 1991, 1998), I have looked at what appears to be a consensus among most economists on the subject of human nature – that 'economic man', or *Homo œconomicus*, is essentially a self-interested species, whose inner life need not concern us greatly – notwithstanding occasional dissenting voices, including the Australian R.F. Irvine, and also John Maynard Keynes. In my article on Keynes, and in a chapter in an earlier edited book (Laurent and Nightingale, 2001), I mentioned that there is a copy of the first printed edition (Rome, 1467) of St Augustine's (i.e. of Hippo, North Africa, 354–430 A.D., to distinguish him from the St Augustine of Canterbury, d. *c.* 605 A.D.) *De Civitate Dei*, or *The City of God*, amongst Keynes's books in the library of King's College, Cambridge, and that, for what it is worth (Keynes read Latin, at least as a student, and the book was in any case available to him in English translation[1]), there is much interesting material on human nature in this work, including the view that sociability is a characteristic feature of the human as well as other species. As mentioned in this article and chapter, among the living creation, according to Augustine, were 'some creatures that love to be alone...and others that had rather live in flocks and companies, as doves, star[ling]s, stags, hinds, and suchlike', and 'there is nothing in the world so sociable by nature...as man is' (Augustine, 1944–5, vol.1, pp. 366, 370).[2] This present chapter will explore this dimension of Augustine's thought further, focusing on his understanding of human nature as presented in Book XIX of *The City of God*—an understanding that can be seen as not only more convincing than the arid '*Homo œconomicus*' of much economic writing, but also as having anticipated fuller and richer evolutionary conceptions of human nature to some extent, including Darwin's.

Augustine would not have used the term 'economic man' as we do, let alone 'economics' (which would appear to have first been used in English in the way that we now commonly employ it in around 1802), though the concept of an 'economy of nature', in the sense of a divinely ordered system (see Hodgson, 1994, Chapter 2), would have been familiar to him.[3] But Augustine was nevertheless deeply interested in questions of human nature, in secular as well as theological contexts, and wrote extensively on the subject in *The City of God* and elsewhere; and it is perhaps worth examining some of his ideas in terms of the historical background to some of our current views on this vexed subject. Specifically, besides having become intrigued by this topic after turning the pages of Keynes's magnificent volume, I was prompted to look into it more closely by an article on 'Platonic deception' in *History of Political Economy* some years ago (Moss, 1996), in which the author argues that the tradition of self-interested 'rational' economic man can be traced ultimately to Plato (whose 'deception' consisted in his advocacy, for the administration of social order, of civic leaders – in *The Republic* – employing trickery to ensure 'that the best of the male stock can be made to mate with the best of the female', quoted Moss, 1996, p. 537), and has been bequeathed to us via such writers as Niccolo Machiavelli, Thomas Hobbes and Bernard Mandeville.

Yet there are other understandings of human nature which can be traced back to Plato and the other ancients, as Geoff Fishburn has shown in the previous chapter. And Machiavelli – best known for such remarks, in *The Prince*, as 'this may be said of men generally: they are ungrateful, fickle, feigners and dissemblers, avoiders of danger, eager for gain' – could nevertheless reserve a place for '*virtù*' in human affairs, albeit in his own conception of the term, which Bernard Crick (1970) describes as having more to do with 'courage, fortitude, audacity, skill and civic spirit' (see also Nederman, 2000), and which Machiavelli probably learnt in part from Plato's student, Aristotle (see Aristotle, 1979, pp.130–1 and *passim*). Machiavelli may also have learnt something from Augustine, who discusses the 'virtues' of the early Romans in Book V of *The City of God*, and who indeed considered their desire for military glory 'a vice closer to a virtue' (Budziszewski, 1986, pp. 161–3). Certainly the idea that there may be similarities between our social nature and that of other species did not originate with Augustine, as quoted above. The idea is at least intimated in Plato's *Republic*, as where Socrates asks Glaucon whether 'community can [not] possibly subsist among men, as it can among other animals?' (Plato, 1997, p. 69), and Aristotle (1979, p. 74), too, believed that 'man is by nature a social being'. But arguably it was Augustine who most fully developed these ideas in antiquity, so that, in this sense as well as others, it may be claimed that the history of Western philosophy can be read as a 'series of footnotes' to both Plato and Augustine (Pelikan, 1987, p. 140).

What was Augustine's view? It is true, firstly, that based on the internal evidence of *The City of God*, the *Confessions* and other surviving writings, Augustine does not seem to have been *directly* greatly influenced by Plato in this matter. Having never learnt to read Greek with facility (see Brown, 1990, p. 36), Augustine was obliged to rely mainly on second-hand versions of Plato's and the other Greeks' ideas from the Latin translations of second and third-century

A.D. Neoplatonists such as Plotinus (as in fact Augustine tells us in the *Confessions* – Augustine, 1961, pp. 144 ff.), as well as other Latin writers, notably Virgil, Sallust and Cicero. But while these writers undoubtedly had distinctive emphases of their own, they nevertheless can in some cases be seen to have more fully developed certain key elements in Plato. Thus, in *The Republic*, there is much incidental reference to the human 'soul' (or, as we might translate, 'mind'), as where Socrates says that the 'soul of each individual [can be] divided into three parts' according to which 'one part [is] the organ whereby a man learns...another that whereby he shows spirit [and a] third...we call appetitive' (Plato, 1997, p. 305). Compare this account with Plotinus' extended discussion of 'On Sense-Perception and Memory' in the *Enneads*, Book IV, chapter 6, which contains such observations as the following: 'It is clear, presumably in every case, that when we have a perception of anything through the sense of sight, we look there where it is and direct our gaze where the visible object is situated in a straight line from us; obviously it is there that the apprehension takes place and the soul turns outwards' (Plotinus, 1984, vol.4, p. 321).

When we turn to Augustine on this subject of the functioning of the 'soul', we find that he has elaborated still further on Plato's rudimentary account. While Plotinus makes no reference to non-human species in Book IV of the *Enneads*, Augustine, in *The Free Choice of the Will*, writes as follows:

> I think it is...clear that the inner sense perceives not only what it receives from the bodily senses but also the senses themselves. For if the beast were not aware of its act of perception, it could not otherwise direct its movements toward something, or away from it...The beast could not open its eyes at all or turn its gaze towards the thing that it wants to see were it not for the fact that while its eyes were closed or not fixed upon the object, it perceived that it was not seeing. But if it is conscious of its not seeing when in fact it does not see, it must also be aware of its seeing when it does see (Augustine, 1968, p. 119).

Today, there would be little discussion about the kinds of psychological processes discussed by Plotinus and Augustine without some reference to comparisons between humans and other species, largely due to the influence of Darwinism. In this, Augustine can be seen to have been remarkably modern in outlook, at least compared with his contemporaries. To describe Augustine as a 'Darwinian' would obviously be a misrepresentation—he is, after all, the same writer who could pen things like 'all Christians holding the Catholic faith believe that the bodily death lies upon mankind by no law of nature, as if God had made man mortal, but as due punishment for sin' (Augustine, 1944–5, vol. 2, p. 11). Yet as Barry Gordon (1975) has pointed out, a common conception of Augustine's time, that the human personality is essentially the pliable subject of external pressures, was overturned to a large extent by Augustine, the commonly accepted view becoming 'no longer a being who can represent human nature in its full dimensions' (Gordon, 1975, p. 103). And there are elements in Augustine's writing that indeed invite comparison with Darwin. One commentator, for example, translates some lines in Book XII, chapter 3 of *The City of God* to read '[I]t is absurd to regard the beasts and trees and other things mutable and mortal...as deserving blame...In the struggle for life, some perish and others succeed; the less give way to the greater, and are changed into the qualities of the predominant type', and describes these words in a footnote as 'an anticipation of the modern theory of "the struggle for life" and natural selection founded most probably on Lucretius' *De Rerum Natura*' (Hitchcock, 1900, p. 79).[4] The authors of a recent biography of Darwin compare Augustine's account of Creation – which he likened to the growth of a tree from its seed (which has the *potential* to become a tree, but only through a long, slow process) – as 'a theory of evolution...in all but name' (White and Gribbin, 1996, p. 31).[5] Augustine also reminds us of Darwin in his treatment of the 'soul' (for which he uses various terms, including *anima, spiritus, mens, ratio, intelligentia* and *intellectus*—seemingly interchangeably: see, e.g., Augustine, 1991, p. 164, footnote 60), as in the last quoted passage from *The Free Choice of the Will*. Three pages further on in this work Augustine refers (through the voice of his interlocutor, Evodius) to 'the inner sense which directs the soul of the beast to open its eyes when they are closed and to supply what it perceives is missing' (Augustine, 1968, p. 122), and earlier he elaborates as follows: 'Now the power enabling the animal to see is one thing, that by which it shuns or seeks what it perceives is something else. The former is located in the eye, the latter within the soul itself' (ibid., p. 116). Elsewhere in *The Free Choice of the Will* Augustine writes:

> We also notice, and admit the fact, that brute animals see and hear and have the power to perceive corporeal qualities by smell, taste, and touch, and that frequently their perceptions are keener than ours...Certainly qualities of this kind are possessed by us in common with the brute animals (ibid, pp. 88–9).

In *The City of God* Augustine (1944–5, vol. 1, p. 336) says of the 'unreasonable creatures' that their senses 'contain no knowledge, yet some likeness of knowledge there is in them', and in a commentary on the Gospel of John (1988, p. 78) he tells his readers 'You do not differ from an animal, except in intellect'. However this may be, Augustine's understanding of 'human nature' clearly encompassed the idea that, whatever else it is, it is something that we share with the other creatures. And prominent in this notion was the propensity for sociality. Augustine wrote most fully on this subject in Book XIX of *The City of God*, that part of the work which most specifically addresses the question of man's *political* nature. As in earlier chapters of the book, Augustine has much to say about the noble qualities of the first Romans, whose 'very unity [was], as it were, the health of the people' (Augustine, 1981, p. 890). Here we see Augustine's use of the *organic* metaphor of society – the 'body politic' – a device later much used by evolutionary writers like Herbert Spencer and A.R. Wallace (who, for example, once asked how long legislators and economists were going to put up with the ills of late nineteenth-century industrial society 'patching here, altering there, now mitigating the severity of a distressing symptom…but never going down to the root of the evil'[6]). For Augustine, civil society was part of the natural order, the 'divine economy', the whole of which he saw as a living organism[7]—and this organic conception of society also owed something to Plato, as in these lines from *The Republic*:

> That city then is best conducted…which comes nearest to the condition of an individual man. Thus, when one of our fingers is hurt, the whole fellowship that spreads through the body up to the soul, and there forms an organised unity under the governing principle, is sensible to the hurt, and there is a universal and simultaneous feeling of pain in sympathy with the wounded part; and therefore we say that the *man* has a pain in his finger: and in speaking of any part of our frame whatsoever, the same account may be given of the pain felt when it suffers, and the pleasure felt when it is easy.
> That same, no doubt…there is very close analogy between such a case and the condition of the best-governed state (Plato, 1997, p. 164).

Besides from Plato, Augustine's 'organicism' also owed much to St Paul (probably the second major influence in his thought), as where he identified the 'City of God' (the Church) with the 'Body of Christ' (Augustine, 1981, pp. 539, 1059; cf. Rom. 12.5, Eph. 5.30, 1 Cor. 12.14–27[8]). In his early work, *Regula*, Augustine told his parishioners at Hippo that they were 'gathered together into one body so that [they] may live in a spirit of unanimity and may have one soul and one heart' (cited White, 1992, p. 215).

But Augustine's organicism, arguably, was a richer conception than that of either Plato or St Paul – or of numerous more recent writers (see Hodgson, 1993, *passim*) – being informed, as it was, by his 'evolutionary' understanding of man's social nature. Organicist views of society – or the economy – have, of course, become fashionable of late in evolutionary economics, beginning perhaps with Alfred Marshall (see Nightingale, 1993) and reaching an art-form in recent years in the writing of people like Peter Weise, as in these assertions: '[E]volutionary economics may study the performance and development of economies, societies, states, institutions, systems of property rights, work teams, or enterprises. If we define economic evolution as a socioeconomic, irreversible, time-consuming process, in which an economy reproduces itself and varies its elements, we see that the principle of self-organisation is responsible for the reproducing part of evolution…[etc.]' (Weise, 1996, p. 718). The trouble with these kinds of arguments is that they are essentially mere words, difficult to tie down to specific entities. Most obviously lacking in the example just given, and in numerous other instances that can be cited (cf., e.g., Bergin and Lipman,

1996; Foster and Wild, 1996, 1999), is a clear reference to human beings. Are these the 'elements' alluded to by Weise? Whatever else an 'economy' may be (a 'system', 'network', 'web' etc.), it is, first and foremost, a collection of *people* – even if on a global scale – interacting with each other in the business of utilizing scarce resources. R.F. Irvine (1914) never tired of criticizing economists guilty of, in his view, 'putting abstractions in place of living men', and more recently Geoff Hodgson has pointed to the shortcomings of 'mainstream' economics in terms of lacking 'an adequate understanding of the human agent and the relationship of agent to social structures' (Hodgson, 1998, p. 869).

Yet even the word 'agent' – at least as it is commonly understood – hardly does justice to the complexities involved in introducing the human 'element' into our equations, and Augustine would have understood this. In fact, this very term, together with some others familiar in economics, has recently come under scrutiny in a review specifically looking at a number of new studies of Augustine's works, the reviewer concluding: '[I]n the present age, the complexity of the full picture Augustine offers may be a needed counterpoint to our contemporary talk of disembodied "agents" and "actors" and "maximizers". The light cast by such general ideas reveals a great deal, to be sure; yet the recent surge of interest in Augustine surely indicates that there is much that is left out by our contemporary accounts' (Mitchell, 1999, p. 699). What are these extra dimensions? Certainly the reviewer believes they are related to Augustine's organic understanding of the Christian community, learnt in part from St Paul: as this reviewer notes concerning one of the books discussed (Hannah Arendt's *Love and Saint Augustine*), for Augustine, the self's relationship with others is resolvable only through a negation of the same in which it ceases 'to be anything but a member, and [its] entire being lies in the connection of all members in Christ' (ibid., p. 702).

But Augustine was thinking of more than the Christian community in *The City of God*, and his 'organicism' took on a more specific meaning. For him, human beings *generally* are necessarily connected with each other as members of earthly society, as social beings. As Arendt's volume is quoted: 'Love extends to all people in the *Civitas Dei*, just as interdependence extended equally to all in the *Civitas Terrena*' (ibid., p. 703). And in this, for Augustine, we shared much of our nature with other social beings, as Darwin was later to show. Augustine, then, in a genuinely innovative contribution to attempts at understanding the human condition, was able to combine the 'organic' metaphor of society (and 'the economy') with generalisations drawn from actual observations of behaviour in humans and other species. Augustine's treatment of this subject is also most fully dealt with in Book XIX of *The City of God*, as in this passage in chapter 12:

Anyone who joins me in an examination, however slight, of human affairs, and the human nature we all share, recognizes that just as there is no man who does not wish for joy, so there is no man who does not wish for peace…[E]ven the most savage beasts…safeguard their own species by a kind of peace, by coition, by begetting and bearing young, by cherishing them and rearing them; even though most of them are not gregarious but solitary—not, that is, like sheep, deer, doves, starlings and bees, but like lions, wolves, foxes, eagles and owls. What tigress does not gently purr over her cubs, and subdue her fierceness to caress them? What kite, however solitary as he hovers over his prey, does not find a mate, build a nest, help to hatch the eggs, rear the young birds, and, as we may say, preserve with the mother of his family a domestic society as peaceful as he can make it? How much more strongly is a human being drawn by the laws of nature, so to speak, to enter upon a fellowship with all his fellow men and to keep peace with them, as far as lies in him? (Augustine, 1981, pp. 866–8).[9]

As explained, the concept of a social instinct in man and other species did not originate with Augustine; it is found in Plato's *Republic*. The idea is also adumbrated in the writing of the Roman jurist and Stoic philosopher Cicero, whose *Hortensius* greatly inspired Augustine in his youth (Augustine, 1961, p. 58) and whose whole corpus of writings, notably *De Officiis* (*On Duty*), is extensively drawn upon in *The City of God* (Brown, 1990, p. 300). *On Duty* opines, for example, that 'a desire for union to produce offspring and a concern for their young' is 'common…to all animate beings'; and Cicero argued further that:

Nature links man to man, by their participation in speech and social intercourse. Above all, she implants in him a special love for his offspring. She impels men to meet and take part in social gatherings and festivals. Thus they are driven to provide not only for their own comfort and livelihood, but also for that of their wives, children, and all others they hold dear and feel bound to protect. This responsibility stimulates their spirits, and encourages them to greater deeds (Cicero, 1948, pp. 324–5).[10]

Elsewhere in *On Duty* Cicero writes: 'As the bees do not assemble in swarms for the sake of making honeycombs, but make their honeycombs because they are gregarious by nature, so – and much more so – do men exercise their genius together in thought and action because they are naturally gregarious' (ibid., p. 383) which, while perhaps being rather dubious biology, is reminiscent of another Roman Stoic, the second-century Emperor Marcus Aurelius, whose *Meditations* argues for things like: 'the instinct for gregariousness' which shows itself 'in its first stage among the creatures without reason, when we see bees swarming, cattle herding, birds nesting in colonies' (Long, n.d., pp. 163, 231). As will be discussed in my chapter on Darwin, below, this idea was to be taken up seriously by Darwin, but for the present, it is important to note its currency amongst much earlier writers (as indeed Darwin was to acknowledge), and how this has undoubtedly had a significant, if not always conscious, influence on the thinking of numerous writers on the human condition over succeeding centuries. Certainly it is acknowledged that Augustine frequently appropriated Stoic insights – indeed it has been argued that Augustine's moral theorizing represents, besides much borrowing from Neoplatonism, 'something of a Christianized brand of Stoicism' (Torchia, 2000, p. 171) – and M. Aurelius (Long, n.d., p. 128) actually uses the phrase 'city of God' for the natural world. But arguably, the concept of a natural proclivity for social living was first treated at length in ways we would now think about this subject by Augustine, whose cogitating about the social instinct in man and the other creatures in fact comes very close to Darwin: that is to say, to the other side of the 'struggle for existence' coin, when Darwin argues for the survival value of 'co-operation' in nature based on instincts for gregariousness and sociability. Darwin elaborates most fully on this subject in chapter 4 – 'The Moral Sense' – in *The Descent of Man*, as in the following lines, in which he suggests, as possibly does Augustine, that the social instinct can be seen as having developed from parental care for offspring:

> Animals of many kinds are social…The feeling of pleasure from society is probably an extension of the parental or filial affections, since the social instinct seems to be developed by the young remaining for a long time with their parents; and this extension may be attributed chiefly to natural selection. With those animals which were benefited by living in close association, the individuals which took the greatest pleasure in society would best escape various dangers; whilst those that cared least for their comrades, and lived solitary, would perish in greater numbers (Darwin, 1875, pp. 100, 105).

Darwin's and Augustine's observations on this persuasiveness of co-operation and 'mutual aid' in nature call to mind the arguments of the anarchist Kropotkin, whose *Mutual Aid: A Factor of Evolution* contains numerous illustrations of the principle (and indeed acknowledges a considerable debt to Darwin on the subject), as Rob Knowles explains below. Augustine, however, was no anarchist (nor, needless to say, was Darwin). Writing amidst the turbulence of the breakup of the Roman Empire (Augustine died as the Vandals were besieging Hippo), Augustine was convinced of the need for strong government. Just a few lines further on from the last quoted passage from *The City of God* he writes of the primary importance of government in ensuring 'temporal peace…the peace that consists in bodily health and soundness, and in fellowship with one's kind, and everything necessary to safeguard or recover the peace' (Augustine, 1981, p. 872)—or, as R.A. Markus (1970) paraphrases, in ensuring the provision of 'economic necessities and public order'.[11] While Augustine has harsh things to say, especially in the first five Books of *The City of God*, about the evils perpetrated throughout the long history of the Roman Empire (and earlier Republic), he was nevertheless convinced (as a proud Roman himself), that the greatness of the Empire and the *Pax Romana* was as it should be, and due to divine providence. Indeed, his very term for 'peace' – Cicero's 'tranquillitas ordinis' – was, as James Hutton (1984) points out, 'thoroughly Roman'. In this view, according to Janet Coleman, Augustine, the Christian, was heir not only to Cicero and other Roman apologists, but also St Paul (another proud Roman citizen), who enjoined his readers to 'be subject unto the powers...ordained by God...Render...tribute to whom tribute is due; custom to whom custom; honour to whom honour' (Rom. 13:1-7, quoted Coleman, 2000, pp. 297–8).

For Augustine, then, society was natural for humans, but the preservation of the same required the maintenance of law and order through appropriate political institutions. While a natural propensity for sociality may not be *sufficient* for social order, it was a necessary *precondition*. Hobbes's version of man's 'natural' state – the *Bellum Omnium, Contra Omnes*, or War of All against All – would have been incomprehensible to Augustine. Such a 'state' simply could not have persisted (even under a 'Leviathan' or Machiavellian 'Prince'). 'Indeed,' Augustine writes in Book XIX of *The City of God*, 'even when men choose war, their only wish is for victory; which shows that their desire in fighting is for peace with glory. For what is victory but the conquest of the opposing side? And when this is achieved, there will be peace. Even wars, then, are waged with peace as their object...Hence it is an established fact that peace is the desired end of war. For every man is in a quest of peace, even in waging war, whereas no man is in quest of war when making peace' (Augustine, 1981, p. 866). Further, in Augustine's view, even a perverted desire for peace – one where a military leader wishes 'to make all men their own people, if they can, so that all men and all things might together be subservient to one master' – assumes the hoped for attainment of a peace 'of some kind or other'. For, as Augustine goes on to say (in another presentiment of the natural selection argument): 'no creature's perversion is so contrary to nature as to destroy the very last vestiges of its nature' (ibid., pp. 868–9). In all, '[E]ven what is perverted must of necessity be in, or derived from, or associated with – that is, in a sense, at peace with – some part of the order of things among which it has its being or of which it consists. Otherwise it would not exist at all' (ibid., p. 869).[12]

Augustine's understanding of *human* nature, then, was a very different one from that of Machiavelli, Hobbes and Mandeville, and ultimately, it may be claimed, from Plato. At least it may represent an enrichment and transformation of the latter, incorporating the insights of Neoplatonism, Stoicism and early Christianity and allowing a more generous assessment of human potentiality than the 'deceptive' version of *The Republic*. But the most interesting element in Augustine's understanding, perhaps, is its focus on comparisons of the behaviour of man and other species, and what this may tell us about underlying natural dispositions. In this, Augustine's writing can be seen to have anticipated Darwinism to some extent (that is, the Darwinism of *The Descent of Man*, not the various 'neo-Darwinisms' of Richard Dawkins and others), and thus to provide interesting, if unexpected, perspectives on the evolution of *Homo œconomicus*.[13]

NOTES

1. Keynes's Latin notes and his answers to papers are in his Eton College records, 1898–1900, Keynes Papers, King's College (PP21/85–100;22/1–3). His Divinity notebooks (PP/22/4–5) contain material about Augustine, such as: 'Between St Paul & Luther there is none that can be measured with Augustine—[Adolf von] Harnack. He shaped the Catholic theory of the church, he gave the great Popes the idea of the City of God, of God's Empire; he was the father of the mystics, the founder of the scholastic philosophy of the Middle Ages, and above all the hero and master of the Renaissance and the Reformation. The Confessions among all books written in Latin stands next to the Aeneid for the width of its popularity and the hold it has upon mankind.'

2. I have used different English translations of *The City of God* according to how clear the meaning seemed to me.

3. The 'Divine Economy' was a common expression in Augustine's time (including in Syriac—see, e.g., Rev. S.G.F. Perry, *The Second Synod of Ephesus, English Version with Notes* [vol. II], 'Printed at Dartford, in the County of Kent', 1877, pp. 327–8). On the possible first usage of the term 'economics' in English see Thorbjørn Knudsen, 'Nesting Lamarckism within Darwinian Explanations: Necessity in Economics and Possibility in Biology?', footnote 17 (p. 157), in J. Laurent and J. Nightingale (2001).

4. The section of Lucretius' *De Rerum Natura* ('On the Nature of Things') that Hitchcock appears to be referring to, and which Augustine may have had in mind, would seem to be Book V, verses 873 f., which read: 'And many races of living things must then have died out and been unable to beget and continue their breed. For in the case of all things which you see breathing the breath of life, either craft or courage or else speed has from the beginning of its existence protected and preserved each particular race.' (H.A.J. Munro, *T. Lucreti Cari, De Rerum Natura, Libri Sex, with Notes and Translation*, London, George Bell and Sons, 1900, pp. 136–7.)

5. Augustine's account is contained in *The Literal Meaning of Genesis, Translated and Annotated by John Harmon Taylor,* S.J., (Vol. 1 (Books1–6), New York, Newman Press, 1982. Both the noted nineteenth-century biologist and student of T.H. Huxley, St George Mivart, and the nineteenth and early twentieth-century American scientist and theologian, John Zahm, thought that Augustine 'had articulated a view of nature expansive enough to allow for evolution' (see Numbers and Stenhouse, 1999, pp. 184–94); and the eminent German entomologist Erich Wasmann (1910) wrote that 'to St Augustine it seemed a more exalted conception, and one more in keeping with the omnipotence and wisdom of an infinite Creator, to believe that God created matter by one act of creation, and then allowed the whole universe to develop automatically by means of the laws which he imposed upon the nature of matter' (ibid., p. 274). See aslo Van Till (1999).

6. A.R. Wallace, 'Economic and Social Justice', in A. Reid (ed.), *Vox Clamantium*, Melbourne; Melville, Mullen and Slade, 1894, pp. 166–97 (178–9).

7. Inge (1918), pp. 130–1. Peter Brown (1990, p. 317), citing *The City of God*, Book X, ch. 14, says that for Augustine 'the human race could be conceived of as a vast organism, like a single man'.

8. In Colossians 2.19, in an elaborated metaphor of the Church, Paul draws on the medical knowledge of his day (see Lightfoot, 1875, pp. 264–7) to speak of Christ as the 'Head' from which 'all the body by joints and bands having nourishment ministered, and knit together, increaseth'.

9. That this recent translation is a tolerably faithful rendition of Augustine's Latin, and not a reading back into it of twentieth-century biological knowledge, is affirmed by a perusal of the

first English translation of *The City of God* (Augustine, 1610), a copy of which is held in the Dean and the Capter Library of Norwich Cathedral and the passage in question in which I here produce:

That the bloudiest warre's chiefe ayme is peace: the desire [for] which is natural in man ...for the very wilde beasts doe preserve a peace each with other in the kinde, begetting, breeding and living together, being otherwise in the insociable births of the deserts: I speake not here of Sheepe, Deere, Pigeons, Stares or Bees, but of Lions, Foxes, Eagles and Owles. For what Tyger is there that doth not nousle her young ones, and fawn upon them in their tenderness? What kite is there, though he fly solitary about for his prey, but will tread his female, build his nest, sit his eggs, feed his young, and assist his fellow in her motherly duety, all that in him lieth? *Farre stronger are the hands that binde man into society, and peace with all that are peaceable* [my emphasis].

10. The late Roman scholar Boethius (*c*. 475–525 A.D.), to whom, like Augustine, the West also owed much of its knowledge of Cicero and other Latin and Greek writers in later centuries, makes much the same point in these lines from *The Consolation of Philosophy* (Boethius, 1999, pp. 45–6):

If love relaxed the reins
All things that now keep peace
Would wage continual war...

Love, too, holds people joined
By sacred bond of treaty,
And weaves the holy knot
Of marriage's pure love.
Love promulgates the laws
For friendship's faithful bond.

11. In a letter to his friend, the tribune Marcellinus, from about 411 A.D. (i.e., at the time he was writing *The City of God*), Augustine wrote, 'For what is a "commonwealth" other than the property of the people? Therefore it is shared property, the property precisely of the citizen body. And what is a city but a group of men united by a specific bond of peace?' (Atkins and Dodaro, 2001, p. 35).

12. Hobhouse (1925, p. 17) succinctly puts the Darwinian argument for the survival value of sociality as follows: 'Instinct...is bound in the main to subserve and not to hinder the needs of the living animal...for if the standard of conduct were so perversely formed as to favour actions tending to the dissolusion of the social bond, it would in the end be self-destructive'.

13. I have borrowed this line from Chris Doucouliagos (1994).

REFERENCES

Aristostle (1979), *Ethics*, Harmondsworth: Penguin.

Atkins, E.M. and R.J. Dodaro (2001), *Augustine—Political Writings*, Cambridge, U.K.: Cambridge University Press.

Aurelius, M. (1964), *Meditations*, Harmondsworth: Penguin.

Augustine, St (1610), *Of the Citie of God: With the Learned Comments of Io. Lod. Vives, Englished by F.H.*, London: Printed by George Eld.

Augustine, St (1944–5), *The City of God (De Civitate Dei)* (2 vols), London: J.M. Dent and Sons Ltd.

Augustine, St (1961), *Confessions*, London: Penguin.

Augustine, St (1968), *The Teacher, The Free Choice of the Will, Grace and Free Will*, Washington, D.C.: Catholic University of America Press.

Augustine, St (1981), *Concerning the City of God against the Pagans*, Harmondsworth: Penguin.

Augustine, St (1988), *Tractates on the Gospel of John 1–10*, Washington, D.C.: Catholic University of America Press.

Augustine, St (1991), *Against the Manichees and On the Literal Interpretation of Genesis: An Unfinished Book*, Washington, D.C: Catholic University of America Press.

Bergin, J. and B.L. Lipman (1996). 'Evolution with state-dependent mutations', *Econometrica*, **64**, 943–56.

Boethius (1999), *The Consolation of Philosophy*, London: Penguin.

Brown, P. (1990), *Augustine of Hippo: A Biography*, London: Faber and Faber.

Budziszewski, J. (1986), *The Resurrection of Nature: Political Theory and the Human Character*, Ithaca and London: Cornell University Press.

Cicero, M. (1948), *Selected Works*, Roslyn, N.Y.: Walter J. Black Inc.

Coleman, J. (2000), *A History of Political Thought from Ancient Greece to Early Christianity*, Oxford: Blackwell.

Crick, B. (1970), 'Introduction', in Niccolò Machiavelli, *The Discourses*, Harmondsworth: Penguin.

Darwin, C. (1875), *The Descent of Man and Selection in relation to Sex*, London: John Murray.

Doucouliagos, C. (1994), 'A Note on the Evolution of *Homo economicus'*, *Journal of Economic Issues*, **28**(3), 877–83.

Foster, J. and P. Wild (1996), 'Economic Evolution and the science of synergetics', *Journal of Evolutionary Economics*, **6**, 239–60.

Foster, J. and P. Wild (1999), 'Econometric modelling in the presence of evolutionary change', *Cambridge Journal of Economics*, **23**(6), 749–70.

Gordon, B. (1975), *Economic Analysis Before Adam Smith—Hesiod to Lessius*, London: Macmillan.

Hitchcock, F.R.M. (1900), *St Augustine's Treatise on The City of God*, London: SPCK.

Hobhouse, L.T. (1925), *Morals in Evolution*, London: Chapman and Hall.

Hodgson, G.M. (1994), *Economics and Evolution*, Cambridge, U.K.: Polity Press.

Hodgson, G.M. (1998), review of M. Storper and R. Salais, *Worlds of Production: The Action Frameworks of the Economy*, *Journal of Economic Issues*, **33**, 869–71.

Hutton, J. (1984), *Themes of Peace in Renaissance Poetry*, Ithaca, N.Y.: Cornell University Press.

Inge, W.R. (1918), *Christian Mysticism*, London: Methuen & Co.

Irvine, R.F. (1914), *The Place of the Social Sciences in a Modern University*, Sydney: Angus and Robertson.

Knowles, R. (2000), 'Political Economy From Below: Communitarian Anarchism as a Neglected Discourse in Histories of Economic Thought', *History of Economics Review*, No. 31, 30–47.

Laurent, J. (1991), 'Evolution and Economic Analogy in R.F. Irvine's Economics', *History of Economics Review*, No. 16, 1–19.

Laurent, J. (1998), 'Keynes and Darwin', *History of Economics Review*, No. 27, 76–93.

Laurent, J. and J. Nightingale (2001), *Darwinism and Evolutionary Economics*, Cheltenham, U.K: Edward Elgar.

Lightfoot, J.B. (1875), *St Paul's Epistles to the Colossians and to Philemon*, London: Macmillan and Co.

Long, G. (n.d.) [1869], *The Meditations of Emperor Marcus Aurelius Antoninus*, London and Glasgow: Collins.

Markus, R.A. (1970), *Saeculum: History and Society in the Theology of St Augustine*, Cambridge, U.K.: Cambridge University Press.

Mitchell, J. (1999), 'The Use of Augustine, after 1989', *Political Theory*, **27**, 694–705.
Moss, L.S. (1996), 'Platonic Deception as a Theme in the History of Economic Thought: The Administration of Social Order', *History of Political Economy*, **28** (4), 533–57.
Nederman, C.J. (2000), 'Machiavelli and Moral Character: Principality, Republic and the Psychology of *Virtù*', *History of Political Thought*, **31**(3), 349–64.
Nightingale, J. (1993), 'Solving Marshall's Problem with the Biological Analogy: Jack Downie's Competitive Process', *History of Economics Review*, No. 20, 75–94.
Numbers, R.L. and J. Stenhouse (1999), *Disseminating, Darwinism: The Role of Place, Race, Religion and Gender*, Cambridge, U.K.: Cambridge University Press.
Pelikan, J. (1987), *The Mystery of Continuity: Time and History, Memory and Eternity in the Thought of Saint Augustine*, Charlottesville, VA: University of Virginia Press.
Plato (1997), *Republic*, Ware, Hertfordshire: Wordsworth Editions Ltd.
Plotinus (1984), 'Enneads', in *Plotinus* (7 vols), Cambridge, Mass.: Harvard University Press (vol.4, pp.319–33).
Torchia, J. (2000), 'St Augustine's Critique of the Adiaphora: A Key Component of his Rebuttal of Stoic Ethics', *Studia Moralia*, **38**(1), 165–95.
Van Till, J. (1999), *Is Special Creation a Heresy?*, Durham, NC: John Templeton Foundation, Science and Religion Resource CD (2 ed.).
Wasmann, E. (1910), *Modern Biology and the Theory of Evolution*, London: Kegan Paul, Trench, Trübner & Co.
Weise, P. (1996), 'Evolution and Self-Organization', *Journal of Institutional and Theoretical Economics*, **152**, 716–38.
White, C. (1992), *Christian Friendship in the Fourth Century*, Cambridge, U.K.: Cambridge University Press.
White, M. and J. Gribbin (1996), *Darwin: A Life in Science*, London: Simon and Schuster.

3. Adam Smith's Theory of Human Nature

Athol Fitzgibbons

Given the extensive scholarly attention that Adam Smith's Wealth of Nations has received over the past two hundred years, it might be thought that its meaning would be clear and resolved. In fact, each age seems to interpret the Wealth in a different way, and we now realize that twentieth-century scholars were wrong to treat it as unambiguously modern. Certainly Smith was a leading figure in the eighteenth-century Enlightenment, and like other Enlightenment thinkers he shared in the project to replace a primarily religious and spiritual view of society with one more attuned to liberty, wealth and science. Nevertheless, the Enlightenment was a fusion of ideas, not all of which were anticipated by Smith, and his system lay on the dividing line between traditional and modern. It was meant to be scientific, but it was also irreducibly spiritual, which is to say based on his understanding of God and human nature.

Modern society draws on two philosophical insights that are attributed to Smith. One is the idea, which is not obvious from experience, nor derivable from economic theory, that the world is not subject to endless transience and change, but is guided by an automatic and invisible hand. The other idea that we attribute to Smith is that morality is an exclusively individual matter, because self-interest will most effectively promote the prosperity and well being of society as a whole. The two ideas are interrelated, because an invisible hand, or at least the sort that the moderns are prepared to countenance, would hardly need assistance from higher states of human nature.

In practice there are frequent references to Smith's authority, partly because no one else seems able to project the same profundity or rhetorical power. Furthermore, there can be no scientific proof of the invisible hand, which is ultimately a matter of faith and belief. I know there are invisible fairies in my garden, you know the invisible hand is in yours; but only you can claim the authority of Adam Smith. And speaking not only of Smith, but in general, though ideas are modified and improved over time, their meaning and life often reside in some original combination of faith and science.

As a result there has always been a temptation to create modern versions of Smith. In the nineteenth century it was necessary to neutralize Smith's preference for agriculture over industrial development, his hostility to entrepreneurship, and his belief that international trade had been artificially over-extended. In the mid-twentieth century neoclassical economics conjured up a 'canonical' Adam Smith, who was supposed to have embraced utility maximization. I admit that pseudo-Smiths can be useful inventions, so long as they are not meant to be historically accurate, but the actuality is that Smith's friend, David Hume, was the first to conceive of utility theory, and Smith was very explicitly opposed to it. He thought that the theory was either meaningless or wrong: either utility maximization meant self-love, in which case it was too narrow to account for experience, or else it meant the pursuit of whatever the individual 'wanted', in which case utility was what Smith called an 'afterthought', that had no meaning:

> The idea of the utility of all qualities of this kind, is plainly an after-thought, and not what first recommends them to our approbation (TMS, p. 20).[1]

More recently there has been renewed interest in what I will call the 'greed-is-good' Smith, who, unlike the canonical version (cf. Lipper, 1988), reflects an important historical truth. Smith believed that self-love, alias low-level greed, had an important role to play in economic life and elsewhere. It might seem paradoxical that the real Smith could stress the importance of self-interest and yet strongly oppose the theory of utility maximization, but Smith believed that utility theory had only one moral dimension. His own system relied on the expression of different moralities, one of which was self-love.

Nevertheless, it can be said at the outset that there would have been a real scandal if the eighteenth-century Smith, who taught Christian students preparing for the ministry, had actually said that society was based on self-love. His own teacher Francis Hutcheson had been subject to a heresy trial merely for advocating the greatest good of the greatest number; which was obviously (to an eighteenth-century Scot) a non-spiritual criterion. Bernard Mandeville (1670–1733) had created just such a scandal, but Smith believed that despite its partial truth, Mandeville's system also contained an important error. Mandeville had recognized nothing *beyond* self-love:

> It is the great fallacy of Dr Mandeville's book [*The Fable of the Bees*] to represent every passion as wholly vicious...in any degree and in any direction (TMS, p. 312).

Smith did not praise self-love as the highest of the virtues. He taught classical moral and political philosophy, the central theme of which, for the past two thousand years, had been the merits of virtue. Virtue was the purpose of life and the main condition for social existence. The State was supposed to encourage virtue through culture and the laws, and the culture and the laws were supposed to be formulated and defended by men of virtue.

However, prosperity was slowly changing eighteenth-century British society, and there were fears that commercial self-interest and the love of money would replace the values required for social commitment. In modern terms, there were fears that economic growth would be at the expense of moral capital. Smith's response to these fears was to argue that society needed a range of moralities, and that there were situations in which self-love was appropriate and desirable. He also believed that it was possible to scientifically formulate the legal principles that would best combine self-interest with values. The enunciation of those principles was the purpose of what Smith called the 'science of jurisprudence'; and economics was supposed to be a branch of that science.

Certainly Smith did reject the black and white distinction (which had been made by the Christians) between the carnal desires and spiritual life. He believed that Christian extremism had given Mandeville an ideal opportunity to promote valuelessness and self-love:

> Some popular ascetic doctrines which had been current before [Mandeville's] time, and which placed virtue in the entire extirpation and annihilation of all our passions, were the real foundations of this licentious system (TMS, p. 313).

Nevertheless, as Smith pointed out, the errors of the Christians did not justify the opposite position. His theme was that higher and lower values could and should co-exist, even in commercial life.

Table 3.1 Relationship of Self-love to Moral Ideas

	System	Socially Beneficial Values
1	18th century Christians	Only higher values needed
2	Mandeville and 'greed-is-good'	Only lower values needed
3	Historical Adam Smith	Higher and lower values combined
4	Utilitarians and Neoclassicals	Only one level of values exists

The different moral systems are compared in Table 3.1. Since Smith primarily opposed position 1, he has been erroneously attributed with position 2. But position 2 is inconsistent with the texts, and so for the past one hundred years scholars have wrestled with the Adam Smith Problem, which is that Smith seems to have contradicted himself. On the one hand Smith said this:

> It is not from the benevolence of the butcher, the brewer or the baker that we expect our dinner, but from their regard to their own interest. We address ourselves, not to their humanity, but to their self-love, and never talk to them of our own necessities but of their advantages (WN, pp. 26–7).

And yet he also said this:

> By the wise contrivance of the Author of nature, virtue is upon all ordinary occasions, even with regard to this life, real wisdom and the surest and readiest means of obtaining both safety and advantage (TMS, p. 298).

Supporters of the Adam Smith Problem conclude that Smith was in two minds, and that he might have changed his mind when he turned from soft moral studies to hard economics. However, the biographical evidence is that Smith didn't change his mind. The supposedly soft *Theory of Moral Sentiments* was published in 1752, and the supposedly hard *Wealth of Nations* in 1776; but the *Theory of Moral Sentiments* was substantially revised, with the earlier editions endorsed but the sections on virtue greatly expanded, in 1790. Not only are there extensive textual connections between the two books, but they overlap in time. And Smith denied that the 1790 version of the *Theory of Moral Sentiments* was substantially different from the earlier editions.

The real role of the Adam Smith Problem has been to protect the greed-is-good Smith from the textual evidence; and, to reply to a reviewer of my book (see References), the artificial distinction between Smith's philosophy and his economics is another such protective device. The evidence is that Smith's economics were *not* exclusively concerned with self-love. It is incorrect to say that there was a greed-is-good Smith and another, more obscure Smith. There was just one Adam Smith, who had, as he made abundantly clear, advanced a single integrated system. That system proposed the acceptance of self-love, subject only to the rules of justice. Nevertheless, it is exegetical nonsense to suggest that self-love was the only motive to play an important role in Smith's system.

THE VIRTUES

Smith's higher values were definitely not Christian, if only because Medieval Christianity was the buttress of the culture that he wanted to change. According to Smith, we are more likely to acquire virtue in the army than in the monastery. And despite his numerous references to God, and though he taught students preparing for the Christian ministry, Smith never once mentioned, in correspondence or his published writings, Christ or the Bible. When he occasionally wrote 'grace', it was with a small 'g'.

He was a classical scholar, and his values were the four cardinal virtues which, though they go back to ancient Greece, he learnt from the ancient Roman Stoics. Smith drew on but modified the Ciceronian version of Stoicism, which had been formulated during the dying days of the Roman Republic and just prior to the Empire.

The cardinal virtues are listed on the left hand side of Table 2, and Smith's virtues are on the right. The fourfold division of the virtues must have seemed arbitrary and rigid even in the eighteenth century, and perhaps Smith tried to enliven it with the argot of the time, but in any event the English language has moved on in the past two hundred years, and his eighteenth century terminology has become obscure. The terms on the right hand side of the table do not have their modern meanings but, when they are examined more closely, correspond to those on the left.

Table 3.2 The Correspondence of Smith's Virtues and the Cardinal Virtues

The Cardinal Virtues	Smith's Virtues
Wisdom	Prudence[b]
Justice	Justice[a]
Temperance	Self-command
Courage	Benevolence[c]

Notes:

a. Justice did not mean distributive justice, or justice in the eyes of God, but black letter (or commutative) justice. It included the protection of property and the enforcement of contracts.

b. 'Prudence' was an Anglicization of Cicero's 'prudentia', or wisdom. It meant having the foresight to take all possible consequences into account. It also meant having the telescopic faculty of being able to see oneself in the future.

c. 'Benevolence' did not primarily refer to charity, but to any motive that went beyond self-love, and especially participation in public life. Smith sometimes used it to include wisdom and temperance, in which case benevolence meant any virtue beyond a minimal and legally enforceable justice.

The *Theory of Moral Sentiments* analysed the tension between self-love and benevolence (virtue), and concluded that each motive was appropriate in its particular sphere. Traditional political philosophy had regarded virtue as a qualification for political life, the army, or the courts, or wherever the internal qualities of individuals were of the essence. Smith drew on the Roman aristocrat Cicero, who was widely read in eighteenth-century Britain. Cicero had taught that justice was the foundation of society and that it generated prosperity by extending the division of labour, but that the higher virtues were necessary in politics, the army and the law:

> Unbecoming to a gentleman, too, and vulgar are the means of livelihood of all hired workmen whom we pay for mere manual labour, not for artistic skill: for in their case the very wage they receive is a pledge of their slavery...least respectable of all are those trades which cater for sensual pleasures—
>
> 'Fishmongers, butchers, cooks, and poulterers'
>
> as Terence says. But the professions in which either a higher degree of intelligence is required, or from which no small benefit to society is derived...are proper for those whose social position they become (Cicero, 1913, p. 155).

Smith's contemporaries would have recognized his famous self-love passage as a variation on the Ciceronian theme. Cicero's conclusion was that since butchery and baking only required self-interest, that it was better for aristocrats to avoid these menial occupations. He implicitly proposed a class-based division of labour.

Smith agreed with Cicero that a particular class of commercial behaviour responded to self-love; the butcher and the baker do not provide the dinner because they are benevolent or, in other words, they do not cook to acquire virtue. But Smith did not extrapolate from butchers and bakers to the whole of life, concluding that society has no need for virtue. To take the most obvious case, Smith thought that philosophers, i.e. thinkers and scientists, should ignore their self-interest and respond only to benevolence:

> For as the establishment of law and government is the highest effort of human prudence and wisdom, the causes cannot have a different influence from what the effects have. Besides that it is by the wisdom and probity of those [philosophers] with whom we live that a propriety of conduct is pointed out to us, and the proper means of attaining it. Their valour defends us, their benevolence supplies us, the hungry is fed, the naked is cloathed, by the exertion of these divine qualities (JB, p. 489).

Indeed Smith went so far as to rebuke Marcus Aurelius, the Stoic philosopher who was also a Roman emperor, for writing his *Meditations* while he was camped out at night with the army. Aurelius had indulged himself with contemplation when he should have kept himself busy with administration or the preparation for war:

> That he is occupied in contemplating the more sublime, can never be an excuse for his neglecting the more humble department...The most sublime speculation of the contemplative philosopher can scarce compensate the neglect of the smallest active duty (TMS, p. 237).

Both the *Wealth of Nations* and the *Theory of Moral Sentiments* considered how to reward work that was needed but that could not, by its very nature, respond to money and self-love:

> But there are also some callings, which, though useful and even necessary in a state, bring no advantage or pleasure to any individual, and the supreme power is obliged to alter its conduct with regard to the retainers of those professions. It must give them publick encouragement in order to their subsistence; and it must provide against that negligence to which they will naturally be subject...The persons employed in the finances [public treasury], fleets [armed forces], and magistracy, are instances of this order of men (WN, pp. 790–91).

The famous passage that praised self-love occurs in Smith's chapter in *The Wealth of Nations* on the division of labour. It moved immediately from butchers and bakers to philosophers because he was changing Cicero's class-based division of labour into a task-based division.

Smith's moral theory was that nearly everyone has mixed motives, depending partly on their experiences and character. Since each task required a different balance of virtue and self-love, different people were suited to these different tasks. Smith differentiated between 'superior' and 'inferior' virtue, superior virtue being mainly relevant to public life, and inferior virtue to commercial life. The wealth of nations would be best and most quickly developed by a mixture of vice and virtue. Virtue in the form of prudence (being able to see oneself in the future) would encourage the propensity to save, and virtue in the form of benevolence would deflect alienation.

Table 3.3 summarizes the system of wealth and virtue. Reading down the left hand column, justice was the most essential virtue, the observance of which meant efficiency and natural liberty. Prudence led to a high savings ratio and so a high rate of capital accumulation; benevolence meant commitment to the work and so the absence of alienation. Reading down the middle column, justice at the political level meant the rule of law, prudence meant a farsighted elite and benevolence (seeing beyond oneself) meant a high degree of social cohesion.

However, justice was the most important virtue, because it was the condition for social survival:

> Justice, on the contrary, is the main pillar that upholds the whole edifice. If it is removed, the great, the immense fabric of human society…must in a moment crumble into atoms (TMS, p. 86).

And only justice could be legally enforced:

> [A] remarkable distinction between justice and all the other social virtues…[is] that we feel ourselves to be under a stricter obligation to act according to justice…We feel, that is to say, that force may, with the utmost propriety, and with the approbation of all mankind, be used to constrain us to observe the rules of the one, but not to follow the precepts of the other (TMS, p. 80).

A society that observed the higher virtues but neglected justice, as ancient Greece had done, would soon collapse. By comparison, a society that observed justice but suppressed the higher virtues, as ancient Rome had done, might carry on, though devoid of art, meaning and ideas, and with a low level of capital accumulation, for centuries. Ancient Rome had been a foundation without a palace, just as ancient Greece had been a palace without a foundation. But eventually Rome too would collapse, through the absence of social commitment and cohesion.

Table 3.3 Social and Economic Implications of Smith's Virtues

The Virtues	Political Implications	Economic Implications
Justice	The Rule of Law	Free Trade
Prudence	A Committed Elite	Capital Accumulation
Benevolence & Self-Command	Social Cohesion	No Alienation

Table 3.4 below describes how the *Wealth of Nations* reflects Smith's moral schemata. Books 1 and 4 of the *Wealth of Nations* discuss free trade (i.e. justice) and self-interest at length. In Books 2 and 3 of the *Wealth of Nations* Smith describes, also at length, how virtue increases the propensity to save. Book 5 is very unfashionable but that is where Smith discusses how education, alienation and religion impact on social cohesion.

It is well known that the alienation passages in Book 5 foreshadow Marx. In this passage Smith complained about the effect of commerce on benevolence and prudence:

> The torpor of [a working man's] mind renders him, not only incapable of relishing or bearing a part in any rational conversation, but of conceiving any generous, noble, or tender sentiment, and consequently of forming any just judgement concerning many even of the ordinary duties of private life. Of the great and extensive interests of his country he is altogether incapable of judging; and unless very particular pains have been taken to render him otherwise, he is equally incapable of defending his country in war. The uniformity of his stationary life naturally corrupts the courage of his mind, and makes him regard with abhorrence, the irregular, uncertain, and adventurous life of a soldier (WN, p. 782).

But whereas Marx predicted that alienation would destroy the capitalist system, Smith's theme was that it was both possible and desirable to combine wealth and virtue.

Table 3.4 Location of the Virtues in The Wealth of Nations

The Virtues	Economic Implications	In *The Wealth of Nations*
Justice	Free Trade	Books 1 and 4
Prudence	Capital Accumulation	Books 2 and 3
Benevolence & Self-Command	No Alienation	Book 5

The Enlightenment thinkers believed that their society could, for the first time in 1,500 years, match the material achievements of ancient Rome. Their new model would differ from the old in two main ways: it would use capital accumulation and technology to replace the need for slaves, and it would soften the old military virtues of the Roman republic. In *The Wealth of Nations* and elsewhere, Smith compared the military capabilities of a commercial society with those of the old Roman republic. He wanted to show that it was feasible to soften the old martial virtue, and redirect its energies into more productive uses.

His goal was to bring virtue into the world, including the world of productive work, and his moral enemy was unworldliness. This redirected virtue away from the world and towards withdrawal and heaven. He was a devout man, but he was also fundamentally opposed to Christian values.

GOD AND THE SOUL

Smith's frequent references to God were based on real belief, though generations of scholars, who have hoped that economics is ultimately a secular and scientific subject, have concluded otherwise. His invisible hand was, of course, the invisible hand of God, and apart from the economy it also guided the planets and other natural phenomena:

> Among savages, as well as in the early ages of Heathen antiquity, it is the irregular events of nature only that are ascribed to the agency and power of their gods. Fire burns, and water refreshes; heavy bodies descend and lighter substances fly upwards, by the necessity of their own nature; nor was the invisible hand of Jupiter ever apprehended to be employed in those matters (EPS, p. 49).

The invisible hand was not and could not have been the hand of the Christian God, because He is transcendent, i.e. beyond this vale of tears and change. The Christian God transforms lives and offers consolation, but He does not guide the economic system. However, the Stoic God did accept responsibility for harmony and order throughout the cosmos. Stoicism was a monotheistic religion that had once appealed to ancient Romans and others who found a transcendent God too remote and austere. It taught that subtly and in ways that were not apparent to human minds, the world was evolving for the best. God was immanent, i.e. within the cosmos, which therefore reflected divine qualities. And Smith, who often referred to God as 'Providence' or 'Nature', was among those eighteenth-century British figures who embraced the Stoic religion.

Smith's impartial spectator was a Stoic version of the soul. His theory, which he believed to be scientific, was that adult life began within a set of conventional rules, but that as individuals came to perceive themselves as others saw them, and grew in self-understanding, an inner self would form. First they saw themselves through the eyes of others and then through the eyes of the impartial spectator. In this way they acquired impartiality towards themselves, which impartiality was the origin of the higher virtues. Smith's theory was that we grow inwardly through participation in the strife and tumult of the world, rather than from withdrawal and an orientation towards heaven; and, as we acquire virtue from the world, so we express it in the world.

He was hostile to Christian fundamentalism because of its stress on the transcendence of God, which he believed had a pernicious effect on the poor. What the poor really needed was a religion that would combine wealth with virtue, i.e. that would combine material growth with inner growth. Fundamentalism redirected their energies away from the world and towards heaven, and it was all the more seductive because of the deprivations that the poor had suffered.

The Stoics believed that self-interest assisted the growth of the individual and conformed to the harmony of the universe. Everyone was referred to their own self-interest because, although everyone is invisibly driven by the objective of inner growth, everyone had to make decisions based on their own insight and understanding.

However Smith used 'self-love' and 'self-interest' in different ways. Self-interest ultimately drove the process of inner growth, whereas self-love meant the ego. The butcher and the baker were self-interested like everyone else, but when they were at work they were necessarily driven by their self-love. Natural liberty meant the liberation of self-interest; society had to restrain self-love within the rules of justice. The self-interested individual must, upon all occasions, 'humble the arrogance of his self-love':

> It is not the soft power of humanity, it is not that feeble spark of benevolence which Nature has lighted up in the human heart, that is thus capable of counteracting the strongest impulses of self-love. It is a stronger power, a more forcible motive, which exerts itself upon such occasions. It is reason, principle, conscience, the inhabitant of the breast, the man within, the great judge and arbiter of our conduct (TMS, p. 137).

There was no concept of grace or inspiration in Stoicism, because God manifested Himself only through Nature and the world, and nothing travelled from beyond the world. Smith was hostile to notions of creativity and genius, and the declared purpose of his *History of Astronomy*, which was his main methodological work, was to demonstrate the pre-scientific nature of 'wonder and surprise'. He believed that irregular events tended to be unduly admired, when in fact everything was part of a hidden pattern:

> It is the design of this Essay to consider particularly the nature and causes of each of these sentiments [wonder, admiration and surprise], whose influence is of far wider extent than we should be apt upon a careless view to imagine (EPS, p. 34).

He saw a parallel between admiration for human genius and admiration for the comets. We tend to admire the comets because of their fiery visibility, without realizing that they are subject to a wider body of rules that steer the planets and everything else. Likewise, we unduly admire genius:

> It is the leader in science and taste, the man who directs and conducts our own sentiments, the extent and superior justness of whose talents astonish us with wonder and surprise, who excites our admiration, and seems to deserve our applause (TMS, p. 20).

But, he believed, we forget that society depends less on the exception than on the observance of the basic rules of justice.

His writings on the arts are disconnected and devoid of feeling because he tried to replace the role of creativity with his own formulistic schemata. He regarded poetry as a relic from the pre-scientific age, and he agreed that Shakespeare's Hamlet was the 'dream of a drunken savage'. Instances of crushing social injustice were, as he admitted, simply outside his system. His was a system of Nature, but the sub-natural and the supernatural were beyond it.

The Stoic system, and the point includes Smith's system, is a philosophy for good times. It has tended to gain adherents during periods of social and economic progress, as during the Roman Republic, eighteenth-century Britain, or, beneath the scientific surface, in the twentieth-century United States. Its concept of human nature is much higher than its admirers have understood, but it is nevertheless limited. It has never been a philosophy for dark times, when society has only an uncertain meaning, and it is not relevant for those who wish to find God in the desert. But then that was never the objective.

NOTE

1. TMS refers to *The Theory of Moral Sentiments*; WN to *The Wealth of Nations*; JB to *Lectures on Jurisprudence*; and EPS to *Essays on Philosophical Subjects*.

REFERENCES

Cicero (1913), *De Officiis*, Cambridge, MA: Harvard University Press.

Fitzgibbons, A. (1995), *Adam Smith's System of Liberty, Wealth, and Virtue: the Moral and Political Foundations of the Wealth of Nations*, Oxford: Oxford University Press.

Lipper, K. (1988), *Wall Street*, New York: Berkley Books.

Smith, A. (1976), *The Theory of Moral Sentiments* (ed. D.D. Raphael and A.L. Macfie), Oxford: Oxford University Press.

Smith, A. (1976), *The Wealth of Nations* (ed. R.H. Campbell, A.S. Skinner and W.B. Todd), 2 vols, Oxford: Oxford University Press.

Smith, A. (1978), *Lectures on Jurisprudence* (ed. R.L. Meek, D.D. Raphael and P.G. Stein), Oxford: Oxford University Press.

Smith, A. (1980), *Essays on Philosophical Subjects* (ed. W.P.D. Wrightman and J.C. Bryce), Oxford: Oxford University Press.

Wood, J.C. (1984), *Adam Smith: Critical Assessments*, 4 vols, London: Croom Helm.

4. Malthus on Indolence

John Pullen

It is common knowledge that Thomas Robert Malthus (1766–1834) regarded excessive population growth as a major impediment to human welfare and happiness, and that his recommended remedy for over-population was 'prudential restraint', or the deferment of marriage until there are reasonable prospects of being able to support the children of the marriage. He recognized that prudential restraint would be a difficult virtue to attain, and that 'moral restraint', i.e. prudential restraint combined with sexual abstinence before marriage, would be even more difficult, and that therefore the universal practice of prudential or moral restraint is unlikely to be a realistic possibility.

In the first edition of his *Essay on Population* (Malthus, 1926 [1798]) he portrayed the human condition in gloomy and melancholic terms, admitting that delayed marriage could often be a form of misery – he himself did not marry until he was 38 years old – and could lead to sexual misconduct during the waiting period. In later editions of the *Essay on Population*, however, he adopted a more optimistic view, arguing that, with proper education, it would be generally accepted that parents who bring into the world children they can not support are guilty of gross immorality, and of inflicting hardship and suffering upon themselves and these children.

While admitting that population pressure is the source of many difficulties and frequently results in misery, vice, and 'much partial evil', Malthus nevertheless argued that it produces 'a great overbalance of good' (Malthus, 1926 [1798], pp. 361–2), and is in fact part of the Divine plan for the progress of mankind. It is one of the 'sorrows and distresses of life' that stimulate human beings to moral, intellectual and economic growth, i.e. to the 'growth of mind' (ibid., p. 367).

It is this struggle with the threat of overpopulation and the other difficulties of life that gives to Malthus's writings a distinctively evolutionary tone. He did not, however, predict that the struggle would result in improvements in the physical condition of the human race. Contrary to the Marquis de Condorcet's view (or hope) that science would cause unlimited improvement in health and longevity, Malthus 'doubted, whether, since the world began, any organic improvement whatever of the human frame can be clearly ascertained' (Malthus, 1989 [1803], Vol. I, p. 314). If the methods of artificial selection used in the propagation of plants and animals were applied to the selective breeding of humans, their physical condition would be enhanced, but the enforced celibacy of those deemed to be inferior would render the process impractical (ibid.).

The evolutionary aspect of Malthus's thought was recognised by Darwin, although the precise nature and extent of his influence on Darwin has been the subject of considerable debate. It has been argued (Pullen, 1987) that the similarity between Malthus's evolutionary ideas and Darwin's is particularly close – and indeed closer than has been realized by much of the secondary literature and by Darwin himself – in the context of Malthus's discussion of the theological implications of his principle of population in the last two chapters of the first edition (1798) of his *Essay on Population*. These two chapters were omitted from later editions of the *Essay*, and it seems that Darwin was unaware of them. They invoke, on the spiritual plane, not only the concept of the struggle for existence and the survival of the fittest, but also the concept of natural selection. Malthus subscribed to the radical theological doctrine of annihilationism, or conditional immortality, according to which those of us who develop morally and intellectually, and thereby achieve a 'growth of mind' through our struggles with the pressure of population and other difficulties in this life, will be rewarded with eternal spiritual life; but those of us who fail in this struggle will cease to exist—both in body and in spirit. By this mechanism of natural selection operating on the spiritual plane, the fit will survive and the unfit will perish, just as in Darwin's theory of evolution, in which natural selection operates on the physical plane amongst plants and animals.

Population pressure[1] was identified by Malthus as a major element in the difficulties of life against which we must struggle in the evolutionary growth of mind, but it was not the only difficulty that he emphasised. Another difficulty – not as major as the pressure of population, but still very significant – was indolence. His concern with the problem of indolence does not appear to have received the attention it deserves.

Unfortunately, Malthus did not undertake a systematic analysis of the problem of indolence. His views on that problem were scattered throughout his writings, and did not always appear under the name 'indolence': 'laziness', 'torpor', 'idleness', and 'sloth' were used as synonyms. This chapter attempts to identify and collate these scattered comments, to show how extensively Malthus's views on indolence permeated his writings, and to highlight the significant role that indolence played in Malthus's system as an impediment to both economic growth and the growth of mind. The paper also attempts a critical appraisal of the validity and relevance of his views on indolence.

THE PREVALENCE OF INDOLENCE IN EARLY SOCIETIES AND IN MODERN EUROPE

In his comments on the 'Checks to Population in the Less Civilized Parts of the World and in Past Times' (Malthus, 1989 [1803], Vol. I, Bk I), Malthus made frequent reference to indolence as a characteristic of the peoples of those places and times and as an impediment to economic growth. For example, the indolence of the American Indians 'is well known' (ibid., Vol. I, p. 438). In not reserving a portion of their food supply to meet future needs, they illustrated the 'ignorance and indolence of the improvident savage'.[2]

In Siberia in past times, according to Malthus, the inhabitants suffered from 'inveterate habits of indolence and want of foresight' to such a degree as to nullify any permanent benefits from improved facilities of production. The Empress of Russia had recourse to encouraging immigration of men and capital, thus substituting 'German industry' for 'Russian indolence', although some of the German settlers also proved to be in 'want of industrious habits'. Because of the richness of the soil, some parts of Siberia produced corn in abundance and had never known a general failure, but this was 'in spite of the indolence and drunkenness of the inhabitants'. The pastoral tribes of Siberia have resisted attempts of the Russian government 'to wean them from their injurious sloth' (ibid., pp. 103–5).

In Tibet witnesses reported 'a mass of indigence and idleness', but attributed it to the 'humane disposition' of 'indiscriminate charity' that attracted more dependants (ibid., p. 120). In Europe in feudal times the landlords could in no other way spend their incomes than by maintaining a great number of 'idle followers'. The 'pernicious power' of the landlords was destroyed when the growth of capital enabled their idle and dependent followers to become 'merchants, manufacturers, tradesmen, farmers, and independent labourers' (ibid., Vol. II, p. 84).

Turning his attention to the 'Checks to Population in the different States of Modern Europe', Malthus again noted the deleterious effects of indolence. He referred, in the case of Norway, to 'the force of habit and natural indolence' of the sons who inherit farms and run them as their forefathers did without introducing any improvements (ibid., Vol. I, p. 154).

With regard to Russia in the eighteenth century, Malthus noted that the system of 'vassalage, or rather slavery, of the peasants' had been accompanied 'almost necessarily' by 'ignorance and indolence'. He believed that this system constituted the 'principal obstacle to...an increase of population astonishingly rapid'. The taxation and land distribution systems likewise encouraged indolence. The boors were taxed according to the productivity of their land. If they improved their land or their methods, they would pay more tax, and in addition run the risk of being deprived by the landowner of part of the improved land at the next redistribution, as each family was granted only sufficient land for its own needs. The result was 'indolent cultivation' (ibid., p. 178). Feudal times in general were characterised by 'indolent cultivation and great waste of labour' (ibid., Vol. II, p. 78).

Indolent habits were also identified as one of the causes of the endemic and epidemic diseases of Scotland – such as scurvy, rheumatism and consumption – the other causes being 'cold and wet situations, meagre and unwholesome food, impure air from damp and crowded houses...and the want of attention to cleanliness' (ibid., Vol. I, p. 288). Quoting the evidence of Humboldt, Malthus said that a similar situation prevailed in New Spain (Mexico). The labouring classes, because of their 'indolence and improvidence', do not take measures to ensure their food supply in unfavourable seasons, and the habits of 'indolence and improvidence which prevail among the people...must necessarily act as formidable obstacles in the way of a rapid increase of wealth and population' (Malthus, 1989 [1820], Vol. I, pp. 384, 388, 575; 1989 [1803], Vol. I, p. 3). Improvidence in matters of marriage and procreation – i.e., the absence of prudential or moral restraint – was of course a central feature of Malthus's political economy; but the juxtaposition of 'indolence' and 'improvidence' in these quotations, and the repeated references elsewhere to the harmful effects of indolence, indicate that he intended the threat of indolence to be taken seriously.

INDOLENCE AND CONSUMER DEMAND

Malthus argued that the appeal of indolence can be so strong as to restrict the growth of demand for new products. Adam Smith had said that there is no limit to the desire for material goods and luxuries,[3] but Malthus considered this to be too strong an expression. He argued that the desire to consume will be 'practically limited by the countervailing luxury of indolence'.[4] In another context, in arguing that the introduction of machinery will not necessarily lead to an increase in demand, he said: 'The peasant who might be induced to labour an additional number of hours for tea or tobacco, might prefer indolence to a new coat' (Malthus, 1989 [1820], Vol. I, p. 405).[5]

Given that Malthus's theory of economic growth was based heavily (but not exclusively) on the role of effective demand – as later acknowledged by Keynes – it follows that anything, like indolence, that discourages the growth of demand must be of serious concern. His statement that '[a] preference of indolence to luxuries, in either of the parties, would immediately occasion a want of demand' (ibid., p. 571) shows how his views on indolence were integrally connected to his theory of effective demand.

INDOLENCE AND PRODUCTIVITY

Malthus argued that a fertile soil provides the greatest possible natural stimulus to wealth,[6] but he also recognised that soil fertility by itself would not guarantee economic progress, and that it might even retard progress. The ease with which food can be obtained might encourage habits of indolence that retard production. He argued that it would be a 'rash and false' conclusion to say a great facility of producing food would necessarily mean that more conveniences and luxuries would be produced. The workman would not have to spend so much time and effort producing food, and would have more time available to pursue luxuries, but that would not happen if he considered indolence as 'a greater luxury than those which he was likely to procure by further labour'. Malthus believed that the historical evidence shows that this preference for indolence is a very common phenomenon:

> [A]s a matter of fact, confirmed by all the accounts we have of nations, in the different stages of their progress, it must be allowed that this choice seems to be very general in the early periods of society, and by no means uncommon in the most improved states (ibid., p. 379).

Malthus argued that a 'crowd of countries' illustrate and confirm that if the facility of getting food creates habits of indolence, people may prefer 'the luxury of doing little or nothing, to the luxury of possessing conveniences and comforts'. The anomalous result could be that they then possess fewer conveniences and comforts than if they had to work harder to obtain food (ibid., p. 382). Relying on the reports by Humboldt of conditions in New Spain, Malthus concluded that the extreme fertility of those countries was not an adequate stimulus to the rapid increase of wealth and population; and, furthermore, 'under the actual circumstances in which they have been placed',[7] this fertility resulted in 'a degree of indolence which has kept them poor and thinly peopled after the lapse of ages'.

A similar argument was presented when he criticised those writers (Say, Mill, Ricardo) who held that savings will always be spent and that capital can never be redundant. According to Malthus, these writers had made a 'fundamental error': they had not taken into consideration '*the influence of so general and important [a] principle in human nature, as indolence or the love of ease*'; and they had 'taken for granted that luxuries are always preferred to indolence'. He repeated that 'it is a most important error to take for granted, that mankind will produce and consume all that they have the power to produce and consume, and will never prefer indolence to the rewards of industry'. If improved machinery causes prices of customary purchases to fall, the farmer, rather than spending more on luxuries, 'might be very likely to indulge himself in indolence, and employ less labour on the land'. Manufacturers also would fall 'almost necessarily into the same indolent system as the farmer' (ibid., pp. 358–9, emphasis added).

Malthus said that those who ignore the motives of indolence and saving, and who argue that 'mankind will always produce and consume as much as they have the power to produce and consume' are guilty of 'a want of knowledge of the human character and of the motives by which it is usually influenced'.[8]

INDOLENCE AND MORALITY

Malthus saw indolence not merely as an impediment to economic growth, but also as a moral evil in itself and one that is likely to occasion further immorality. He spoke of the 'bad moral effects of idleness' and, in describing the disastrous attempt by the French to establish a colony in Guiana in 1663, he referred to 'the irregularities which idleness produces among the lower classes of society'. He regarded 'dirt', 'squalid poverty', and 'indolence' as being 'in the highest degree unfavourable to happiness and virtue'. He added that 'squalid poverty, particularly when joined with idleness, is a state the most unfavourable to chastity that can well be conceived'. He believed that if the squalid poverty a girl is brought up in exceeds a certain degree, it would be an 'absolute miracle' if she were 'really modest' at the age of twenty (Malthus, 1989 [1803], Vol. I, pp. 342, 369; Vol. II, pp. 89, 114).

Malthus thus seems to have been implying that, as the moral character of a people is affected by their economic condition, those who are responsible for setting a nation's economic conditions must also bear a share of responsibility for its moral character. It would be easy, but not correct, to attribute Malthus's fear of indolence to the influence of a puritanical version of Protestantism, according to which working assiduously in one's calling is a moral duty and the enjoyment of more leisure than is necessary for health is sinful. Malthus's eulogies of leisure – for example, his statement that a wider distribution and enjoyment of leisure would constitute a marked improvement in society – show that his remarks on indolence cannot be interpreted as an expression of what is now known as the Protestant work ethic.

INDOLENCE OF THE HIGHER CLASSES

When Malthus spoke of the harmful consequences of indolence, his comments were generally directed at vassals, serfs, savages, labourers and other 'lower classes'. However, the lower classes were not the only targets of his criticisms. He recognised that indolence is not unknown amongst other classes. In describing conditions in Siberia in past times, he argued that the 'natural indolence' of the farmers would prevent them from expanding production simply in order to provide food for the extra employees (ibid., Vol. I, p. 102). In more recent times, according to Malthus, the progress of Russia was being hindered by the indolence of landowners. A Russian nobleman had told him that he cared little about the proper cultivation of his land, as long as he received his rents and taxes—an attitude that Malthus described as one of 'indolence and present convenience' (ibid., p. 178). Using information contained in Humboldt's *Essai Politique*, he said that the failure of the large landowners of Mexico to cultivate their land fully was attributable to their 'natural indolence' and 'caprice' (ibid., pp. 390, 391). In arguing against the over-employment of labourers merely in order to provide food for the extra labourers, Malthus said that the employers would be 'quite indifferent' to whether the labourers worked in an industrious manner, and as a result both masters and servants would acquire 'the most indolent habits'. Indolence is generated amongst the lower classes by the desire of the upper classes to distinguish themselves by employing a great number of 'idle retainers' (Malthus, 1989 [1820], Vol. I, pp. 377–8).

INDOLENCE AND CONTRACEPTION

Malthus's fear of the scourge of indolence was one of his reasons for objecting to contraception. James Grahame (in *An Inquiry into the Principle of Population*, 1816) accused Malthus of recommending recourse to the restraints prescribed by Condorcet. In a new Appendix in the 1817 edition of the *Essay*, Malthus replied: 'This is an assertion entirely without foundation. I have never adverted to the check suggested by Condorcet without the most marked disapprobation' (cited in Malthus, 1989 [1803], Vol. II, p. 235). His reasons for rejecting any 'artificial and unnatural modes of checking population' were 'their immorality', 'their tendency to remove a necessary stimulus to industry', and the 'fear that the indolence of the human race would be very greatly increased':

> If it were possible for each married couple to limit by a wish the number of their children, there is certainly reason to fear that the indolence of the human race would be very greatly increased; and that neither the population of individual countries nor of the whole earth, would ever reach its natural and proper extent (ibid., Vol. I, p. 235).

Malthus, being a minister of the Church of England at a time when the Church had not approved of contraception, would presumably have rejected contraceptive practices on the grounds of their perceived immorality, even if he had not been convinced that contraception would increase indolence and reduce the stimulus to industry. The immorality argument would have stood even if the indolence and industry arguments had been set aside. For Malthus, they were supporting rather than convincing arguments. But the fact that he made use of the indolence argument to support his criticism of contraception shows that the indolence problem occupied an important place in his overall theory of population.

INDOLENCE AND PRUDENTIAL RESTRAINT

Although he obviously intended to give great emphasis to the problem of indolence, Malthus did not adopt the extreme position of arguing that it was the only or the greatest evil confronting the human race. In this he differed from David Hume:

> Hume fell into a very great error when he asserted that 'almost all the moral, as well as natural evils of human life, arise from idleness'; and for the cure of these ills required only that the whole species should possess naturally an equal diligence with that which many individuals are able to attain by habit and reflection.[9]

For Malthus, the industry and diligence of the whole human species would not succeed in 'rescuing society from want and misery'. That would require 'another virtue', which he left unnamed in that context, but which we can reasonably assume was intended to be the virtue of prudential (or moral) restraint.

INDOLENCE AND EQUALITY

Malthus also invoked the threat of indolence in his response to the 'systems of equality' proposed by Robert Wallace (1697–1771), Condorcet and others. Condorcet had proposed that credit could be made more widely available, and should not be the exclusive privilege of great fortunes, in order that the progress of industry and commerce would then be less dependent on great capitalists. Malthus's response was to argue that economic activity would slow down if the 'idle and negligent' were to be granted credit:

> [I]f the idle and negligent be placed upon the same footing with regard to their credit…as the active and industrious, can we expect to see men exert that animated activity in bettering their condition, which now forms the master-spring of public prosperity? (ibid., p. 308).

The same argument was used to oppose Condorcet's proposal for a nationally guaranteed social insurance policy to provide assistance for the old, widows, and young families. Malthus believed that such a policy would remove the 'goad of necessity' (ibid.). The indolence argument was also extended to welfare assistance by means of the Poor Laws, and even by means of compulsory sub-scriptions to benefit clubs and friendly societies. Malthus argued that such relief measures would fail because they would inevitably cause the number of the 'idle and dissolute' to proliferate (ibid., Vol. II, pp. 164–5).

In these comments on the availability of bank credit and social insur-ance, Malthus recognised the principle that indolence is susceptible to institutional forces. There are no doubt some who, while agreeing with the principle, would challenge his interpretation of the direction of these insti-tutional effects. Malthus did not consider the possibility that, if credit-granting institutions were reformed as Condorcet suggested, many of the poor might avail themselves of business opportunities, and forsake their idle ways. As noted above, Malthus had elsewhere recognised that it was through the growth of capital that the 'idle followers of the landlords' were able to become 'merchants, manufacturers, tradesmen, farmers, and independent labourers', and that this was a change of 'prodigious advan-tage to the great body of society, including the labouring classes' (ibid., p. 84). If this were true of the idle followers of the landlords, might it not also be true of the idle poor? Likewise, it might be argued that a social insur-ance scheme that guaranteed a minimum standard of living might encourage the poor to aspire to more than mere survival. As argued below, the desire to better one's condition and the goad of consumerism could prove to be even stronger motives for industriousness than the goad of necessity. Malthus used the threat of indolence to oppose the socialistic or redistributionist proposals of Condorcet, but the same threat of indolence could be used to support Condorcet's proposals.

INDOLENCE *VERSUS* LEISURE

A theme that was left insufficiently developed in Malthus's treatment of indo-lence was the distinction between indolence and leisure. Having been so critical of the prevalence of indolence in his discussion of savage life, he surprisingly concluded that 'the only advantage in [savage life] above civilized life, that I can discover, is the possession of a greater degree of leisure by the mass of the people' (ibid., Vol. I, p. 58). By comparison with 'the incessant toil to which the lower classes of society in civilized life are condemned', he regarded the greater leisure of savage life as 'a striking advantage'. He did not suggest that savage life was therefore to be preferred over civilized life. He acknowledged that the advantage of leisure is probably overbalanced by the much greater disadvan-tages of primitive life—he mentioned, in that context, a most tyrannical distinction of rank, blows, violation of property, and the comparative degrada-tion of the lower classes. It is nevertheless clear that, in Malthus's mind, leisure is of itself a desirable goal, and is not to be equated with indolence or idleness. We are not, however, given any clear criteria for distinguishing between desirable leisure and undesirable indolence.

Further statements in praise of leisure can be found in his eulogy of the surplus produce or rent of agricultural land. The quality of the earth is such that it can produce more food and more of the materials of clothing and lodging than are necessary to feed, clothe and lodge those employed in their production. Because of this surplus produce, 'leisure has been given to a greater number of persons to employ themselves in all the inventions which embellish civilized life' (ibid., Vol. II, p. 30). This surplus produce of agriculture 'will always increase, and furnish funds for arts, sciences, and leisure' and 'will always afford a fund for the enjoyments and leisure of the society, sufficient to leaven and animate the whole mass'. If this surplus is small, a large portion of society will be employed in producing the mere necessaries of life, and society will be 'most scantily provided with conveniences,[10] luxuries and leisure'; but if the surplus is large, 'manufactures, foreign luxuries, arts, letters and leisure may abound'. Malthus added that 'there is every reason to believe' that these benefits 'may be divided among a much greater number of persons' (Malthus, 1989 [1820], Vol. I, pp. 237–8, 554).

Not only did Malthus believe that increased leisure was highly desirable; he also argued that the enjoyment of leisure was a moral obligation, one that was ordained by natural law, and that a refusal to accept a life of greater leisure would have adverse economic consequences:

> [T]he great laws of nature have provided for the leisure of a certain portion of society...[I]f this beneficent offer be not accepted by an adequate number of individuals, not only will a positive good, which might have been so attained, be lost, but the rest of the society, so far from being benefited by such self-denial, will be decidedly injured by it...and if it be not accepted, the progress of wealth will be impeded rather than accelerated (ibid., pp. 463–4, 585).

It is difficult to understand how Malthus could argue that the progress of wealth would be enhanced if more people were leisured and fewer people worked, and would be retarded if more people worked, and fewer were leisured. A possible resolution of this paradox is that, when he advocated a greater degree of leisure, he thought of leisure not as a state of inactivity and inertness, but as a situation where the leisured members of society would be engaged in the provision of services – such as, doctors, teachers, actors – rather than in the production of material goods. The provision of services could cause the production of goods to be maintained, or even increased. The producers of goods would be motivated to produce more goods in order to purchase services, and although the providers of services were no longer producing goods, they would generate a demand for the goods that made up their necessaries, comforts and conveniences.

That Malthus did not intend 'leisure' to be synonymous with 'idleness' can also be inferred from his statement that if statesmen and their principal advisers do not have the leisure to devote time to the study of political economy, they should be guided by those who do have the leisure; and those who have the leisure and ability to pursue researches in political economy should not be deterred by any 'common difficulty or obscurity' (Malthus, 1989 [1803], Vol. I, pp. 17–18). Malthus had the leisure to study political economy, but he probably would not have described his life of leisure as one of indolence, idleness or sloth.

The idea that 'leisure' was intended to mean not a state of indolence and inactivity, but a situation where the leisured would be actively engaged in the provision of services, could also be inferred from a statement added to the second edition of Malthus's *Principles of Political Economy*, where it is said that in a country with fertile land 'a larger proportion of its population might enjoy leisure, or be engaged in personal services without prejudice to its wealth'.[11] Malthus perceived that the leisure and luxuries enjoyed by landlords would motivate others to advance their rank in society. The man of business would not submit to long hours of clerical drudgery – 'It is not the most pleasant employment to spend eight hours a day in a counting-house' – unless motivated by a desire to contend with the landlords in the 'enjoyment of leisure, as well as of foreign and domestic luxuries' (Malthus, 1989 [1820], Vol. I, p. 470).

As well as justifying those whose leisure is financed by land rents, Malthus spoke favourably (albeit briefly) in favour of those whose leisure is financed by mortgages and by dividends received on public loans. In a letter in 1816 to William Smith, MP, he was critical of Smith's proposal to cancel the national debt, reminding Smith that 'a great body of the most helpless portion of society, whom it is our duty to protect, rely almost solely on the funds for their incomes'.[12] He also said in the first edition of his *Principles* that, with a more favourable distribution of a nation's produce, numerous people 'could live nearly at leisure upon their mortgages', adding that this would contribute to an 'improved structure of society'. For Malthus, living at leisure on one's investment income was an honourable estate.[13]

Malthus's views on whether the labouring classes can expect increased leisure were left unclear. In one passage in the first edition of his *Principles* (1820) he expressed the view that many among the labouring classes work too hard, and that they should be given a 'greater degree of relaxation from severe toil', even if this meant a reduction of national wealth and populousness; but he immediately said: 'I see no probability, or even possibility, of accomplishing this object,' adding that it would be 'an act of gross injustice' to legislate for shorter hours, in contravention of 'the principle of competition' (ibid., pp. 473–4). A little later in the first edition of the *Principles* this view was reinforced by the statement: 'it would not be possible, under the principle of competition (which can never be got rid of) to secure much more leisure to those actually engaged in manual labour' (ibid., p. 483). Thus he was saying in 1820 that increased leisure for the labouring classes was desirable, but unlikely to occur; but his final position on this issue was left unclear, because these statements were omitted from the second (posthumous) edition of the *Principles* in 1836.[14] He gave no explanation for the omission. Nor do we know whether he himself was responsible for the omission, or whether the omission was made on the initiative of John Cazenove, the editor of the second edition.[15] We cannot conclude therefore that the omission represents a recantation.

Another statement that some labourers work too hard and too long, and should have more leisure, can be found in his *Inquiry into the Nature and Progress of Rent* (Malthus, 1815, p. 49n):

> To work really hard during twelve or fourteen hours in the day, for any length of time, is too much for a human being. Some intervals of ease are necessary to health and happiness: and the occasional abuse of such intervals is not valid argument against their use.

The statement is made with conviction and appears to express genuine concern, but it was omitted (without explanation) when the *Inquiry* of 1815 was incorporated into Chapter III of the *Principles* (1820), and we are again faced with the problem of deciding whether the omission represents a recantation.

INDOLENCE AND CHARITY

As already noted, one of the arguments used by Malthus against the Poor Laws was that they encouraged indolence. He applied that argument also to indiscriminate private charity. He believed that the poor man should be taught to depend on 'his own exertions, his own industry and foresight', and that he should not expect assistance from private charity if his difficulties have arisen from his own 'indolence or imprudence'. The poor do not have a right to support, and their best entitlement to support should be their not having brought distress upon themselves by their 'own idleness or extravagance'. Citing the reports of travellers, he stated (as noted above) that in Tibet the 'mass of indigence and idleness' was due to the 'indiscriminate charity' resulting from a humane but misguided disposition. More generally, he spoke of 'the evil habits which might be generated by depending for a considerable time on mere alms'. He approved of 'discriminate and occasional assistance' for the distress of the poor, but did not approve of assistance for distress caused by 'idle and improvident habits' (Malthus, 1989 [1803], Vol. I, pp. 120, 369; Vol. II, pp. 161, 189, 216).

INDOLENCE AND SECTORAL BALANCE

The indolence factor also figured in Malthus's argument for sectoral balance; that is, for an economy in which agriculture, manufacturing and commerce would be optimally balanced, as opposed to an economy where manufacturing occupies a dominant place and which depends for its food supply on the vagaries of the export market in manufactures. A nation that is excessively dependent on manufacturing exports could not survive if its customers, 'from indolence and want of accumulation', would not, or could not, purchase its manufactures. Their demands for its manufactured exports would be affected by their 'indolence, industry or caprice'. Its economic progress, instead of being under its own control, would be affected by the 'ignorance and indolence of others' (ibid., Vol. II, pp. 34–5, 42).

INDOLENCE AND ORIGINAL SIN

The problem of indolence permeated not only Malthus's economic, social and political deliberations, but also his theology. In the final chapters of the first edition of the *Essay* he presented a novel interpretation, based on the concept of indolence, of the Christian doctrine of Original Sin.

He did not reject the explanation of Original Sin given in the Book of Genesis. From the accounts of friends and colleagues, and from his own words, particularly those of his surviving sermons, it is clear that he remained throughout his life a devout and sincere Christian clergyman. His alternative version of Original Sin was derived from Natural Theology, or from what we can know through reason, rather than from Revelation. It would not have been intended as a rejection of Revelation, given that since reason and Revelation both come from God, the truths derived from one could not be inconsistent with those derived from the other.

In his naturalistic version, he said that 'The original sin of man, is the torpor and corruption of the chaotic matter, in which he may be said to be born'. He described man's original state as 'the sluggishness of original matter'.[16]

INDOLENCE—NATURAL OR ACQUIRED?

Is indolence the product of nature or of nurture? In some statements Malthus seemed to argue that indolence is a basic trait of human nature, and therefore universal, unavoidable, and irremediable. In other statements he seemed to suggest that it was caused by adverse environmental and institutional conditions, and was therefore remediable. Whether his view of human destiny is to be ultimately classified as positive and optimistic, or as negative and pessimistic, will depend (at least in part) on which of these two positions is preponderant. That Malthus believed indolence to be part of human nature would seem to be implied by his use of expressions such as 'natural indolence', 'inveterate indolence', 'inveterate habits of idleness' and 'the acknowledged indolence of man', and in his assertion that 'a state of sloth, not of activity' is 'the natural state of man' (ibid., Vol. I, pp. 60, 93, 102, 154, 434–5). He also believed that man, as he really is, is 'inert, sluggish and averse from labour, unless compelled by necessity', and that without the stimulus of necessity, the 'savage would slumber forever under his tree' and would 'sink into listless inactivity' (Malthus, 1926 [1798], pp. 357, 363).

However, Malthus also recognized that indolence can be either engendered or exacerbated by environmental, political and institutional forces. For example, he accepted Humboldt's view that, although the Mexican Indians were indolent by character, their indolence was aggravated by their political situation.[17] He added: 'That the indolence of the natives is greatly aggravated by their political situation, cannot for a moment be doubted'. Elsewhere, he asserted that 'ignorance and indolence...almost necessarily accompany' a state of vassalage or slavery (Malthus, 1989 [1803], Vol. I, pp. 177, 388). This suggests that indolence is not a necessary human characteristic, but is the product of the political system.

Indolence can be exacerbated not only by political conditions, but also by economic factors. Once again using Humboldt's account of New Spain, Malthus noted that the opening up of a new mine in an area will create an 'animated and effective demand' for labour, thus overcoming the indolence that had previously characterised the workers of the area. Speaking more generally he held that indolence 'yields to excitement and demand' (Malthus, 1989 [1820], Vol. I, pp. 388, 575). The influence of economic determinants is also apparent in his account (noted above) of the Russian boors. The taxation system and the land distribution system took away their incentive to work productively, and reinforced their indolence. As also noted above, he believed that the system induces indolence in the landowners as well as in the farmers and vassals.

Perhaps the clearest and strongest evidence for Malthus's belief that indolence is institutionally determined is to be found in his criticisms of the Poor Laws. Their effect, he argued, was to encourage indolence and dependence, and thus to create the poor they were intended to maintain. His recognition that indolence can be institutionally determined is also apparent in his statement that the 'practice among labourers of not working more than three or four days in the week' would adversely affect population growth whether it arose 'either from inveterate indolence, or any other cause' (Malthus, 1989 [1803], Vol. I, p. 434). This suggests that, in his mind, 'inveterate indolence' was not the only possible cause of a short working week, and that causes arising from institutional factors, rather than from the nature of man, could also be responsible.

The question of whether indolence is natural or acquired was highlighted in Malthus's discussion of Ireland. He stated that the 'indolence of the country-labourers in Ireland has been universally remarked', but he left unanswered the question of 'whether this arises from there being really little for them to do in the actual state of things, or from a natural tendency to idleness, not to be overcome by ordinary stimulants'. The fertility of the land of Ireland, and the adoption of the potato as the staple food of the lower classes, have meant that the land can support 'a much greater population than it can employ',[18] and that the 'natural and necessary effect...is the very general prevalence of habits of indolence'. The redundant population generates 'an excessive degree of poverty and misery as well as indolence'. Malthus thus seems to attribute the indolence of the Irish labourer more to social circumstances than to human nature, and to suggest that such indolence would be replaced by industriousness given the proper stimulants:

> In defence, however, of the Irish peasant, it may be truly said, that in the state of society in which he has been placed, he has not had a fair trial; he has not been subjected to the ordinary stimulants which produce industrious habits (Malthus, 1989 [1820], Vol. I, p. 396).

When it is a question of providing themselves with new clothing, then the cost of the materials, their low wages, the difficulty of preparing new clothes, and the custom of wearing old clothes a little longer, combine to make the 'temptations to indolence...too powerful for human weakness' (ibid., p. 397). Malthus believed that the indolent habits of the Irish peasant 'might soon change' if he were given 'constant employment at a fair money price'; and that, more generally, industrious habits can never occur without constant work: 'it may be doubted whether any large body of people in any country ever acquired regular and industrious habits, where they were unable to get regular and constant work'. As in the case of the Mexican Indians, the indolence of the Irish is affected by the lack of demand for their labour: 'If the labour of the Irish peasant, whether in the house or in the field, were always in demand, his habits might soon change' (ibid., pp. 397–8, 576).

This relationship between indolence and the demand for labour was also clearly stated in a new footnote added by Malthus to the second edition of his *Principles*. In that footnote he said that the practice of the labourers working only two or three days a week could have arisen 'partly from indolence, and partly from the want of demand for labour', thus admitting that external or institutional factors might be as important as any innate or natural factor in explaining the occurrence of under-employment. In other words, under-employment and indolence could be either involuntary or voluntary.[19] More significantly, Malthus added that, in old states, the want of demand for labour is 'the great parent of indolence' (ibid., Vol. II, pp. 186, 388), which implies that the external institutional factor is even more important than any innate moral fault. This is also significant because it implies that moral attitudes are affected by economic conditions.

Malthus concluded his discussion in the *Principles* of the 'state of Ireland' by saying that, although an 'immense capital' would be required to develop fully her national resources, the premature supply of capital would be less beneficial than a change in the 'tastes and habits of the lower classes of people' (ibid., Vol. I, pp. 400–401, 576). This raises the question of the order of causation. Should the investment of capital precede the change of tastes and habits, or vice versa? If indolence is affected, at least to some extent, by environmental factors such as the demand for labour, and if the demand for labour is a function of the supply of capital, it would seem that capital investment must come first. However, since investment will be ineffectual if habits of indolence prevail, then it would seem that a change of tastes and habits must come first. Malthus did not explicitly address this issue. If he had done so, he would probably have invoked the concept of the mutuality and reciprocity of causation—a concept that was a frequent and distinctive feature of his methodology.

The question therefore is: Can Malthus's views on the natural and the institutional bases of indolence be reconciled? If he had devoted a chapter or an essay to the question of indolence, perhaps that question would have been answered. Unsympathetic critics will see his statements on indolence as further evidence of his muddle-headedness and self-contradiction, and will draw unfavourable comparisons with the (alleged) logic of David Ricardo. A less unsympathetic interpretation might be that there is in human nature a tendency or proclivity towards indolence, but one that can be either exacerbated or minimized by institutional determinants. The fact that Malthus identified ways in which indolence could be overcome implies that, in saying that it is natural, he did not mean that it is an essential, irremediable, invincible, and a permanent feature of all humankind.

The question of whether, in Malthus's view, indolence is natural or acquired, is also relevant to the question of whether Malthus was 'Darwinian' (or, placing them in their chronological order, whether Darwin was Malthusian). If indolence is an essential, invincible, irremediable feature of all humankind, neither created nor increased nor diminished in interplay with environmental circumstances, there can be, with respect to indolence, no struggle, no change, and no evolution.

However, although Malthus emphasised the utility of external or institutional forces in overcoming indolence, it would not be correct to conclude that he attributed progress to external forces only. As already noted, he attributed great significance to the 'desire to better one's condition', which he regarded as a 'laudable' internal force that is 'strongly implanted in the human breast' (ibid., pp. 476, 517).

REMEDIES FOR INDOLENCE

Malthus explicitly recommended two main policies for ridding the world of indolence, but further policy recommendations can be inferred from his views on the institutional causes of indolence.

The first explicit policy recommendation was to refuse poor relief to those whose poverty was the result of their own indolence, thus forcing them to abandon their indolent ways and discouraging others from becoming indolent. He believed that the indolent should be allowed to bear the full consequence of their indolence. Unless indolence brings its own punishment, there will be a decline in 'animated activity' and 'public prosperity': 'if industry did not bring with it its reward, and indolence its punishment; we could not expect to see that animated activity in bettering our condition which now forms the master-spring of public prosperity' (Malthus, 1989 [1803], Vol. II, p. 194).

The second explicitly recommended policy was the more general adoption of 'economical and industrious habits, particularly among unmarried men'. He hoped that this would prevent that 'indolence, drunkenness, and waste of labour, which at present are too frequently a consequence of high wages' (ibid., p. 196). However, he did not enter into a discussion of the methods and feasibility of persuading unmarried men and others to adopt 'economical and industrious habits'. Presumably, he hoped that this could be achieved through education, and that his own writings would contribute to that educational process.

Malthus thus seems to have believed that, to the extent that economic progress depends on the elimination of indolence, the economic progress both of the individual and of society as a whole requires a moral transformation at the level of the individual. It is a clear statement of Malthus's belief in the intimate connection between ethics and economics. Additional cures for indolence can be inferred from the many institutional factors mentioned by Malthus as causes of indolence. As noted above, these included a combination of geographical, social, psychological and economic factors—such as systems of land tenure, taxation policies, political structures, the demand for labour, the constancy of employment, the fertility of the soil, the choice of staple food, the tastes and habits of the people, etc.[20]

The principal economic determinant of indolence – and, hence, the principal economic cure for indolence – was the demand for labour; and the question of the determinants of the demand for labour, and of effective demand in general, was the subject of Malthus's (1820) *Principles of Political Economy*, in particular chapter VII, 'On the Immediate Causes of the Progress of Wealth', Sections

VI–X, where he argued that effective demand is generated by a wider (but not too wide) distribution of wealth and income. In this way, whether his economic theories are correct or not, Malthus was obviously attempting to show the causal reciprocity between the economic and the ethical, and to establish an integrated theory of economic and ethical growth.

It is clear therefore that, insofar as Malthus can be described as an evolutionist, his evolutionism was of the pro-active, hands-on, interventionist variety. He was not content for society to evolve slowly by its own internal struggles. Rather, he envisaged a conscious and deliberate policy of social melioration, through education, political reform, land tenure reform, and any other measures that would encourage industrious and prudent behaviour.[21]

SOME CONCLUDING COMMENTS

Malthus's remarks on indolence leave a number of questions unanswered. For example, he argued that the struggle to overcome natural indolence would contribute towards the evolutionary progress of those involved in the struggle. The poor would be obliged by 'the goad of necessity' to undertake the struggle, but he did not say what would happen to the rich, who, by definition, are not subject to the goad of necessity. If they are not obliged to struggle, how will their natural indolence be overcome? Will they be deprived of the beneficial effects of evolutionary progress? What will happen to their 'growth of mind'? Their riches would also exclude them from the beneficial effects to be achieved by the struggle involved in the practice of prudential restraint. If they are sufficiently wealthy, they can marry as early and have as many children as they like.

Another issue not explicitly addressed by Malthus was the possible conflict between the indolence problem and the population problem. If through moral reform and/or the goad of necessity, people become less indolent, and begin to work harder, they will then produce or purchase more food, and be able to marry earlier and raise more children—thus exacerbating the threat of over-population. If Malthus had addressed this question, he probably would have asserted, as he did in reply to similar criticisms, that he was not 'an enemy to population', and that an increased population was desirable, provided that it could occur without reduction in the quality of life.

Another way of expressing the same paradox is to ask: If, as Malthus argued, population pressure is part of the Divine Plan for raising man from his natural, slothful condition and for the growth of mind, and if population pressure has existed for such a long time in so many countries, why does large-scale indolence still exist? This dilemma was unfortunately not explored by Malthus. A possible solution might lie in the distinction between a winnable struggle and an unwinnable struggle. If the struggle for survival is too severe, it will not result in evolutionary growth, but will generate a spirit of hopelessness and fatalistic despair. If the economic and social circumstances render it impossible to better one's condition, population pressure will not succeed in counteracting indolence.

A further theme left unsatisfactorily treated by Malthus is the seeming contradiction between natural indolence and the natural desire to better our condition. Levin (1966, p. 95n) has recognised that, in Malthus's view, man's innate desire to better his condition prods him to overcome his innate indolence, and to raise himself to a higher level of living. But, as well as noting the countervailing effect of the two forces, we could ask whether in fact there is a paradox or a logical inconsistency in asserting that the two forces can co-exist within human nature. One possible way of resolving the paradox would be to argue that these two conflicting tendencies do in fact co-exist within human nature; and that to assert their co-existence is not to indulge in self-contradiction but rather to accept the reality of the internal contradiction. However, as far as I am aware, Malthus did not address the paradox, and we therefore have no textual guide to his possible response.

Another possible way of resolving the paradox would be to argue that, if some persons judge that their condition will be bettered by becoming more indolent, then for those persons there is no logical conflict between the instinct to be indolent and the instinct to better their condition. However, although that resolution of the paradox removes a logical dilemma, it would hardly be acceptable to Malthus, in whose judgment indolence was abhorrent.

Finally, if Malthus was correct in saying, in his case against contraception, that if people could limit the size of their families at will, they would become indolent, then the widespread practice of contraception in many countries today should have resulted in a great increase in indolence. But it does not seem to have had that effect. This suggests either that Malthus might have been wrong in declaring mankind to be naturally indolent, or that he had overlooked the existence of some powerful institutional forces that can effectively counter any innate tendency towards indolence when the child-support motivation has been removed or diminished. It is not difficult to suggest what these alternative motivational forces might be in modern society. Conspicuous consumption, as Veblen taught us, is an obvious one; and the emulation effect, or the urge to 'keep up with the Joneses', is just as pressing as the goad of necessity.

The ever-increasing range of consumption possibilities provides another powerful anti-indolence motivating force. Malthus could never have envisioned the vast array of useful and useless consumer goods that modern technology has made available even for people of moderate means. Their desire to possess cars, refrigerators, television sets, computers, foreign travel, etc., is sufficiently strong to raise most people from their natural torpor. These wants are further stimulated by the persuasive arts of advertising that have succeeded in 'educating' us out of our natural inertia. Malthus recognized that one of the ways to overcome indolence was to stimulate the 'wants and tastes' of the people, a process that he deemed to be both slow and difficult. He would be astounded to find the extent to which wants and tastes have expanded, and how quickly and easily they can be manipulated. Even those who make a deliberate decision to 'drop out' of our consumption-led modern society, usually retain a modicum of comfortable consumer goods that far exceeds what Malthus could have dreamt of, and that ensures that their owners do not succumb to utter indolence.

Property prices and mortgage obligations provide yet another motivational force that successfully drives many of us away from a life of delightful sloth into forty years or more of hectic work and saving. The fact is that, unsuspected by Malthus, consumerism in many societies today is at least as powerful as population pressure as a cure for indolence, although some would argue that an over-generous welfare state could be removing the goad of necessity, encouraging indolence, and creating the poor it seeks to maintain. The goad of necessity still exists, even in affluent economies, although it might have changed from a concern with biological survival to the self-inflicted 'necessity' of ever-expanding consumption. The problem of indolence may therefore have taken on new dimensions since Malthus wrote, but there can be no doubt that – whether it be called indolence, torpor, sluggishness, laziness, inertness, listlessness, idleness, sloth, or an aversion to labour – the problem of indolence was a persistent preoccupation for Malthus, and one that he deemed to be of vital concern for economic progress and human welfare.

NOTES

1. It is perhaps worth noting that, for Malthus, though not for many so-called Malthusians, population pressure is not always harmful. Up to a point, it can be an important, and even a necessary, cause of economic, social and intellectual growth.
2. The idleness of the men was in contrast with the 'wretched state' of the women: 'A wife is no better than a beast of burthen. While the man passes his days in idleness or amusement, the woman is condemned to incessant toil' (Malthus, 1989 [1803], Vol. I, pp. 30, 32).
3. 'The desire of the conveniences and ornaments of building, dress, equipage, and household furniture, seems to have no limit or certain boundary' (Adam Smith, *Wealth of Nations*; cited in Malthus, 1989 [1820], Vol. I, p. 468).
4. ibid. See also ibid., p. 586: 'the tendency to consume is powerfully counteracted by the love of indolence.'
5. Although Malthus argued that indolence was an important impediment to the growth of consumption, he did not argue that it was the only important impediment. Other impediments included the desire to better our condition and the desire to provide for a family, both of which stimulated the desire to save. He said, for example, that consumption would be limited by 'the general desire of mankind to better their condition, and make provision for a family.' and by 'the desire to save in order to better our condition' (ibid., pp. 468, 586). See also ibid., p. 503: 'We should constantly keep in mind that the tendency to expenditure in individuals has most formidable antagonists in the love of indolence, and in the desire of saving, in order to better their condition and provide for a family.' For his frequent emphasis on the 'desire to

better one's conditions', see Malthus, 1989 [1803], Vol. I, pp. 62, 308, 363, 439; Vol. II, pp. 145, 187, 198, 202; and 1989 [1820], Vol. I, pp. 468, 476, 503, 517, 586.

6. See Malthus, 1989 [1820], Ch. VII, Sec. IV: 'Fertility of the Soil, considered as a Stimulus to the continued Increase of Wealth'.

7. Presumably a reference to the great inequalities in the distribution of land.

8. Ibid., Vol. I, p. 503. Such statements could be used to support a claim that Malthus was an early exponent of economic humanism, if that term is taken to mean an economics that gives great emphasis to the role of human character and human motivation in its theory of economic growth.

9. Malthus, 1989 [1803], Vol. II, pp. 188–9, citing David Hume, *Dialogues Concerning Natural Religion*. Hume's statement continues:

    and were our species, by the original constitution of their frame, exempt from this vice or infirmity, the perfect cultivation of land, the improvement of arts and manufactures, the exact execution of every office and duty, immediately follow; and man at once may fully reach that state of society, which is so perfectly attained by the best-regulated government (Hume, 1963 [1779], p. 183).

    Despite Malthus's criticism of Hume on this point, he was fully in accord with, and might have been influenced by, Hume's comment that '[Nature] has so contrived [man's] frame, that nothing but the most violent necessity can oblige him to labour; and she employs all his other wants to overcome, at least in part, the want of diligence, and to endow him with some share of a faculty, of which she has thought fit naturally to bereave him' (ibid.).

10. 'conveniences' was printed as 'convenients' in the first edition, but was corrected in the second edition (Malthus, 1989 [1820], Vol. I, p. 230; Vol. II, p. 193).

11. Ibid., Vol. II, p. 267. However, the added statement is not unambiguous. It could be interpreted in a way that would allow 'leisure' to include 'indolence', as well as 'personal services'.

12. Malthus (1816). Extracts from the letter were contained in a sale catalogue in 1960. Malthus supplemented his salary from the East India College with dividends from his investments in the funds, and he assisted his sister to make investments. Their father, Daniel Malthus, had independent means; there is no record of his ever having to engage in paid work.

13. The passage was omitted from the second edition of the *Principles*, but there is no evidence that the omission meant a retraction. See Malthus, 1989 [1820], Vol. I, p. 483; Vol. II, pp. 280, 461–2.

14. Ibid., Vol. II, pp. 278, 459–60.

15. On the part played by Cazenove in editing the second edition, see ibid., Vol. I, pp. lxi–lxiv; and Pullen (1978).

16. Malthus, 1926 [1798], pp. 354, 357. As already stated, this theological material in the last two chapters of the first edition of the *Essay* was omitted from later editions, but there is no convincing proof that the omission was a recantation.

17. 'Les Indiens Mexicains…indolens par caractère, et plus encore par suite de leur situation politique, les natifs ne vivent qu'au jour le jour' (Humboldt, *Essai Politique*; cited by Malthus, 1989 [1820], Vol. I, p. 387).

18. The work required of a man on a small farm is less than a single day in the week, with the result that 'they are generally seen loitering about, as if time was absolutely of no value to them' (ibid., pp. 396–7).

19. Although Malthus was clearly aware of the distinction between voluntary and involuntary indolence, he could perhaps have given the latter greater emphasis. Much of what he said about indolence as an inveterate and natural phenomenon would not be applicable to the involuntary indolence resulting from an inadequate demand for labour.

20. Malthus regarded tastes as 'more the children of accident & education than nature'. See Vol. II, forthcoming, of Malthus (1997). In other words, natural indolence can be overcome by suitable tastes, and suitable tastes arise more from external environmental forces than from nature.

21. In this respect it might be possible to see Malthus as a precursor of the so-called 'Baldwin effect', according to which in the evolutionary process the capacity to acquire particular char-

acteristics can be inherited even though the particular characteristics themselves are not inherited. Improvements in the educational and material circumstances of families would hopefully mean that the children who inherit these conditions would be more receptive to the adoption of industrious and prudent habits. I am grateful to John Laurent for suggesting this possible link with the 'Baldwin effect'. See Introduction in Laurent and Nightingale (2001).

REFERENCES

Hume, D. (1963) [1779], *Dialogues Concerning Natural Religion*, reprinted in R. Wollheim (ed.) *Hume on Religion*, London: Collins.

Laurent, J. and J. Nightingale (eds) (2001), *Darwinism and Evolutionary Economics*, Cheltenham, U.K. and Northampton, MA, U.S.A.: Edward Elgar.

Levin, S.M. (1966), 'Malthus and the idea of progress', *Journal of the History of Ideas*, **27**, 92–108.

Malthus, T.R. (1926) [1798], *An Essay on the Principle of Population*, reprinted in *idem*, *First Essay on Population*, London: Macmillan.

Malthus, T.R. (1989) [1803], *An Essay on the Principle of Population*, reprinted in P. James (ed.) *An Essay on the Principle of Population*. Variorum edn, Cambridge: Cambridge University Press for the Royal Economic Society, 2 vols.

Malthus, T.R. (1815), *An Inquiry into the Nature and Progress of Rent*, London: John Murray and J. Johnson and Co.

Malthus, T.R. (1989) [1820], *Principles of Political Economy*, reprinted in J. Pullen (ed.) *Principles of Political Economy*. Variorum edn, Cambridge: Cambridge University Press for the Royal Economic Society, 2 vols.

Malthus, T.R. (1997), *T.R. Malthus: The Unpublished Papers in the Collection of Kanto Gakuen University*, J. Pullen and T. Hughes Parry (eds), Cambridge: Cambridge University Press for the Royal Economic Society, Vol. I.

Pullen, J. (1978), 'The editor of the second edition of T.R. Malthus's Principles of Political Economy', *History of Political Economy*, **10**(2), 286–97.

Pullen, J. (1987), 'Malthus, Jesus, and Darwin', *Religious Studies*, **23**, 233–46.

5. Charles Darwin on Human Nature

John Laurent

In December 1857 Charles Darwin wrote to fellow naturalist Alfred Russel Wallace, then in the Celebes islands (Sulawesi), concerning Darwin's long awaited book on the 'species question': 'You ask whether I shall discuss "man". I think I shall avoid the whole subject, as it is so surrounded with prejudices— though I fully admit that it is the highest and most interesting problem for the naturalist' (Darwin, 1995, p. 183). True to his word, when Darwin was jolted into hurriedly putting together the 'abstract' of his work which was to go on sale as *The Origin of Species*, after receiving Wallace's letter independently outlining a theory of natural selection (see Darwin and Wallace, 1958, pp. 268– 79), Darwin wrote no more on the subject than to say, on the second last page of the book, 'In the distant future I see open fields for far more important re-searches. Psychology will be based on a new foundation, that of the necessary acquirement of each mental power and capacity by gradation. Light will be thrown on the origin of man and his history' (Darwin, 1901, p. 375).

It was to be a little over 11 more years before Darwin finally overcame his reticence and published the treatise on 'man' (Darwin's term) that everyone was expecting; and again it was Wallace who played a major part in this. Among Darwin's books and papers held in the Cambridge University Library is a copy of the May 1864 issue of the *Anthropological Review* containing Wallace's 'The Development of Human Races under the law of Natural Selection', a number of passages of which have been heavily marked by Darwin, including the following:

> Capacity for acting in concert, for protection and for the acquisition of food and shelter; sympathy, which leads all in turn to assist each other; the sense of right, which checks depredations upon our fellows; the decrease of the combative and de-structive propensities; self-restraint in present appetites; and that intelligent foresight which prepares for the future, are qualities that from their earliest appearance must have been for the benefit of each community, and would, therefore, have become the subjects of 'natural selection' (Wallace, 1864, p. clxii).

And Darwin went on to double-mark these lines:

Tribes in which such mental and moral qualities were predominant, would therefore have an advantage in the struggle for existence over other tribes in which they were less developed, would live and maintain their numbers, while the others would decrease and finally succumb (ibid.).

Darwin does not add marginal comments, but his whole-hearted agreement with Wallace is clear: he wrote to Wallace (now back in England) congratulating him for his 'grand and most eloquently done' paper; and to his (Darwin's) American friend, the botanist Asa Gray, Darwin commended Wallace's 'most suggestive article on the natural history of man' (Darwin, 2001, pp. 212, 216). When Darwin's *The Descent of Man and Selection in Relation to Sex* (henceforth shortened to *The Descent of Man*) finally appeared in early 1871 (with a second edition in 1874), Darwin was quick to acknowledge Wallace's contribution, which in the meantime had appeared as a chapter in Wallace's book, *Contributions to the Theory of Natural Selection* (Wallace, 1870). Ironically, Wallace had also, by this time, sought to *diminish* the role of natural selection in the development of man's mental and 'moral' faculties—as in his essay, 'The Limits of Natural Selection as Applied to Man', which also became a chapter in *Contributions to the Theory of Natural Selection*.

Whatever Wallace's later position on human evolution, a perusal of *The Descent of Man* – especially of chapter IV on 'The Moral Sense' – shows that Darwin had fully embraced Wallace's earlier suggestions and had expanded upon them, making the link with pre-human species:

All animals living in a body, which defend themselves or attack their enemies in concert, must indeed be in some degree faithful to one another...Although man...has no special instincts to tell him how to aid his fellow-men, he still has the impulse, and with his improved intellectual faculties would naturally be much guided in this respect by reason and experience (Darwin, 1875, pp. 104, 109).

Darwin elsewhere describes animals 'living in a body' as 'social' animals. He writes (p. 100): 'Animals of many kinds are social...Everyone must have noticed how miserable horses, dogs, sheep, etc., are when separated from their companions, and what strong affection the two former kinds, at least, shew [sic] on their reunion';[1] and for 'mutual affection' Darwin sometimes uses the term 'sympathy', which he says may have evolved in part from instinctive feelings associated with parental care for offspring (which, as we saw in my earlier chapter, was also noted by Augustine):

With those animals which have benefited by living in close association, the individuals which took the greatest pleasure in society would best escape various dangers, whilst those that cared least for their comrades, and lived solitary, would perish in greater numbers. With respect to the origin of the parental and filial affections, which apparently lie at the base of the social instincts, we know not the steps by which they have been gained; but we may infer that it has been to a large extent through natural selection (Darwin, 1875, p. 105).

Natural selection, then – as with Wallace – lay at the basis of *social* evolution, and what would today be described as 'altruism', as in books like *Unto Others: The Evolution and Psychology of Unselfish Behaviour* (Sober and Wilson, 1998). Darwin elaborates from a few lines further down the same page in *The Descent of Man*:

> [W]ith all animals, sympathy is directed...towards the members of the same community, and therefore towards known, and more or less beloved members, but not to all the individuals of the same species...With mankind, selfishness, experience, and imitation probably add...to the power of sympathy; for we are led by the hope of receiving good in return to perform acts of sympathetic kindness to others; and sympathy is much strengthened by habit. In however complex a manner this feeling may have originated, as it is one of high importance to all those animals which aid and defend one another, it will have been increased through natural selection; for those communities who included the greatest number of the most sympathetic members, would flourish best, and rear the greatest number of offspring (Darwin, 1875, pp. 106–7).

At least two important topics in current debates in evolutionary theory are touched on in this extract written 130 years ago by Darwin. Firstly, as can be seen, Darwin has not forgotten the centrality of *competition* in his and A.R. Wallace's theory of natural selection. This factor is not overruled by Darwin's emphasis here on 'sympathy', or 'affection': it is simply shifted so as to operate *between* communities (or groups) of animals or humans. 'Group selection' may be currently out of favour with many theorists who wish to focus on the individual, or even gene (e.g. Dawkins, 1989) as the unit of selection, but the idea is by no means extinct, as is witnessed in the continuing appearance of books and articles on the topic such as Sober and Wilson's (above), V.C. Wynne-Edwards's (1986) *Evolution through Group Selection* and Samir Okasha's (2001) 'Why Won't the Group Selection Controversy Go Away?' The arguments for and against group selection will not be examined at length here (for a good discussion see Hodgson, 1993, pp. 186–94); what is important at this juncture is that *Darwin*, anyway, certainly believed in group selection, and that this strongly informed his understanding of human nature (and so, in turn – consciously or unconsciously – continues to influence our understanding of the same).

A second major point made by Darwin in the above extract (a third relates to his use of the term 'habit', of which more will be said below) is less controversial, but also is a helpful corrective to some of the less persuasive arguments of today's evolutionary theorists. In a recent article, the eminent geneticist John Maynard Smith (2001) discussed the so-called phenomenon of 'reciprocal altruism' in nature—the 'you scratch my back and I'll scratch yours' argument. This has been around for a long time: it was made much of by writers such as

Robert Trivers in the 1970s (e.g., Trivers, 1971)—though even then the case made for operation of the principle in species such as ants drew heavy criticism for what was seen as unrealistic assumptions concerning the capabilities (memory, etc.) of these species (see, e.g., 'Why You Do What You Do', *Time*, 1 August 1977). In the economics sphere, the theory continues to attract game theorists, who look for evidence of its operation in Prisoner's Dilemma and suchlike game situations.

The kinds of criticisms directed at Trivers may still hold, to some extent at least, for Maynard Smith's arguments. Maynard Smith discussed the possibilities of 'cheating' associated with 'signalling' in some species (where an animal indicates it is ready to receive, but avoids returning, some favour), and concludes that this is minimal where animals live in small and stable groups and 'are able to recognize other members of the group as individuals, and which are intelligent enough to remember whether a particular individual's signals have been honest in the past and to respond accordingly' (ibid., p. 12). Perhaps, but as can be seen above, Darwin does not ask us to accept such claims for the abilities of non-human species. He limits 'reciprocal' altruism to humans: it is we who are 'led by the hope of receiving good in return to perform acts of sympathetic kindness to others.' 'Altruism' (or at least mutual assistance) in other species is made possible by the instinctive promptings of 'sympathy' alone.

This term 'sympathy' is also, of course, a crucial one in Adam Smith's *The Theory of Moral Sentiments* (Smith, 1984)—the other side (to self-interest) of Smith's vision of economic man, as is explained in Athol Fitzgibbons's chapter in the present volume. And indeed Darwin fully acknowledges a debt to Smith on this subject in the same paragraph in *The Descent of Man* from which the last quote is taken; and in a footnote to the same Darwin directs his readers to 'the first and striking chapter in Adam Smith's "Theory of Moral Sentiments" ' (Darwin, 1875, p. 106). Darwin cites Smith in describing sympathy as involved in, for example, 'the sight of another person enduring hunger, cold, fatigue, [which] revives in us some recollection of these states, which are painful even in idea', so that '[w]e are thus impelled to relieve the sufferings of another' (ibid.). Besides from Smith directly, Darwin was also able to learn of Smith's ideas from Sir James Mackintosh, a distinguished philosopher and historian who was related by marriage to Darwin's aunt, Elizabeth (Betty) Wedgwood, and with whom Darwin enjoyed conversations in his youth at the Wedgwoods' home, at Maer Hall ('I listened with much interest to everything which he said, for I was as ignorant as a pig about his subjects of history, politics and moral philosophy'). In later years, Darwin read and copiously annotated his own copy of Mackintosh's *Dissertation on the Progress of Ethical Philosophy*, and marked passages including 'Perhaps there is no ethical work since Cicero's *Officiis*, of which an abridgement enables the reader so inadequately to estimate the merit, as the *Theory of Moral Sentiments*'. Beside the lines, 'mankind are [sic] so constituted as to sympathise with each other's feelings', and that this is the principle 'on which' [in Smith's view] 'are founded all the high virtues of self-denial and self-command,' Darwin has written: 'common to animals' (Darwin, 1995, p. 16; Mackintosh, 1837, pp. 233–4).

Mackintosh's comparison of *The Theory of Moral Sentiments* with Cicero's *Officiis* is not accidental, as the reader will know from Athol Fitzgibbons's chapter. Smith draws extensively on the Latin jurist and Stoic philosopher (there are 24 pages devoted to him in *The Theory of Moral Sentiments*), and as Fitzgibbons (1995) notes, this is not surprising given Cicero's conception of 'mutual helpfulness' being the 'key to civilization'. Without the operation of this principle, Fitzgibbons summarizes Cicero as saying, there could be 'no medicine, no agriculture, no metals, no cities, no laws, and no trade' (Fitzgibbons, 1995, p. 48). Darwin doesn't cite Cicero, but he does the other Roman Stoic cited in my earlier chapter—the Emperor, Marcus Aurelius Antoninus, whose *Meditations* clearly drew upon Cicero (Long, n.d., pp. 33, 36, 58) and is cited three times in Darwin's chapter on 'The Moral Sense' in *The Descent of Man*. In a summary of his argument for the evolution of a moral sense in man at the end of his chapter, Darwin quotes Marcus Aurelius as referring to 'the social instincts—the prime principle of man's moral constitution' (Darwin, 1875, p. 126, quoting Long, n.d., p. 191), and in an expansion of what he means elsewhere in *Meditations* Marcus Aurelius shows that his conception of this principle was indeed very close to Darwin's:

> [A]mong the animals devoid of reason we find swarms of bees, and herds of cattle, and the nurture of young birds, and in a manner, loves, for even in animals there are souls [mind?], and that power which brings them together is seen to exert itself in the superior degree, and in such a way as never has been observed in plants nor in stones nor in trees...[I]n rational animals [i.e., man] there are political communities and friendships, and families and meetings of people; and in wars, treaties and armistices...Thus ascent in the ranks of creation can induce *sympathy* [Stanisforth, 1964, has 'fellow-feeling'] even where there is no proximity (Long, n.d., p. 231, my emphasis).

At the beginning of his chapter on 'The Moral Sense' Darwin outlines his position in these terms: 'The following proposition seems to me in a high degree probable—namely, that any animal whatever, endowed with well marked social instincts, the parental and filial affections being here included, would inevitably acquire a moral sense or conscience, as soon as its intellectual powers had become as well, or nearly as well developed, as in man'; and he goes on to add that 'Similar ideas have probably occurred to many persons, as they did long ago to Marcus Aurelius' (Darwin, 1875, p. 98). However this may be, the 'sympathy' concept is of obvious importance in both Darwin's and Marcus Aurelius' understanding of the origin of morality, as it is in Adam Smith's thought on the subject. And Smith's ideas, especially (as well as Darwin's), were not lost on another important theorist on human nature—Kropotkin, whose *Mutual Aid: A Factor of Evolution* and various other writings (see, e.g., Kropotkin, 1892, 1992) drew extensively on both Smith and Darwin and also Cicero (see Rob Knowles's chapter in this volume). Cicero's 'mutual helpfulness', then, or *co-operation*, is as much a part of nature, including human nature, as competition for all of these authors.

But lest this juxtaposition of co-operation and competition jar with some readers, perhaps more should be said about Darwin's conception. In the first edition of *The Origin of Species*, at the beginning of chapter III, on 'The Struggle for Existence', Darwin (1901, p. 58) writes: 'I should premise that I use the term Struggle for Existence in a large and metaphorical sense, including dependence of one being on another'; and further on in the book Darwin makes it clear that he could envisage this principle extending to self-sacrifice for the good of the community in at least some species, for example bees:

> If we look at the sting of the bee, as having originally existed in a remote progenitor as a boring and serrated instrument, like that in so many members of the same order, and which has been modified but not perfected for its present purpose, with the poison originally adapted to cause galls subsequently intensified, we can perhaps understand how it is that the use of the sting should so often cause the insect's own death: for if on the whole the power of stinging be useful to the social community, it will fulfil all the requirements of natural selection, though it may cause the death of some few members (Darwin, 1901, p. 162).[2]

Such talk of 'self-sacrifice' rings somewhat hollowly today perhaps, used as we are to 'selfish genes' and suchlike expressions, but the principle was clearly seen by Darwin, anyway, as part and parcel of his theory of what more recent authors (e.g., Montague, 1952; Ardrey, 1977) would call 'collective fitness'. Darwin took up the argument and expanded upon it in *The Descent of Man*: 'With strictly social animals, natural selection sometimes acts on the individual, through the preservation of variations which are beneficial to the community...Associated insects have thus acquired many remarkable structures, which are of little or no service to the individual, such as the pollen-collecting apparatus, or the sting of the worker-bee, or the great jaws of soldier-ants' (Darwin, 1875, p. 62–3). In the case of vertebrates, according to Darwin, similar arguments can apply: '[T]he horns of ruminants and the great canine teeth of baboons appear to have been acquired by the males as weapons for sexual strife, but they are used in defence of the herd or troop' (ibid.). And with man: 'As no man can practice the virtues necessary for the welfare of his tribe without self-sacrifice, self command and the power of endurance, these qualities have been at all times highly and most justly valued' (ibid., p. 118).

Robert Ardrey (1977, p.190) succinctly stated the 'collective fitness' argument thus: 'If competition takes place not only between individuals but between groups, then the group with greater endowments of loyalty, co-operation, self-sacrifice and altruism concerning social partners will be selection's survivor. Both Darwin and Wallace foresaw the possibility over a century ago'. Jules Verne also accepted the validity of the principle: his hero, Captain John Branican, who early in life had saved children from drowning, in later life 'had not belied the instincts of self-sacrifice which had marked his youth' (Verne, 1970, p. 2); and in an economics context, Alfred Marshall (see Peter Groenewegen's chapter), in the same decade that Verne was writing, could aver – evidently with Darwin's writing in mind[3] – that 'the struggle for existence causes in the long run those races of men to survive in which the individual is most willing to sacrifice himself for the benefit of those around him' (Marshall, 1898, p. 322).[4]

The most obvious relevance of this aspect of Darwin's thinking on human nature to economic theory is in relation to co-operation vis-à-vis competition (see also Introduction to this volume). As we have seen, there is no necessary conflict here, at least not for Darwin: these are the complementary principles – the Janus faces (cf. Koestler, 1967) as it were – of the human condition. But not all economists have seen things in this way. Jack Hirshleifer (1977; in Hodgson, 1995), for example, in a paper on 'Economics from a Biological Viewpoint', takes a strongly genetic approach, influenced by the sociobiology of E.O. Wilson (1975), which was much discussed around Hirshleifer's time of writing (see, e.g., *Time*, 1 August 1977). As with Wilson's (1975) landmark *Sociobiology*, most of which is concerned with the 'social insects'—the Hymenoptera (Wilson being an entomologist by training), much of Hirshleifer's paper searches for analogies between human institutions and these simple societies. Hirshleifer also draws upon the 'reciprocal altruism' arguments of Robert Trivers and others. Thus, for Hirshleifer (as well as his sociobiology mentors), '[f]rom the evolutionary point of view the great analytical problem of altruism is that, in order to survive the selectional process, altruistic behaviour must be profitable in fitness terms' (Hirshleifer, 1977; in Hodgson, 1995, p. 106). To illustrate his case, Hirshleifer goes on to cite instances of so-called 'selfish altruism' in various species, from the Hymenoptera to American wild turkeys. Why, Hirshleifer (after Wilson) asks, are parents more altruistic to offspring than offspring to parents, given that the extent of gene sharing is the same? The answer, according to both authors, is that offspring have greater 'productive value'—they are more efficient at producing future descendants for parents than parents are in producing future relatives (sibs and their descendants) for offspring, especially when parents are close to completing their reproductive life.

Such arguments have a certain level of cogency, but as with many other similar scenarios in Wilson and like-minded authors, the impression often left is one of mathematical neatness rather than reality—of the order of the biologist J.B.S. Haldane's famous reply, when once asked in a pub who he would be prepared to sacrifice his life for: 'two brothers or eight cousins' (i.e., those with whom he shared most genes in common—see Rose and Rose, 2001). More convincing, surely, is Darwin's conception of an underlying drive for altruistic behaviour, a *generalized* altruistic impulse, which would very likely have evolved from its *coincidental* effectiveness in maximizing the survival chances of near-relatives (especially offspring), as with a troop of baboons (whose protective males, characteristically patrolling the periphery of the troop, are undoubtedly the sires of at least some of the juveniles[5]). Darwin, as seen, emphasized the fundamental importance of the 'parental and filial affections' in the probable evolution of social instincts. He makes the point a number of times in *The Descent of Man*;[6] but with 'man' especially, and to some extent other species, he is able to expand the operation of the altruistic principle enormously, so that, coupled with reason, 'sympathy' can be extended well beyond the confines of a breeding group:

> The feeling of pleasure from society is probably an extension of the parental and filial affections...and this extension may be attributed in part to habit [see below], but chiefly to natural selection...[T]he social instincts, which no doubt were acquired by man as by the lower animals for the good of the community, will from the first have given to him some wish to aid his fellows...and have compelled him to regard their approbation and disapprobation...As man gradually advanced in intellectual power, and was able to trace the more remote consequences of his actions...his sympathies became more tender and widely diffused, extending to men of all races (Darwin, 1875, pp. 105, 124).

Thus we have a total contrast to the 'selfish gene' theories of Richard Dawkins, E.O. Wilson and others. Especially is Darwin more convincing with our own species. As was noted earlier, Darwin specifically singled out 'man' as a special case in terms of sociability, in that although we may, in common with other species (and he includes insects, even the genus Forficula, or earwigs), experience a general impulse for mutual assistance, especially in times of danger, we, unlike other species (with the possible exception of some other primates), are able to *direct* our social behaviour through *reason and experience*. Human beings are not 'lumbering robots' (to use Richard Dawkins's [1989, p. 19] colourful but misleading phrase), driven by our genetic 'instructions'. As we all know, *pace* Dawkins, human beings are capable of *novel* solutions to problems, be they survival-threatening or far more trivial. This is the enormous advantage in the 'struggle for existence' that evolution has produced in our species through the crucible of natural selection. And these solutions often involve collective behaviour. It *makes sense*, for example, for humans to band together in the face of a common enemy, and to implement rational means to deal with such a crisis. As the political theorist and later British Prime Minister J. Ramsay MacDonald once well expressed it: '[W]ith man it is different...He finds out many inventions first of all to defy nature and then to exploit her. In common with some other animals he protects himself by forming groups, and these groups carry on the war of nature. But they nourish and nurture within themselves both individual intelligence and personal and group laws of existence, ethics, customs, justice, religion. And thus a new path…is discovered, the path which consists of an intelligent conception of ends and purposes and an adoption of rational means to those ends' (MacDonald, 1911, p. 246).

Actually, Darwin's thinking along these lines – the importance of a coupling of human sociability with inventiveness – was very likely stimulated in part by another economist, the widely respected editor of *The Economist* and author of *Lombard Street*, Walter Bagehot. Besides the latter book, Bagehot wrote another less-known volume with the long title, *Physics and Politics, or, Thoughts on the Application of the Principles of 'Natural Selection' and 'Inheritance' to Political Society* (Bagehot, 1873[7]), which first appeared as a series of articles in *The Fortnightly Review* in 1867–9, Darwin's copies of which are also held in the Cambridge University Library. Darwin's debt to Bagehot's articles is fully acknowledged, Bagehot being cited in a number of places in *The Descent of Man*. On page 130 (of the second edition) of chapter IV, for instance, Darwin summarizes Bagehot's argument for the crucial role of co-operation and 'coherence' in human evolution, the full original text of which reads as follows:

> The progress of *man* requires the co-operation of *men* for its development. That which any one man or any one family could invent for themselves is obviously exceedingly limited…The rudest sort of co-operative society, the lowest tribe and the feeblest government, is so much stronger than isolated man, that isolated man (if he ever existed in any shape which could be called man), might very easily have ceased to exist. The first principle of the subject is that man can only make progress in co-operative groups (Bagehot, 1873, p. 212–13).

Earlier on in *The Descent of Man* Darwin (1875, p. 117) quotes Bagehot thus: 'No tribe could hold together if murder, robbery, treachery, etc., were common; consequently such crimes within the limits of the same tribe "are branded with everlasting infamy" '; and then expands on Bagehot in a reiteration of Darwin's vision of the gradual *universalization* of such principles as applied to man:

> In order that primeval man, or the ape-like progenitors of man, should become social, they must have acquired the same instinctive feelings which impel other animals to live in a body; and they no doubt exhibited the same general disposition. They would have felt uneasy when separated from their comrades, for whom they would have felt some degree of love; they would have warned each other of danger, and have given mutual aid in attack or defence…Obedience, as Mr. Bagehot has well shown, is of the highest value [in this process], for any form of government is better than none. Selfish and contentious people will not cohere, and without coherence nothing can be effected. A tribe rich in the above qualities would spread and be victorious over other tribes; but in the course of time it would, judging from all past history, be in its turn overcome by some other tribe still more highly endowed. Thus the social and

moral qualities would tend slowly to advance and be diffused throughout the world (Darwin, 1875, pp. 129–30).

Of course, the obverse of this argument is the role of warfare in this process.[8] This is the other side of Darwin, the side highlighted by militarist and racialist 'social Darwinism', which has so negatively coloured many people's perception of Darwin's ideas. Unfortunately it is undoubtedly true that some passages *could* be quoted from *The Descent of Man* which could be distorted and utilized in support of such destructive ideologies: Nazi Germany being the most extreme case to spring to mind. Just such a misuse of Darwin's writing was in fact recognized by Darwin's son, Leonard Darwin, during World War I,[9] and a perusal of *The Descent of Man* can lend force to Leonard Darwin's fears—as with the following lines:

> Of the high importance of the intellectual faculties there can be no doubt, for man mainly owes to them his predominant position in the world. We can see that in the rudest state of society, the individuals who were the most sagacious, who invented and used the best weapons, and who were best able to defence themselves, would rear the greatest number of offspring. The tribes, which included the largest number of men thus endowed would increase in number and supplant other tribes...At the present day civilized nations are everywhere supplanting barbarous nations...and they succeed mainly, though not exclusively, through the arts, which are the products of the intellect (Darwin, 1875, p. 128).

Unless it be thought, however, that Darwin's apparent hard-line 'social Darwinist' position here so seriously disfigures the broader complexion of his writing on human nature as to discredit it, numerous other paragraphs in *The Descent of Man* can also be adduced to demonstrate a more complex understanding. As already shown, Darwin could envisage man's 'sympathies', with the development of his intellect, extending to all people. This was not an idle remark: Darwin repeats it as has been seen, and he does so again in a remarkable passage (allowing for nineteenth-century European notions of 'advances in civilization') towards the end of chapter IV that should, it is suggested, be read by all who believe that Darwinism is entirely about cut-throat competition and the 'survival of the fittest':

> As man advances in civilisation, and small tribes are united into larger communities, the simplest reason would tell each individual that he ought to extend his social instincts and sympathies to all the members of the same nation, though personally unknown to him. This point being once reached, there is only an artificial barrier to prevent his sympathies extending to the men of all nations and races (Darwin, 1875, p. 122).

Together with his talk of 'barbarous races' then, Darwin could take a more enlightened view of non-European peoples, a relatively uncommon attitude among his countrymen of the time (compare, for example, some of the views of his contemporary, Herbert Spencer[10]). A very significant experience for Darwin in this respect was his getting to know three Fuegians on board the *Beagle* who were returning to their country after having travelled to England a few years before on the ship. In chapter VII of *The Descent of Man* Darwin (1875, p. 178) writes: 'I was incessantly struck, whilst living with the Fuegians on board the "Beagle", with the many little traits of character, showing how similar their minds were to ours' (to which he adds: 'and so it was with a full blooded negro with whom I happened once to be intimate'). Elsewhere in *The Descent of Man* Darwin (1875, p. 65) notes: 'The Fuegians rank amongst the lowest barbarians; but I was continually struck with surprise how closely the three natives on board H.M.S. "Beagle", who had lived some years in England, and could talk a little English, resembled us in disposition and in most of our mental faculties.' Notwithstanding Darwin's impression, recorded in his diary, of the natives met on the shore at Tierra del Fuego – 'I believe if the world was searched, no lower grade of man could be found' (quoted Desmond and Moore, 1991, p. 133) – he could nevertheless speak of the 'good intellect' of the Fuegians on board the *Beagle* (the young woman, 'Fuegia Basket', especially, 'was very quick in learning anything, especially languages'—Darwin, 1898, p. 208; Hazlewood, 2000, p. 112) and enjoy their company. On reflection, Darwin felt he could recognize that:

> Their country is a broken mass of wild rocks, lofty hills and useless forests...The habitable land is reduced to the stones on the beach...How little can the higher powers of the mind be brought into play: what is there for imagination, for reason to compare, for judgement to decide upon? to knock a limpet from a rock does not require even cunning, that lowest power of the mind (Darwin, 1898, pp. 215–16).

Again, for Darwin, humans are not prisoners of their heredity: given the right environment, they can develop strategies to meet material and other needs in ways not possible for other species, and this capacity is universal in our species.[11]

These facts have major consequences for evolutionary theory. If humans can learn from their experiences, and moreover pass on that learning to others and later generations through oral and written language, a new level of evolution – *cultural* evolution – becomes possible. Darwin was well aware of this, as he was of the apparent independence of various discoveries and inventions in human history (he instances stone tools and the boomerang), which was further evidence of the universal capacities of the human species. For Darwin, novelty of invention and transmission of knowledge have been made possible by the prior and continuing development of the intellect, whereas for our nearest living relatives, for instance, '[t]he fact of the higher apes not using their vocal organs for speech, no doubt depends on their intelligence not having been sufficiently advanced' (Darwin, 1875, p. 89).

It must be said here, though, that Darwin also somewhat confuses the issue of what probably most biologists today would consider to be essential differences between biological and cultural (or sociocultural) evolution. The current view is lucidly explained by Stephen Jay Gould (1992, pp. 217–30), who points to what he calls the 'major fact of our history'—that there is no evidence that the brain of *Homo sapiens* has physically changed at all in the past 100,000 years or so, certainly in the last 30,000 years, as is witnessed in the magnificent cave paintings of mammoths and other extinct fauna in the caves of Altamira, Lascaux and elsewhere (some of which have been dated at over 30,000 years B.P.—see Casteret, 1940; Clottes, 2001).[12] Yet, Gould goes on to remind us, even 15,000 years ago no human social grouping had produced anything that would conform to standard definitions of civilization—no agriculture, permanent cities, use of metals, etc. The *capacity* to do such things was evidently there, yet they were not done: they came later and in an instant of time, evolutionarily speaking. Gould, then, would presumably not agree with the British biologist Sir Alister Hardy, who once said (1965, p. 29) that 'evolution is still proceeding, only now we call it history'.

Darwin, however, does not draw Gould's sharp distinction between biological, or organic, evolution, and human cultural development. This is evident in his further discussion of language. Notwithstanding his above apparent ruling out of the possibility of any extant non-human primate learning vocal language, Darwin could surmise that through 'the principle of the inherited effects of use':

> the continued use of language and the development of the brain, has no doubt been…important. The mental powers in some early progenitor of man must have been more highly developed than in any existing ape, before even the most imperfect form of speech could have come into use; but we may confidently believe that the continued use and advancement of this power would have reacted on the mind itself, by enabling and encouraging it to carry on long trains of thought. A complex train of thought can no more be carried on without the aid of words, whether spoken or silent, than a long calculation without the use of figures or algebra (Darwin, 1875, pp. 87–8).

Is Darwin suggesting that exercise of the vocal cords can directly affect the physical development of the brain? He seems to be. Moreover, there is a clear suggestion by Darwin here that such effects are *inherited*—an idea more usually associated with Darwin's predecessor, Jean Baptiste de Lamarck (1744–1829), and to which few, if any, biologists would subscribe today (though see Steele et al., 1998). Darwin's 'Lamarckism' has in fact long been recognized. In 1909, a Professor G. Schwalbe of the University of Strasbourg noted an 1876 letter by Darwin in which he regretted that 'the greatest error which I have committed has been not allowing sufficient weight to the direct action of the environment…independently of natural selection' (Schwalbe, in Seward,

1909, p. 125)—an opinion which may have been influenced to some extent by Darwin's earlier enthusiasm for Henry Buckle's (1858) *History of Civilisation in England*, a book which emphasizes the role of the physical environment in human history, and of which Darwin wrote to his friend, the botanist Joseph Hooker in March 1858: 'Have you read Buckle? I think you would be interested in it. I have been, extremely' (Darwin, 1991, p. 59).

But even under this 'error' Darwin could write the above, and could include a section of a chapter (II) in *The Descent of Man* headed 'Effects of the Increased Use and Disuse of Parts' which contains such remarkable observations as: 'In infants, long before birth, the skin of the soles of the feet is thicker than any other part of the body; and it can hardly be doubted that this is due to the inherited effects of pressure during a long series of generations' (Darwin, 1875, p. 33). Of course, there is another explanation for such phenomena, also coming from Darwin: natural selection (babies expressing such a faculty during foetal development will after birth be at an advantage in the 'race of life' and will be more likely to survive and transmit their fortuitous faculty to offspring). Darwin himself wrote, specifically in the context of human evolution, that there is 'a large class of variations which may be provisionally called "spontaneous", for to our ignorance they appear to arise without any existing cause...such variations...depend much more on the constitution of the organism than on the nature of the conditions to which it has been subjected' (Darwin, 1875, p. 44); and the sufficiency of natural selection of such chance 'variations' (mutations) was well argued a few years after Darwin's death by his fellow-discoverer of the principle, A.R. Wallace:

> The American naturalists lay much stress on the evolution of the teeth of mammals in complete palaeontological series, alleging that the successive modifications of the cusps conform strictly to lines of use and disuse. To this [I reply]...[I]n such vitally important organs as the teeth of mammals, natural selection will necessarily keep them on these lines, because *use* implies *utility*, and *disuse*, *disutility*, and utilities necessarily survive. If, then, variations occur in the forms of cusps – and they certainly do – natural selection will modify them along these lines of utility; and it will be absolutely impossible, from a study of the series of fossil forms, to prove that they have been *directly* modified by use and that the modifications have been inherited, and that they are not the result of normal variations accumulated by survival of the fittest (Wallace, 1900, vol. 1, p. 323).

We return, then, to the basic tenets of natural selection in the biological world, as originally proposed by Darwin and Wallace. But what of the relevance of this principle to human institutions, including economic institutions? Here we must introduce another idea discussed by Wallace in the volumes just quoted and which, while it moves somewhat beyond Darwin's writing and is therefore strictly outside the confines of this chapter, needs to be looked at briefly (for further discussions see Richards, 1987; and Hodgson, 1993, 2001) for its importance in the thinking of certain late nineteenth- and early twentieth-century economists interested in Darwin.

Wallace's 1900 volumes, *Studies Scientific & Social*, contain a review of the animal behaviourist C. Lloyd Morgan's (1896) *Habit & Instinct*, in which Wallace looks closely at two chapters towards the end of the book titled 'Are Acquired Characters Inherited' and 'Modification and Variation'. These chapters contain in outline an idea which Lloyd Morgan thought was an original contribution to evolutionary theory, but which history was to remember as the 'Baldwin effect', after its apparent independent discovery by the American social psychologist James Mark Baldwin in the same year (1896). As Wallace explains, the argument hinges on the relationship of 'instincts', or inherited behavioural predispositions, and 'habits' (a term used by Darwin—as seen above), or learned behaviours. In this scheme, adaptation can be seen as a product of *both* sources of behavioural modification in that survival enhancing habits can assist congenital change by allowing time for the necessary behavioural *variation* (or, as we would say today, genotype) to be selected. Wallace quotes Lloyd Morgan's summary of the argument thus: '[Learned] modification *as such* is not inherited, but is the condition under which congenital variations are favoured and given time to get a hold on the organism, and are thus enabled by degrees to reach the fully adaptive level' (Wallace, 1900, vol. 1, pp. 507–8). At a time when natural selection as a theory to account for all evolutionary change was coming under increased question (see, e.g., Bowler, 1983). Wallace, at any rate, was satisfied that Lloyd Morgan's concept did not violate the essentials of natural selection theory and that 'all the...objections to the adequacy of natural selection have been theoretically answered'.

As indicated, the Baldwin effect is important in the history of economics for its influence on certain key economists. Notable among these is Thorstein Veblen, a 'father figure' in evolutionary and institutional economics who early in his career rejected classical economics' 'faulty conception of human nature' (quoted Potts, 2001, p. 42) and began reading Darwin and other evolutionary writers. As Geoffrey Hodgson (1998) notes, Veblen was at the university of Chicago when Lloyd Morgan gave a lecture there in 1896, and from that time on the latter's influence on Veblen was 'decisive'. The end result for Veblen was a sophisticated appreciation of the place of both instinct and 'habits' in human evolution (see also Twomy, 1998), so that, in Robert Richards's (1987, p. 480) words summarizing the significance of the Baldwin effect, 'consciousness and intelligence [are] allowed...a role in directing evolution.' In 1914 Veblen expressed his understanding of the relative importance of instincts and habits in the human domain in these terms: 'It is a distinctive mark of mankind, that the working out of the distinctive proclivities of the race is guided by an intelligence not approached by the other animals. But...it is only by the prompting of instinct that reflection and deliberation come to be...employed' (Veblen, 1964 [1914], p. 6).

More could be said about the Baldwin effect and its obvious relevance to questions concerning the relative roles of biological and cultural evolution in human affairs. But I will conclude by asking whether *Darwin*, in the lines from *The Descent of Man* about the development of speech quoted above, can be seen to have glimpsed, to some extent at least, the insight of Baldwin and Lloyd Morgan? When Darwin wrote of the continued use of rudimentary speech in man's immediate 'progenitors' enabling and encouraging mental development, could he not be interpreted as suggesting that such activity might contribute towards an individual's *survival*, which in turn would allow that individual's genotype for this ability to be transmitted to offspring? Be this as it may, there is no doubt that Darwin, unlike some of his more recent votaries (see, especially, chapters by Dover and Gould in Rose and Rose, 2001), was clearly aware of 'the difference of man and the difference it makes' (to borrow a phrase from Mortimer Adler[13]), as this chapter has attempted to show—and perhaps, if it is not overstating things, would have been sympathetic with attempts by Kenneth Boulding and others (see Richard Joseph's chapter, below) to allow for human uniqueness in the broader evolutionary picture.

NOTES

1. In his *Autobiography* (Darwin, 1995, p. 10), Darwin relates how Gilbert White's *Natural History of Selborne* was one of his favourite books in his youth, and there is an 1845 edition (London: 'Printed for C. & J. Rivington') in Darwin's library. It too, like Darwin, notes that 'There is a wonderful spirit of sociability in the brute creation, independent of sexual attachment...Oxen & Cows will not fatten by themselves; but will neglect the finest pasture that is not recommended by Society...[T]his propensity seems not to be confined to animals of the same species' (Vol. 1, pp. 328–9). Among Darwin's books, also, is his annotated copy of A.R. Wallace's *The Malay Archipelago* (2 vols, London: Macmillan, 1869), and in the margin beside Wallace's observation (Vol. 2, p. 460) that 'I have lived with communities of savages in South America and the East, who have no laws or law courts but the public opinion of the village freely expressed. Each man scrupulously respects the rights of his fellow, and any infraction of those rights rarely or never takes place', Darwin has written: 'like a herd of animals'.

2. The social Hymenoptera and Isoptera (ants, bees, wasps and termites) are, of course, special cases, in that in their 'societies' of thousands, only one individual – the queen – is a fertile female. The 'workers' are sterile, thus it is in their 'interest' to attend to the welfare of the queen, whose genes they share. (That is to say, those communities that *have* operated in such a way are those which have survived in the 'struggle for existence' and are observable today.) See H. Frauca, *Animal Behaviour* (Melbourne: Lansdowne Press, 1971), p. 110.

3. Marshall's copies of *The Origin of Species* and *The Descent of Man* are held in the Cambridge University Library. (Peter Groenewegan, personal communication to John Nightingale, 10 November 1998.)

4. In his copy of Mackintosh's (1837) *Dissertation on the Progress of Ethical Philosophy*, Darwin has a pencil mark beside the passage (p. 265) which reads: '[A] man is ready to sacrifice his life for him who has shewn [sic] generosity, even to others; and persons otherwise of

common character are capable of cheerfully marching in a forlorn hope, or of almost instinctively leaping into the sea to save the life of an entire stranger'; and in a letter to his cousin Hensleigh Wedgwood (9 March 1871) Darwin wrote that 'We seem to agree about what may be called instinctive moral actions, as in impulsively saving a drowning man.' (Thanks to the Editors of the Darwin Correspondence Project for access to this unpublished letter and to the Syndics of Cambridge University Library for permission to quote it.) Kropotkin, similarly, in an address in Bradford in 1887, is reported to have said: 'Supposing a child were drowning in the river...the simple and popular moralist would see the child drowning and hear the cries of the mother, jump like a good dog into the water, and save the child. That was the simple morality which acted without reasoning, and was ready to suffer with the suffering of others' (*Bradford Observer*, 28 March 1887).

5. I am indebted to Jill Bowie for reminding me of this point.

6. The Roman poet Horace (65–8 B.C.), whose odes Darwin (1995, p. 9) had 'admired greatly' at Shrewsbury School, was also well aware of this natural phenomenon: 'Do you not see, Pyrrhus', the poet asks, 'at what grave personal risk you touch the cub of this North African lioness?' (Horace, 1983, p. 152).

7. I have David Edmunds of John Drury Rare Books to thank for my fine copy of Bagehot's volume.

8. In one of his articles, Darwin's copy of which I have before me, Bagehot argues as follows: '[W]hat makes one tribe...to differ from another is their relative faculty of coherence. The slightest symptom of legal development, the least indication of a military bond, is then enough to turn the scale. The compact tribes win, and the compact tribes are the tamest. Civilisation begins, because the beginning of civilisation is a military advantage' (*Fortnightly Review*, Vol. III, New Series, 1 January to 1 June, 1868, p. 457).

9. In a review of David Starr Jordan's *War and the Breed: The Relation of War to the Downfall of Nations* (Boston: Beacon Press, 1915) in the *New York Times Book Review*, 3 October 1915, it is noted: 'Major Leonard Darwin, son of Charles Darwin and the President of the Eugenics Education Society of London, is quoted in a vigorous protest against the connecting of his father's name with the pseudo-scientific theory of "social Darwinism".'

10. See, e.g., Spencer's *First Principles* (London: Williams and Norgate, 1900, first published 1862), pp. 289–90.

11. Notice should perhaps be taken here of the observations of Robert Fitzroy, the Captain of the *Beagle,* on revisiting Tierra del Fuego: 'Disagreeable, even painful, as is even the mental contemplation of a savage, and unwilling as we may be to consider ourselves even remotely descended from human beings in such a state, the reflection that Caesar found the Britons painted and clothed in skins, like these Fuegians, cannot fail to augment an interest excited by their childish ignorance of matters familiar to civilized man, and by their healthy, independent state of existence' (R. Fitzroy, *Narrative of the Surveying Voyages of His Majesty's Ships* Adventure *and* Beagle *between the Years of 1826 and 1836, Describing Their Examination of the Southern Shores of South America and the* Beagle's *Circumnavigation of the Globe*, London: H. Colburn, 1839. Vol. 1, p. 121). See also J. Moore and A. Desmond, 'Introduction' to forthcoming Penguin edition of *Descent of Man*.

12. G.K. Chesterton, who knew what he was talking about, having trained at the Slade School of Fine Art, London, early recognized the essential humanity of the Altamira cave artists: The paintings 'showed that love of the long sweeping or the long wavering line which any man who has ever drawn or tried to draw will recognise; and about which no artist will allow himself to be contradicted by any scientist. They showed the experimental and adventurous spirit of the artist, the spirit that does not avoid but attempts difficult things; as where the draughtsman had represented the action of the stag when he swings his head clean round and noses towards his tail, an action familiar enough in the horse. But there are many modern animal-painters who would set themselves something of a task in rendering it truly. In this and twenty other details it is clear that the artist had watched animals with a certain interest and, presumably, a certain pleasure' (Chesterton, 1928, pp. 30–32).

13. See M. Adler, *The Difference of Man and the Difference it Makes* (New York: Rinehart and Winston, 1956). (I am grateful to Fr Joe Martins for drawing my attention to this volume.) For

a good discussion on the place of language in human sociocultural evolution, see also Derek Bickerton, *Language and Human Behaviour* (Chicago: University of Chicago Press, 1995) pp. 4–6.

REFERENCES

Ardrey, R. (1977), *The Hunting Hypothesis*, London: Fontana.

Bagehot, W. (1873), *Physics and Politics, or, Thoughts on the Application of the Principles of Natural Selection' and 'Inheritance' to Political Society*, London: Henry S. King & Co.

Bowler, P.J. (1983), *Evolution: The History of an Idea*, Berkeley and Los Angeles: University of California Press.

Buckle, H.T. (1858), *History of Civilisation in England* (2 vols.), London: John W. Parker.

Casteret, N. (1940), *Ten Years Under the Earth*, London: Readers Union.

Chesterton, G.K. (1928), *The Everlasting Man*, London: Hodder & Stoughton.

Clottes, J. (2001), 'Chauvet Cave', *National Geographic*, **200** (2), 104–21.

Darwin, C. (1875), *The Descent of Man and Selection in Relation to Sex*, London: John Murray.

Darwin, C. (1898), *Journal of Researches into the Natural History and Geology of the Countries Visited During the Voyage of H.M.S. "Beagle" Round the World*, London: Ward, Lock & Co.

Darwin, C. (1901), *On The Origin of Species by means of Natural Selection, or, The Preservation of Favoured Races in the Struggle for Life*, London: Ward, Lock & Co.

Darwin, C. (1991), *The Correspondence of Charles Darwin*, Vol. 7 (1858), Cambridge, U.K.: Cambridge University Press.

Darwin, C. (2001), *The Correspondence of Charles Darwin*, Vol. 12 (1864), Cambridge, U.K.: Cambridge University Press.

Darwin, C. and A.R. Wallace (1958), *Evolution by Natural Selection*, Cambridge, U.K.: Cambridge University Press.

Darwin, F. (1995), *The Life of Charles Darwin*, London: Senate.

Dawkins, R. (1989), *The Selfish Gene*, Oxford: Oxford University Press.

Desmond, A. and J. Moore (1991), *Darwin*, London: Michael Joseph.

Fitzgibbons, A. (1995), *Adam Smith's System of Liberty, Wealth and Virtue: The Moral and Political Foundations of 'The Wealth of Nations'*, Oxford: Clarendon Press.

Gould, S.J. (1992), *Life's Grandeur: The Spread of Excellence from Plato to Darwin*, London: Vintage.

Hardy, A. (1965), *The Living Stream: A Restatement of Evolution Theory and Its Relation to the Spirit of Man*, London: Collins.

Hazlewood, N. (2000), *Savage: The Life and Times of Jemmy Button*, London: Hodder & Stoughton.

Hodgson, G.M. (1993), *Economics and Evolution: Bringing Life Back into Economics*, Cambridge, U.K.: Polity Press.

Hodgson, G.M. (ed.), (1995), *Economics and Biology*, Aldershot, Hants, U.K.: Edward Elgar.

Hodgson, G.M. (1998), 'On the Evolution of Thorstein Veblen's Evolutionary Economics', *Cambridge Journal of Economics*, **22**, 415–31.

Hodgson, G.M. (2001), 'Is Social Evolution Lamarckian or Darwinian?', in J. Laurent and J. Nightingale (eds), *Darwinism and Evolutionary Economics*, Cheltenham, Glos., U.K. and Northampton, MA, U.S.A.: Edward Elgar.

Horace (1983), *The Complete Odes and Epodes*, London: Penguin.

Koestler, A. (1967), *The Ghost in the Machine*, London: Hutchinson.

Kropotkin, P. (1892), *Anarchist Morality*, London: Freedom Press.

Kropotkin, P. (1992), *Ethics: Origins and Development*, Montreal and New York: Black Rose Books.

Long, G. (n.d.) [1869], *The Meditations of the Emperor Marcus Aurelius Antoninus*, London and Glasgow: Collins.

MacDonald, J.R. (1911), *The Socialist Movement*, London: Williams and Norgate.

Mackintosh, J. (1837), *Dissertation on the Progress of Ethical Philosophy*, Edinburgh: Adam & Charles Black.

Marshall, A. (1898), *Principles of Economics*, Fourth Edition, London: Macmillan.

Montague, M.F.A. (1952), *Darwin, Competition and Cooperation*, New York: Henry Schuman.

Morgan, C. L. (1896), *Habit and Instinct*, London: and New York: Edward Arnold.

Okasha, S. (2001), 'Why Won't the Group Selection Controversy Go Away?', *British Journal for the Philosophy of Science*, **52**, 25–50.

Potts, J. (2001), *The New Evolutionary Microeconomics: Complexity, Competence and Adaptive Behaviour*, Cheltenham, Glos, U.K.: Edward Elgar.

Richards, R. (1987), *Darwin and the Emergence of Evolutionary Theories of Mind and Behaviour*, Chicago: University of Chicago Press.

Rose, S. and H. Rose (2001), *Alas Poor Darwin: Arguments Against Evolutionary Psychology*, London: Vintage.

Seward, A.C. (ed.) (1909), *Darwin and Modern Science: Essays in Commemoration of the Centenary of the Birth of Charles Darwin and of the Fifteenth Anniversary of the Publication of 'The Origin of Species'*, Cambridge: U.K.: Cambridge University Press.

Smith, A. (1984) [1759], *The Theory of Moral Sentiments*, Indianapolis: Liberty Fund.

Smith, J. Maynard (2001), 'Why Fruitflies Dance: The Variety and Reliability of Animal Signals', *Times Literary Supplement*, 3 August 2001, 11–12.

Sober, E. and D.S. Wilson (1998), *Unto Others: The Evolution and Psychology of Unselfish Behaviour*, Cambridge, MA: Harvard University Press.

Staniforth, M. (tr) (1964), *Marcus Aurelius—Meditations*, London: Penguin.

Steele, E.J., Lindley, R.A. and R.V. Blanden (1998), *Lamarck's Signature: How Retrogenes are Changing Darwin's Natural Selection Paradigm*, St Leonards, N.S.W.: Allen & Unwin.

Trivers, R. (1971), 'The Evolution of Reciprocal Altruism', *Quarterly Review of Biology*, **46**, 35–57.

Twomy, P. (1998), 'Reviving Veblenian Economic Psychology', *Cambridge Journal of Economics*, **22**, 433–48.

Veblen, T. (1964) [1914], *The Instinct of Workmanship, and the State of the Industrial Arts*, New York: Augustus Kelley.

Verne, J. (1970), *Mistress Branican*, Melbourne: Sun Books.

Wallace, A.R. (1864), 'The Origin of Human Races and the Antiquity of Man deduced from the theory of "Natural Selection" ', *Journal of the Anthropological Society*, **2**, clviii–clxxxvii.

Wallace, A.R. (1870), *Contributions to the Theory of Natural Selection*, London: Swan Sonnenschein.

Wallace, A.R. (1900), *Studies Scientific and Social* (2 vols), London: Macmillan.

Wilson, E.O. (1975), *Sociobiology: The New Synthesis*, Cambridge, MA: Harvard University Press.

Wynne-Edwards, V.C. (1986), *Evolution Through Group Selection*, Oxford: Blackwell Scientific Publications.

6. Alfred Marshall on *Homo œconomicus*: Evolution versus Utilitarianism?

Peter Groenewegen

I [Alfred Marshall] now differ from you both [J.S. Mill and J.N. Keynes] in holding (what I did not always hold) that the economic man does so little good service & causes so much trouble that on practical & tactical (not theoretical) grounds, it is best to do without him. (Alfred Marshall to John Neville Keynes, 17 November 1889, in Whitaker, [1996], I, letter 278, p. 305.)

Marshall's letter to John Neville Keynes quoted above indicates that the issue of 'economic man' was a difficult one for him at the time of writing his Principles of Economics, as it had been during the formative period of Marshall's studies in economics. He then appears to have quarrelled with his friend and colleague, Henry Sidgwick on this matter (Henry Sidgwick to Alfred Marshall, July or August 1871, in Whitaker, 1996, I, letter 7, pp. 13–14; cf Groenewegen, 1995, p. 664). This letter had juxtaposed 'economic man' and evolution, indicating the need in Marshall's mind at the time to supplement the Benthamite utilitarian view of human nature with 'some historical sociology'. In the early 1870s, Marshall had been teaching utilitarianism to Moral Science students at Cambridge, and his criticism of the utilitarian perspective on human nature appears at least in part to have derived from his contemporaneous study of Marx's Capital (Groenewegen 1995, p. 664 n.*)

It should be emphasized that Marshall's objections to using the concept 'economic man' were 'practical and tactical, not theoretical'. The meaning of 'tactical' in this context is illustrated in a subsequent letter to J.N. Keynes (31 January 1902, Whitaker, 1996, II, letter 675, p. 350). Amidst 'this weary and oppressive work for the liberation of economics from the incubus by which I believe it to be oppressed [i.e. the Moral Sciences Tripos]', during which Marshall had to fight against even old friends such as J.N. Keynes from among his former students – 'whom I have loved' – the issue of 'economic man' also cropped up. The relevant part of the letter may be quoted, and follows almost immediately from the introductory material of the letter which has just been paraphrased:

And it has grieved me increasingly to feel compelled to protest against doctrines, especially to those relating to 'the economic man', & c. which I once taught myself under the baneful spell of Mill's Logic & of which I know the studious members of the class will find traces of in your Logic of Political Economy. But I have been utterly convinced that the hostility wh[ich] businessmen & men of affairs have to economics, is due not to anything which is really done by economists, but to things which logicians & especially Mill have said they did; and have been echoed or reechoed millions of times. *Amicus Plato, sed magis amice veritas.*

Tactical considerations concerning the issue therefore arose from the fight Marshall had been waging for a significant part of his life to make economics more acceptable to leading sections of the community including businessmen. He was trying to win the support of such people, especially businessmen and men of affairs, for the introduction of an Economics and Politics Tripos, a goal he finally achieved in 1903 (the full story of this is told in Groenewegen, 1995, chapter 15). Business men apparently found the notion of 'economic man' of-fensive, because the general public frequently believed such an individual to be an actual person, or an accurate description of actual persons, and not 'the crea-ture of hypothesis and analysis' as it was, and was intended to be, understood by public men and economists (Goschen, 1905, pp. 332–3). Goschen's modest defence of 'economic man' on this occasion (his 1893 Presidential Address to the British Economic Association), as a proper object of hypothesis and analy-sis, was even too much for Marshall. As seconder of the formal vote of thanks to Goschen, he strongly distanced economics from both the *abstract* notion of 'economic man' and from the utilitarian theory of ethics with which Goschen had (indirectly) associated it. Utility in economics, according to Marshall, re-ferred to 'satisfactions', not to Benthamite notions of pleasure; and economics 'was then not utilitarian… she left such questions to be decided by her mistress ethics' (Marshall, 1893, p. 389; Groenewegen, 1995, p. 467).

Marshall's hostility to 'economic man' was therefore strong and manifested itself on various occasions. The nature of this opposition is an issue of consid-erable interest, if only because it relates in part to contemporary debates on the implications for economics of suppositions of 'rational economic man' or 'eco-nomic rationalism'. To explore these issues comprehensively, the argument of this chapter is sub-divided into the following sections. The first looks at the specific background to the debate over 'economic man' by surveying the posi-tion on it of some of the major British literature from the second half of the nineteenth century. The second section reviews Marshall's position on 'eco-nomic man' as visible in his writings, partly to test the validity of his position that he had abandoned acceptance of this notion during the early years of his life as an economist. The third section explores Marshall's decidedly evolution-ary views as an explicit rationale for this criticism of 'economic man' on 'practical' rather than theoretical grounds, and examines the manner in which

Marshall tried to resolve the problem left by his criticism for abstraction within the pages of his *Principles*. A final section then draws some conclusions.

I

A survey of the notion of 'economic man' as portrayed by economic writers of the nineteenth century is best started with J.S. Mill. In his 'On the Definition of Political Economy; and on the Method of Investigation proper to it' (Mill, 1844, pp. 120–64), the notion of abstract human beings whose objects of desire are confined to wealth, is broadly introduced as part of the abstract method most suitable, in Mill's opinion, for the development of economic laws (Mill, 1844, esp. pp. 137–40, 146). Mill's position is simply the following. Political Economy 'does not treat of the whole of man's nature as modified by the social state, nor of the whole conduct of man in society. It is concerned with him solely as a being who desires to possess wealth, and who is capable of judging of the comparative efficacy of means for obtaining that end' (Mill, 1844, p. 137). Hence political economy entirely abstracts for 'every other human passion or motive'; it only 'considers mankind as occupied solely in acquiring and consuming wealth' subject to the two constraints of 'aversion to labour, and desire of the present enjoyment of costly indulgences' (Mill, 1844, pp. 137–8). Hence economic man (or rather the conception of man implied by economic science, since Mill himself did not use the term, 'economic man') abstracts from all facets of human nature except those relevant to the formulation of economic laws, or laws relating to the production and distribution of wealth.

Mill's essay on scope and method was written (and published) more than a decade before its appearance in the 1844 *Essays on some Unsettled Questions in Political Economy*, so it is not surprising that much of its content had previously appeared in Mill's textbook on scientific method, *A System of Logic*.

In the argument of Mill's *Logic* (Mill, 1843, 1896, Book VI, chapter X, §3), which separated political economy from the other moral sciences, Mill explained his reasons for this separation by referring to the narrow set of circumstances with which Political Economy concerns itself. Citing his earlier essay on scope and method, Mill restricted these circumstances to the 'pursuit of wealth', thereby legitimizing the high degree of abstraction appropriate to the subject. This procedure, Mill hastened to add, did not imply that political economists ever seriously believed that human beings were constituted in this way; but only that 'this is the mode in which science [political economy] must necessarily proceed' (Mill, 1843, 1896, p. 588). By implication, political economy can say nothing about 'those parts of human conduct of which wealth is not even the principal object' (Mill, 1843, 1896, p. 589). However, Mill failed to qualify the usefulness of this mode of abstraction in political economy, for example, by indicating its effects on limiting the generality of the conclusions reached through its use. The problem of the laws of distribution, where the arrangements of society are not immutable but evolving, thereby making their conclusions 'local' rather than 'general', had nothing to do, in his view, with the 'method of investigation' which is 'applicable universally' (Mill, 1843, 1896, p. 590). Mill, therefore, staunchly adhered to the usefulness of the notion of 'economic man' for the limited range of inquiry with which political economy was concerned. In this way, Political Economy was to be sharply distinguished from the 'infant science of political ethology' which sought to elucidate the diverse causes of 'national character' (Mill, 1843, 1896, p. 590). It was this type of doctrine that Marshall had apparently been teaching during the early 1870s, as he confessed in the 1902 letter to J.N. Keynes previously quoted.

Given the subject matter of this chapter, it is useful at this stage to interrupt this survey of the artefact of 'economic man' as used in abstract political economy, by linking it briefly to its utilitarian antecedents. Mill's utilitarian credentials need little elaboration. He had absorbed them in his youth, and had reiterated them in his various writings. Utilitarian doctrine itself rested on a set of rather simple, 'abstract' propositions. These viewed happiness as the sole aim of man, with the motives for human action expressed in terms of their positive and negative consequences for happiness, that is, pleasure and pain. Happiness in short was represented by the sum of pleasure and pain, implying their measurability and addibility. This picture of the 'spring of action' for humanity was devoid of many other human motives – such as 'conscience', 'principle', 'moral rectitude' or 'moral duty' – as prescribed either by religious or by secular moral codes. Hence utilitarianism tended to view man simply as a pleasure machine, searching for the greatest possible happiness by minimising pain and maximising pleasure. This constituted the essence of the felicific calculus, as the main principle of the utilitarians was sometimes described. For Bentham and his followers, the calculus also provided a case for action based on the analysis of human conduct stripped down to these bare essentials. The parallels between this abstract view of human nature in its moral dimensions, and that encapsulated by the concept of 'economic man' in its 'commercial' dimensions, are so close that they need no further justification. This association would have been very evident to British moral scientists of the second half of the nineteenth century, who had all immersed themselves in utilitarian philosophy and its methods of abstraction. It is, therefore, no wonder that 'economic man' became an almost automatically acceptable abstraction for use in the science for which it had been developed by the major authority on logic and scientific method of the mid-nineteenth century, J.S. Mill, who had first put it on the agenda of economic method.

J.E. Cairnes (1875, 1888) largely followed Mill in his depiction of the limited view of human nature necessarily taken by Political Economy. He reiterated that Political Economy treats men in terms of extensive and constant motivations relating to the acquisition of wealth, motivations almost infinite in number but among which some are 'of so marked and paramount a character' that they are of particular relevance to Political Economy as the science of wealth (Cairnes, 1875, 1888, pp. 56–7). However, Cairnes (1875, 1888, pp. 62–4) warned, more fully than Mill had done, that such abstraction by means of 'conditioning' (*ceteris paribus*) clauses somewhat limited the generality of Political Economy's conclusions when predicated on this rather narrow view of human nature.

Two widely known methodological essays by Walter Bagehot (1879, 1908) also drew attention to the frequent use made by political economists of the concept of economic man as a stratagem of abstraction. In describing political economy as the science of commercial society, commercial practices are isolated so as to be more easily explained and better understood. Bagehot continued:

> [A]nd it ['economic man'] deals too with the men who carry on that commerce, and who make it possible. It assumes a sort of human nature such as we see everywhere around us, and again it simplifies that human nature; it looks at one part of it only. Dealing with matters of "business", it assumes that man is activated only by motives of business. It assumes that everyman who makes anything, makes it for money, that he always makes that thing which makes him most at least cost, and that he will make it in the way that will produce most and spend least; it assumes that everyman who buys, buys with his whole heart, and that he who sells, sells with his whole heart, each wanting to gain all possible advantage. Of course, we know that this is not so, that men are not like this; but we assume it for simplicity's sake, as an hypothesis (Bagehot, 1879, 1908, pp. 6–7).

This precise picture of the abstraction of 'economic man' was restated in more Millian fashion in the second essay of Bagehot's *Economic Studies*. Talking about the role of abstraction in political economy, Bagehot indicated that this even applied to the manner in which the science dealt with people: 'The abstract man of this science is engrossed with one desire only – the desire of possessing wealth, not of course that there ever was a being who always acted as that desire would dictate...' (Bagehot, 1879, 1908, pp. 97–8). It is interesting to note that in 1885 Marshall wrote a brief preface, at the request of Bagehot's widow, for a special edition reprinting Bagehot's methodological essays designed to introduce them to student readers. He later regretted this action even though he himself had initially suggested it (see Groenewegen, 1995, p. 406 n.*, cf. p. 173), something he likewise confessed to John Neville Keynes (Marshall to J.N. Keynes, 27 August 1889; Whitaker, 1996, vol. I, Letter 270, p. 298).

Bagehot, not surprisingly, became a target of Cliffe Leslie who, in two of his economic essays, criticised the notion of economic man, as implied by the political economists' devotion to deducing a theory of commercial values from 'the love of money ... [based on a] universal desire for wealth' (Leslie, 1888, p. 2, cf. p. 8), and argued moreover that they had never bothered to analyse 'the demand of consumers', which gives 'the love of money all its force and all its meaning'. A subsequent essay on 'the Philosophical Method of Political Economy' repeated this type of criticism, especially directed at the use Nassau Senior and Mill had made of this notion (Leslie, 1888, pp. 166, 167, 169–72). Henry Sidgwick's *Principles*, as hinted previously, supported Mill on the notion of 'economic man' as a necessary abstraction for political economy (Sidgwick, 1887, p. 5). Sidgwick explicitly rejected Leslie's criticism of Mill on this point as mistaken, because it rested on a misinterpretation of Mill's views (Sidgwick, 1887, pp. 35–6).

In his authoritative *Scope and Method of Political Economy*, John Neville Keynes defended the abstraction of 'economic man' as 'both legitimate and necessary' (J.N. Keynes, 1891, pp. 16, 119), in this context reviewing the opinions on the subject of J.S. Mill (J.N. Keynes, 1891, pp. 19, 116), of Bagehot (p. 117 n.1) and in a long note criticising Leslie's negative views thereon (J.N. Keynes, 1891, p. 120 n.1). Of special relevance to this chapter, Keynes approvingly quoted Marshall's view that Mill's theoretical position on the use of economic man as a theoretical position was not matched by his practice in the later *Principles of Political Economy* (J.N. Keynes, 1891, p. 116 n.1), and that, moreover, there was merit in Mill's position because the motivations of 'economic man' are more easily measurable in economics than those of 'altruistic man' (J.N. Keynes, 1891, p. 127). Keynes (1891, pp. 127–8) also reviewed the opinions on economic man of several German economists (Knies, Roscher and Wagner). By way of conclusion, Keynes came down emphatically in favour of the use of the concept in deductive economic reasoning, which to his mind invariably necessitated the frequent use of a *ceteris paribus* assumption. On this last point, he cited Marshall's proposition that 'the function of pure theory is to deduce definite conclusions from definite premises' (J.N. Keynes, 1891, pp. 218, 240 n. and 243 n.), which implied a need to review the position of several economic writers on the nature of political economy's necessary postulates. Keynes therefore sided with Mill (and without naming it, Sidgwick's defence of Mill) on the acceptability of the notion, 'economic man', in abstract political economy reasoning.

Another Cambridge logician, W.E. Johnson (1897), concisely summarised the differences of opinion on the subject of 'economic man' for the *Palgrave Dictionary of Political Economy*. Much of this summary relied explicitly on J.N. Keynes's treatment of the matter, but its neat and useful bibliography listed the major treatments of 'economic man' in the literature in use at the end of the nineteenth century. Of particular interest is Johnson's reference to 'the idea of *semi*-economic man' as suggested by Edgeworth (1882), usefully employed by Marshall (1891, Book V chapter XII) and elegantly, and concisely, presented by Maffeo Pantaleoni's treatment of the subject (Pantaleoni, 1898, 1957, chapters I–III). Having now explicitly introduced Marshall's position on 'economic man' into the discussion on two separate occasions in these last two paragraphs, it has clearly become time to review Marshall's views on the subject more systematically.

II

Few traces remain, it has to be said, in the written record of Marshall's initial treatment of 'economic man'. Marshall's early philosophical writings which have been preserved are silent on this issue even though they were associated with scientific abstraction and argument, a matter occasionally broached in these writings. The same applies to Marshall's early economic writings, including the two editions of Economics of Industry written jointly with his wife, and the privately printed *Pure Theory of Foreign Trade and of Domestic Value*. Some of this material, however, contained hints that Marshall had implicitly dropped any thoughts of discussing the actions of an 'economic man' in his writings, and instead was looking at people who, as he was to put it in the later editions of his Principles, were decidedly creatures 'of flesh and blood' (e.g. Marshall, 1920, p. 27). Moreover, and in accordance with his methodological stance of treating economic motivation as an attribute of actual people as members of a social group, there is reference to evolving character and differentiated personal characteristics in the various categories of people including both working men and business men (see e.g. Whitaker, 1975, I, pp. 198, 207–9; II, p. 55–6, 197–8).

The first explicit reference by Alfred Marshall to 'economic man' in his published writings occurs in his 1885 inaugural lecture. In three paragraphs, following a brief remark on the inevitable presence in economics of 'pure or abstract theory', Marshall discussed 'economic man' as one of 'the modes of expression adopted by the older economists'. These paragraphs stressed the term's rationale with respect to measurability and strongly rejected its popular association with selfishness and egoism. The paragraphs can therefore be quoted in full since some of their contents resurfaced (increasingly in modified form) in the pages of the *Principles*. They also link 'economic man' with the 'tactical' in Marshall, because his inaugural lecture was designed in part to impress upon his Cambridge audience both the importance of economics as a science and the need therefore to give it a wider exposure than it received in the Moral Sciences syllabus, the metaphysical content of which deterred good minds from the study of economics (Marshall, 1885, pp. 171–3; and see Groenewegen, 1995, pp. 310–13):

> For indeed, when they [the older economists] spoke of the "economic man" as governed by selfish or rather self-regarding motives, they did not express their meaning exactly. For example, Mill says that in economic phenomena "the psychological law

chiefly concerned is the familiar one that greater gain is preferred to a smaller"; and argues that science gets a better hold in economics than in other social phenomena because it deals with motives that can be compared quantitatively and measured one against another. It is this notion of measurability that he really takes as the basis of his work, though he does not sufficiently emphasize it.

Whenever we get a glimpse of the economic man he is not selfish. On the contrary he is generally hard at work saving capital chiefly for the benefit of others. The fact is that the desire to make provision for one's family acts in a very regular way and is eminently capable of being reduced to law: it is prominent in all economic reasoning, because, though unselfish, it is measurable. Again, if with Cliffe Leslie, we analyse all the infinite variety of motives that are commonly grouped together under the term "love of money", we see that they are of all kinds. They include many of the highest, the most refined and the most unselfish parts of our nature. The common link that binds them together is that they can be more or less measured; and in this world they are measured by money.

But, though in wording our economic organon this idea of measurability should be always present, it should not, I think, be prominent. For practical purposes, and in order to keep the better in touch with real life, it will be best to go on treating it as chiefly concerned with those motives to which a money price can be directly or indirectly assigned. But motives that are selfish or self-regarding have no claim to more consideration than others except in so far as they may be more easily measurable and may more easily have a money price assigned to them (Marshall, 1885, pp. 160–1).

As already indicated, much of the contents of this inaugural lecture on 'economic man' was transposed onto the pages of the first edition of the *Principles of Economics* (Marshall, 1890). Its Book I, chapter VI, designed to explain 'economic motives', devoted its first sub-section to 'economic man'; the 'popular error' of viewing this conception as equivalent to the proposition that man 'is governed only by selfish motives'; and the advantages economics had over the other social sciences in terms of its opportunities for dealing with measurable motives. However, the last proposition entailed a warning: human motivation was based on a variety of factors, many of them not measurable. The meaning of this was further pursued in a long footnote at the end of §1, in which Marshall explained that in this context the individual is a member of a social group, and measurement requires a degree of applicability to the whole of that group of the motive to be measured. (This remark can be seen, incidentally, as anticipating the notion of a 'representative' individual, firm, or business, as Marshall explicitly did in later editions of this book, when this condition appeared to be met.) In the present world, Marshall continued, money is the yardstick of economic motive, since 'when we want to induce a man to do anything for us, we offer him money', notwithstanding the fact that a 'system of honours' (as implied in the 'use of the letters C.B., or to wear a star or a garter') may induce some types of action. A hypothetical society is then conjured up in which money is replaced by a finely gradated scheme of honours and for which a 'treatise of economic theory very similar to the present' needs little reference to material things, 'and no mention at all of money' (Marshall, 1890, pp. 78–9 and n. 1). Earlier, the preface to the first edition of the *Principles* claimed that 'efforts to construct an abstract science with regards to the action of an "economic man"… have not been successful', both because 'economic man' cannot be seen as 'perfectly selfish' and because 'altruistic motives' to action can never be totally excluded from explanations of human action (Marshall, 1890, p. vi).

It should be noted in this context that this brief, critical treatment of 'economic man' is nowhere explicitly associated with utilitarianism, or with its founder, Jeremy Bentham. Some indirect association between the two are, however, made. For example, Bentham's 'harsh' and one-sided treatment of motives 'on the supposition that everyone was always on the alert to find out what course would best provide his own interest' is depicted as incomplete, because of its lack of concern, among other things, with the influence of 'custom' (Marshall, 1890, pp. 38–9). Bentham's discussion of 'pleasure', 'its duration', 'intensity', and 'propinquity' is approvingly quoted in connection with the theory of consumption, while the possibility of an 'impure pleasure' is explicitly ascribed to him (Marshall, 1890, pp. 152–3, 747). However, neither utilitarianism as a doctrine or guide for action, nor its synonym hedonics was explicitly mentioned in the first edition of the *Principles*.

The second edition of the *Principles*, published in 1891 made some significant changes to this treatment. Book I chapter VI on economic motives disappeared. Its contents, however, were partly transferred in a much revised form to a new Book I chapter V, §5 which was headed, 'economic motives are not exclusively selfish' (Marshall, 1891 pp. 77–8). Apart from the reference to 'economic man' in the preface to the first edition (which this, and all subsequent editions, reprinted in full), 'economic man' and his characteristics disappeared from the text. However, the benefits of being able to measure personal motives 'by the sum of money which he will just give up in order to secure a desired satisfaction or… to undergo a certain fatigue' (Marshall, 1891 p. 73) remained; and in a footnote were acknowledged to J.S. Mill (Marshall, 1891 p. 73 n. 1). Money and command over wealth remained likewise as 'the centre around which economic science clusters', together with the warning that nothing could be inferred from this about 'the main aim of human effort' or the 'main subject matter' of study for the economist. Systems of honours as inducements to action were also retained as alternative forms of motivation, together with the implications of this for the writing of an economic treatise in a world without money (Marshall, 1891, p. 76 n. 1).

The treatment of the role of utilitarianism and Bentham in economics was also much downgraded in the new edition, both in terms of space and the nature of the comments they received. Marshall now stated that Bentham himself 'wrote little on economics', but that he influenced 'the young economists around him' and steered them away from a 'concern with custom' as an explanatory force in human action (Marshall, 1891 p. 58). Bentham was now also charged with a failure to discuss 'wants' and their nature in his political economy (Marshall, 1891, p. 149). Marshall, however, acknowledged some indebtedness to Bentham (together with Cournot and von Thünen) in discovering the notion of 'consumer's rent' (later rechristened to 'consumer surplus'); though their relative importance in this is not indicated. An argument on discounting future pleasures introduced as a new mathematical note V (Marshall, 1891, p. 747) was explicitly stated to belong 'to hedonics, and not properly to economics', a further explicit thrust to divorce the rigidities on human action of utilitarianism from the broader study of this subject of which economics was inherently capable.

It would be tedious to pursue these minutiae through all the editions of Marshall's *Principles*. In the relatively long lasting fourth edition, Book I chapter V retained a strong disclaimer (introduced in the third edition—Marshall, 1895, p. 178 n.) of 'the belief that economists are adherent of the philosophical system of hedonism', while the advantages and drawbacks of using money as a measuring rod of economic motivation were considerably enlarged upon. The problems in such measurement (particularly those arising from inequalities in money income) were more fully discussed and (with an eye to the criticisms of Ruskin and Carlyle of the careless remarks on this subject by 'the older economists') motives from 'man's higher nature' were explicitly distinguished from those of his 'lower nature'. Both of these tended to be somewhat indifferently mingled together in economics by the necessity for the economist to deal with the 'manifestations' of 'mental states' in the market place as compared with psychologists who analysed the mental states themselves (Marshall, 1898, p. 77).

Many of these sentiments were retained in the final, eighth, edition. There they featured largely in Book I chapter II as a result of the reorganisation (in the fifth edition) of the contents of Book I necessitated by the creation of Appendices A–D from the contents of Book I chapters II, III and IV and parts of V and VI of the first four editions. Appendix C now contrasted Ricardo's mechanical analogies with the use of some more appropriate biological ones (Marshall, 1920, p. 777) and gave even more attention to the need to qualify human motivation from the narrow perspective which Mill had given it ('man solely occupied in acquiring and consuming wealth') through the emphasis given on this by the German economists. In particular, Marshall now emphasised Adolph Wagner's four fold division of economic motives, sub-divided as they were into egoistic and altruistic. The first of these was subdivided in turn into 'economic advantages', 'hope of reward' (fear of punishment), 'honour and striving for recognition', and fourthly, 'the pleasure of activity', or work, or 'the thrill of the chase' (Marshall, 1920, pp. 783–4).

References to Bentham and utilitarianism were by then even more reduced in scope. Bentham's views, interestingly, were themselves partly separated from the view that the pleasure–pain principle could give rise to an 'ethical creed'

(Marshall 1920, p. 17 n.), while recognition continued to be given to Bentham's vision of 'impure pleasures', but now in the context of Mathematical Note V, with its explicit disassociation of economics from hedonics (Marshall, 1920 p. 841). As in the inaugural lecture, economics was firmly presented as a completely separate and distinct social science from utilitarian doctrine.

Marshall's Presidential Address to the 1890 Economics and Statistical Section of the British Association dealing with 'aspects of competition' briefly used this public forum to correct popular misgivings about the motives underlying business competition being confined to the 'love of money'. This, Marshall stated, was only one of many of such motives, even though it was the most measurable of them and therefore frequently was given undue emphasis (Marshall, 1890a, pp. 281–2). A subsequent public address claimed the advance for economics of recognising the need to 'deal with the whole of man's nature...[even if] chief stress [was laid] on certain aspects of it' (Marshall, 1897, p. 299). In particular, this lecture drew attention to the inconstancy of human nature: rather than being static, it was continuously developing, and social science, of which economics was an important part, found its 'unity in the forces of human character' which it systematically studied (Marshall, 1897, pp. 299–300). Marshall's famous 1907 essay on economic chivalry dwelt in detail on the latter's association with the 'highest work in industry', and the need for adequately recognising and honouring this, rather than concentrating, as so often was the case, on the 'common place or even the sordid sides of business work' (Marshall 1907, pp. 331–2). However, these sorts of remarks were already far removed from the use of the notion of 'economic man' in economic reasoning, though they reveal the continuous 'tactical' importance for Marshall of what constituted economic motivation for the sake of preserving the good name of economics and of the economist.

It was therefore appearance rather than substance that characterised Marshall's changed perspectives on the notion of economic man as an apt instrument for discussing economic motivation. As in the case of the strong associations economics was alleged to have with utilitarianism, this type of association with simplistic abstraction tended to give economics a bad name. For Marshall, as the above has demonstrated, both associations were unnecessary and overdrawn, if not irrelevant or incorrect. 'Economic man' could easily be by-passed in economic discourse; utilitarianism was completely distinct from economics. Moreover, such static pictures of motive to action, whether economic or ethical, were particularly deficient once time and the process of evolutionary change were fully taken into consideration, as they had to be in any economic science with claims to realism. Marshall's rejection of static abstraction, except when it was used in the most preliminary way, was fully evident in this matter, as it was in others. Man's character and motivation, diverse as they were, were also continuously in a state of flux, just as the general environment which influenced, if not created, them, was continuously changing. Such evolutionary aspects of change in their various ramifications were only ignored by economists at their peril.

III

Marshall's decided evolutionary views do not need detailed demonstration. As I have indicated elsewhere (Groenewegen, 2001), Marshall had become sufficiently interested in the subject during the second half of the 1860s to study Darwin's two major works, Origin of Species and Descent of Man, as well as, and much more thoroughly, the evolutionary writings of Herbert Spencer (see also Laurent, 2000). It has already been mentioned in the introduction to this chapter that Marshall appears to have criticised the concept of 'economic man' on evolutionary grounds in discussions with Sidgwick in 1871. The *Principles* in particular, and various parts of the later books as well, exhibit evolutionary perspectives and clearly see evolutionary processes as central to explaining and understanding the course over time of human activity, human nature, human organization and human institutions. This is particularly evident in Book VI, chapters XII and XIII, of the later editions of the Principles of Economics. Marshall's considerable grasp of evolutionary theory made excessive reliance on static theory not only repugnant to him, but also highly misleading because of the over-simplification it forced on the observer of social and economic behaviour. Neglecting evolution in developing reasoned economic argument was just not on for him. (For a more detailed discussion, see Groenewegen, 2001, esp. pp. 52–9).

Marshall's early recognition of a changing human nature as partly the direct result of industrial and economic progress, together with his equally early interest in the improvement of human character, made him oppose a static notion of 'economic man'. His reasons were probably similar to those reported to J.N. Keynes in 1889. It gave 'little good service' to analysis in these areas and, in addition, was very unsuitable as a practical tool for use in such discussions. His quarrel with Sidgwick in the early 1870s was more than likely along such evolutionary lines. By then, Marshall was also already heavily drawn into historical, and other factual research in economics, mainly under the influence of the German economists whom he admired, such as Wagner and Schmoller and on this point, perhaps even Marx (see Groenewegen, 1995, p. 664). Given that the utilitarianism of Bentham, Mill and Sidgwick was essentially static in nature, and only paid lip service to factual and empirical research, such disaffection with 'economic man', as there was in the early 1870s on Marshall's part on 'evolutionary grounds', was capable of creating tensions between him and Sidgwick. From 1869 onwards, Sidgwick had been working on his first book, *The Methods of Ethics*, not published until 1874, even though, as Schneewind (1986, pp. 40–41) suggests, its utilitarian foundations would have been firmly in place well before then. Hence hedonics, and its creature, 'economic man' (which had, after all, in essence been a creation of J.S. Mill) fell foul early on in Marshall's academic life through the historical, analytical and sociological demands made by a vibrant and evolutionary political economy. All this is highly speculative, and rests on the single Sidgwick letter of 1871 cited at the start of this chapter, as well as on the mass of circumstantial and harder evidence on Marshall's expanding economic horizons in the early years of his 'economic apprenticeship'.

Perhaps, and again this is highly speculative, Marshall's lectures on utilitarianism for the Moral Sciences Tripos, possibly assigned to him by Sidgwick through his dominant position among the Moral Sciences teachers at this time, may have given him cause to link tactical considerations of course organization reforms for economics with a 'practical' opposition to aspects of hedonism and 'economic man' as handmaidens of economics. However, as Mary Paley Marshall later recalled about his 1870s Cambridge lectures, these were still praising Bentham and his utilitarianism as 'an influence on economics [greater] than any other non-economist' because of the stress [which Bentham] laid on measurement' (cited in Groenewegen, 1995, p. 271). A number of other rifts between Sidgwick and Marshall also started to appear at this time, even though their relations, generally speaking, were still very cordial (see Groenewegen, 1995, pp. 663–5, esp. p. 664).

Having already traced the evolution of Marshall's views in print on the subject of 'economic man', and noted his desire to replace such an artificial and potentially damaging abstraction with representations of real human beings 'of flesh and blood', the manner in which this substitution was carried out in the pages of the *Principles* is of some interest. If its pages are successively scanned for examples of human life and activities, a veritable parade of specific producers and consumers passes in steady progression before the reader of this book. Confining such scanning to the eighth, definitive edition, this parade presents itself as follows, Book by Book, page by page.

After the opening two chapters, with their identification of political economy or economics with 'the study of mankind in the ordinary business of life' (p. 11) in which families, slaves, poets, the poor, producers and traders, make initial appearances, a full and quite specific array of the human subject matter of economics begins in earnest in chapter 3. On turning the pages, their presence is made felt by bricklayers (p. 34), stockbrokers (p. 35), matchbox makers and cattle breeders (p. 36), employers and the employed, middle men and producers, bankers and their clients (p. 51), bondholders (p. 60), cabinet makers and furniture makers (p. 63), ploughmen (p. 64), bakers, cooks and confectioners (p. 66), agricultural and town labourers (p. 69), borrowers and lenders (p. 73), undertakers (that is, entrepreneurs) and businessmen (pp. 74–5), drivers, piano dealers and the Commissioner of Taxation (p. 77), domestic servants (p. 79), land owners, private secretaries (p. 80) and this is just the cast of the short two introductory Books of the *Principles*. Book III expands this parade of human economic actors further. It starts, historically appropriately, with 'savages' (p. 86), and then continues with eighteenth century well-to-do labourers (p. 87), fishermen (p. 89), West-Indian negroes (p. 90), traders and manufacturers (p. 92), tea drinkers with different levels of income (pp. 94–7), expert surgeons (p. 98), rich wine drinkers (p. 103), sugar consumers over the last two centuries (pp. 105–6), persons with high musical sensibility (p. 108), shop keepers (pp. 113–14), a primitive housewife (p. 117), clerks (pp. 118–19), mountain climbers (p. 121), while in conclusion the Book re-introduces tea drinkers (pp. 125–8) and discusses the special case of low income bread purchasers (p. 132), renters (p. 134), Buddhists (p. 136), and those addicted to luxury consumption (pp. 136–7).

For Book IV, the parade almost becomes an avalanche of human actors, differentiated from the previous Book in that its various classes of consumers are replaced by various types of producers. It starts with agriculturists (p. 145) and continues with biblical shepherds (p. 151), farmers in general and English farmers in particular (p. 152), peasant owners (p. 153), cultivators (p. 154), settlers in a new country (p. 164), parents (p. 173), lawyers (p. 174), religious orders (pp. 174–5), unskilled labourers (p. 182), agricultural labourers, farmers and peasant proprietors (p. 183), artisans (p. 186), manufacturers (p. 188), business men and university men (p. 194), a skilled housewife (p. 195), puddlers and navvies (p. 196), Americans and Chinese (p. 201 n.), mothers and fathers (p. 207), technical school masters (p. 209), apprentices (p. 210), manufacturers (p. 210), artisans (pp. 213–14), Frenchmen, Indian and Persian masters of colour (p. 215), professional men (p. 218 n.), errand boys (p. 219), husbandmen, blacksmiths, merchants, farmers (p. 221), Indian Ryots and Lowland farmers (p. 222), women and child workers (p. 223), travellers and primitive tribesmen (p. 224), misers, Indian, Irish and English savers (p. 225), French peasants (p. 226), hoarders (p. 228), professional men and wage earners (p. 229), prophets, priests and legislators (p. 243), Jewish and Armenian money-dealers, Chinese labour (p. 244), artists (p. 251 n.), merchants, lawyers, physicians, men of science (p. 252), medical men, child cotton workers (p. 253), watchmakers, gun makers (p. 258), newspaper editors, 'readers', engineers, machinists, pressmen, compositors (p. 259), artists, engravers, photographers, electrotypers, stereotypers (p. 261), house carpenters, machine attendants (p. 262), weavers (p. 263), agriculturalists, agricultural labourers (p. 264), producers, consumers (p. 267), canary breeders (p. 268 n.), kings, dyers (p. 269), artisans (p. 273), trained businessmen, skilled artisans, agriculturalists, bakers, spinners, brewers, weavers, bricklayers, carpenters, dressmakers, tailers (p. 274), agriculturalists, coal miners, agricultural labourers (p. 275), public servants, entertainers, doctors, actors, musicians, domestic servants (p. 276), hotel proprietors, confectioners, grocers, fishmongers (p. 277), manufacturers (p. 280), masters and heads of large business (p. 284), small shopkeepers (p. 289), country carriers, cabmen (p. 289), businessmen and handicraftsmen (p. 291), solicitors and educators (p. 292), capitalists, traders, artists, master builders (p. 293), warehouse men, designers (p. 295), employers (p. 297), undertakers, managers, directors (p. 302), shareholders (p. 303), taxpayers (p. 304), co-operators (p. 308), foremen and superintendents (p. 310), founders of businesses (p. 316) and even 'representative producers' (p. 317) whose presence in this list of actual people is tainted by being at least partly dressed in the unwelcome garb of 'economic man'.

Without going on to present the parade which it is possible to extract from Books V and VI, the type of people featuring on the pages of Marshall's *Principles* make an impressive list, even if there are the occasional duplications of certain types. These are, however, few and far between. They reflect Marshall's awareness from observation, particularly during his summer holiday travels (see Groenewegen, 1995, chapter 7, esp. pp. 208–14) of the nature of work and industry, of occupations, and of the manner by which the economic activities of actual human beings in consumption and production can be disaggregated into narrow sub-sections. Even the set of tea drinkers we meet in Book III can be further de-homogenised in terms of the type of tea they drink and their specific brand preference. The extent to which these sub-sets of human actors are flesh and blood substitutes for 'economic man' can be clarified by looking at a number of specific case studies in which Marshall went into more detail. In the manner in which his parade of economic actors has been presented so far, his intention of portraying them as people of flesh and blood seems fully realised.

The following cases suggest themselves. Take first the example of the 'primitive housewife', who is reverted to in Book V, chapter IV, §4, designed to illustrate the 'principle of substitution'. On her first appearance in the *Principles* (p. 117) she is presented as a maximiser of her family's well-being in the context of allocating her 'limited number of hanks of yarn' among alternative clothing requirements (socks or vests). Best allocative results are obtained when the marginal utility of yarn applied to sock knitting equals that from the application of yarn to vests. Her subsequent appearance (p. 357) complicates her choices by introducing two methods of producing vests (one is more wool using but less labour intensive than the other). Hence her 'marginalist' decision making practice to secure maximum benefits (returns) from her given stock of yarn gradually approach the decision making required in 'the larger business world'. Without spelling out the rule, it can be asked whether this is simply 'economic man' the rational, maximising decision maker, translated purely for illustrative purposes into a 'primitive housewife' in order to demonstrate the 'generality' of the substitution principle underlying the economics of choice in the sphere of production.

Another famous person 'of flesh and blood' inhabiting the pages of the *Principles* is the 'boy [picking] blackberries for his own eating' designed as a simple illustration of 'equilibrium between desire and effort'. Here the boy is said to balance an 'eagerness for play' and a 'disinclination for the work of picking' (the cost side) with 'the desire for eating' blackberries. So long as the act of picking a blackberry, and eating it almost simultaneously, adds more to his 'pleasure' than the cost subtracts, the boy will continue to pick and eat. However, eventually costs will equal benefits (the point of maximum satisfaction for this young blackberry aficionado) and after this point, costs increasingly outweigh the diminishing pleasure of eating additional blackberries for a gradually replete stomach (p. 331). Here is the essence of rational economic decision making – the equalising of marginal benefits and costs – illustrated by the homely example of a boy in the bush enjoying an environment of blackberries. Again, it may be asked, is this a simple transposition of the essentials of the behaviour of 'economic man' into the seemingly normal behaviour reflected in the common occurrence of a boy picking and eating blackberries during a stroll or game in the bush? The abstract nature of the treatment may be gauged from the fact that nothing is said about the staining qualities on clothing of blackberry juice, the hazards of the thorns on blackberry bushes or the risk of sore stomachs when fruit insufficiently ripe is devoured, or similar complications.

A third and final example of Marshall's practice is the case of the 'alert business man' grazier, 'ever seeking the most profitable application of his resources' and the choice of the 'marginal shepherd'. It provides a simple application of the principles guiding young amateur blackberry pickers to a feature of the rural labour market. Additional shepherds will be employed, so long as their marginal benefit (product) in terms of sheep effectively protected outweighs the given cost (in terms of the wage rate and auxiliary on-costs such as shepherds crooks). Equilibrium is produced when marginal benefit (product) equals cost (wage rate). Marshall exhaustively indicated the various additional assumptions required for a satisfactory analysis of this problem of choice in a grazing society and, in addition, was very emphatic in his warning that this resource allocation exercise could never constitute a theory of wages (pp. 515–18). Here the 'alert' grazier is the 'flesh and blood' replica of 'economic man' interested in maximising wealth through maximising profit by making the best use of his resources through efficient choices about offering employment opportunities to shepherds.

These three fairly well known 'flesh and blood' examples from the *Principles* represent illustrations of the application of rational economic resource allocation principles to secure maximum benefits for specific actions. Hence they formally replace the activities of 'economic man' by more concrete, everyday examples of human behaviour. The examples from the three previous paragraphs illustrate what Marshall had claimed in his letter to John Neville

Keynes quoted at the start of this chapter, i.e., that explicitly ignoring the device of 'economic man' entailed no theoretical loss. The substituted 'flesh and blood' decision makers (housewives, playing children, alert graziers) act as simple proxies who, by assumption, act as 'economic man' would have done in a rational, maximising manner to solve their own individual problems (more vests versus more socks, more play and less work versus more blackberries, hiring an additional shepherd).

For Marshall, it seems, such a switch in form of presentation and illustration had practical and tactical benefits. First of all, they showed the generality of the rules he was developing in the key action in rational economic decision making, that is, choosing among alternatives in order to maximise satisfaction from using the resources at hand. This thereby dressed the principles of economics with their implications for explaining the actions of everyday life, thereby imparting both reality and relevance to these principles. Simultaneously, and this was a major contribution, Marshall generally indicated the potential problems in application of these principles when motives were more complex, when the data were incomplete, and when, for specific and individual reasons, the actors in the human economic drama behaved in peculiar (or non-normal) ways. Marshall's strategy in his *Principles* implicitly preserved all the theoretical benefits derivable from using the abstract construct of a rational 'economic man' without paying the 'practical' and 'tactical' price from openly parading such a narrow, theoretical construction, for all to see and scoff at. The qualities he gave to his 'flesh and blood' creations precisely resembled those of discredited 'economic man' and secured the general decision-making results he wanted to obtain without any disadvantages.

It should also be indicated that some of Marshall's economic actors discussed at greater length exhibit certain hedonistic qualities in the sense that they attempt to maximise 'net pleasure' (e.g., the blackberry-picking boy). The knitting housewife maximises benefits in terms of family well-being at least possible cost to herself, hence possessing a degree of altruism conspicuously absent in conventional 'economic man'. The grazier-cum-alert businessman is the closest to 'Millian economic man': he maximises profit through his rational economic hiring practice, which equates wage costs to returns at the margin. However, a cost–benefit calculus underlies the practice of all three decision makers as maximisers even if their maximands are different, and an altruistic motive can be ascribed at least to the primitive but rational house wife. Both the housewife and blackberry-picking boy examples were little changed during the eight editions of the *Principles*; that of the marginal shepherd (a longer and more complex example) shows considerable variation. Marshall (1890, pp. 548–9) gave it less than a full paragraph, Marshall (1891, p. 567) added a footnote, Marshall (1898, pp. 586–8) expanded the example considerably, and it was not until the sixth edition that it came close to its final, definitive version.

There is, of course, a more general reason why Marshall preferred to deal with actual people rather than with an artificial construct. Only the former as objects of study could shed light on the study of 'man's character as moulded by every-day work' (p. 1), the basic aim and objective of Marshall's economic study. This, as Talcott Parsons (1931, p. 284) perceptively argued, makes activities a topic of general interest for Marshall additional to the analysis of 'wants'; an aspect fully reflected in the relative space devoted to these topics in the *Principles*. For this wider agenda, the human agents were better presented as actual persons, with a capacity to act, grow and evolve through the influence of their activities, including economic activities. However, as Marshall also realised, theoretically this choice was unimportant. It was immaterial in developing and explaining economic principles, whether a simplified version of 'economic man' was used for explanatory purposes or a more realistic creature 'of flesh and blood'. For reasons already explained, the matter was seen as crucial on practical and tactical grounds.

Evolving man, benefiting from changes in economic and social environment, makes an appearance towards the end of the book, particularly its final chapter (Book VI, chapter XIII), which was not included until the fifth edition. This examines 'progress in relation to standards of life', where standard of life refers to 'standard of activities adjusted to wants' (p. 689). The last implies, as Marshall also explained, 'an increase of intelligence and energy and self respect'. This included 'greater care and judgement in expenditure', food and drink as proper nourishment rather than indulgence, and 'avoidance ... of unwholesome' physical and moral actions. This type of improvement can be universal in a country as part of its development, or limited to specific groups of trades. It has major implications for economic efficiency (p. 689). The chapter thereby raised the possibility that material improvement may have wider consequences for general advancement in standards moral, social and cultural. Such broad-based social change would also reduce the importance of the 'residuum', Marshall's expression for the social flotsam of unemployables from moral, physical or mental causes, so that 'mechanical' progress, aided by government intervention in education and poverty relief, can effect a genuinely progressive evolution of man. This is the utopian vision Marshall associated with real progress for the future, though he appreciated that with reference to the past a great deal of such real progress had already been achieved.

IV

What other conclusions can be drawn from this paper? Many of these parallel Talcott Parsons's (1931) findings on the subject. Marshall rejected the selfish element in 'economic man' but kept his qualities as rational economic decision-maker. However, these were presented as a general endowment of the modern individual, whether businessman, housewife or school-age youngster. This approach transcended occupation and class. Marshall's practice matched his precepts on the use of 'economic man' in economic discourse. For practical and tactical reason, such a use is easily disguised by substituting creatures of flesh and blood, while this does not impose any costs whatsoever in terms of theoretical application.

This approach leaves room in Marshall's economics for character development as well as for a technical and applied analysis of economic motivation and its consequences in consumption, production, exchange and distribution. Economics could therefore be presented as a study of wealth and as a study of man. Evolution and social change in such an account could co-exist with rationality and economic calculation based on measurable consequences. Its partial equilbrium/caeteris paribus framework enabled every important aspect of each economic problem to give due weight to all relevant factors for solving a problem even if, in practice, only the most relevant of them could be effectively included.

Marshall's eclecticism enabled him to maintain the abstract nature of utilitarian constructs side by side with evolutionary flourishes as part of what he considered to be a realistic, historical and factual method. In contrast to Parsons, this can now be depicted as one of Marshall's strengths in economic analysis. The positivist fiction of a 'value free' economic science was an alien and unproductive world for Marshall. Analysis can and should mix with ethical concerns if a particular problem is to be truly illuminated. Economic rationalism in some things need not preclude a just society. What was wrong with 'economic man' in general was its narrowness in conception in depicting the motivation and striving of people in the modern world of work, business and living the 'full life'.

REFERENCES

Bagehot, W. (1879, 1908), *Economic Studies*, R.H. Hutton (ed.), London: Longmans, Green and Company.
Cairnes, J.E. (1875, 1888), *The Character and Logical Method of Political Economy*, second edition, London: Macmillan and Company.
Edgeworth, F.Y. (1882), *Mathematical Psychics*, London: C. Kegan Paul.
Goschen, Viscount G.J. (1905), 'Ethics and Economics' in idem, *Essays and Addresses on Economic Questions*, London: Edward Arnold, pp. 328–41.
Groenewegen, P. (1995), *A Soaring Eagle. Alfred Marshall 1842–1924*, Aldershot: Edward Elgar.
Groenewegen, P. (2001), 'The Evolutionary Economics of Alfred Marshall', in *Darwinism and Evolutionary Economics*, J. Laurent and J. Nightingale (eds), Cheltenham: Edward Elgar, pp. 49–62.

Johnson, W.E. (1897), 'Economic Man' in *A Dictionary of Political Economy*, R.I. Palgrave (ed.), London: Macmillan, first edition, Volume I pp. 676–7.

Keynes, J.N. (1891), *The Scope and Method of Political Economy*, reprinted New York: Augustus M. Kelley, 1986.

Laurent, J. (2000), 'Alfred Marshall's Annotations on Herbert Spencer's *Principles of Biology'*, *Marshall Studies Bulletin,* **VII**, 1–6 (http://www.cce.unifi.it/dse/marshall/laure7.htm).

Leslie, C.T. (1888), *Essays in Political Economy*, second edition, London: Longmans, Green & Co.

Marshall, A. (1885), 'The Present Position of Economics', in *Memorials of Alfred Marshall*, A.C. Pigou (ed.), London: Macmillan, 1925, pp. 152–74.

Marshall, A. (1890), *Principles of Economics*, first edition, London: Macmillan.

Marshall, A. (1890a), 'Some Aspects of Competition' in *Memorials of Alfred Marshall*, A.C. Pigou (ed.), London: Macmillan, 1925, pp. 256–91.

Marshall, A. (1891), *Principles of Economics*, second edition, London: Macmillan.

Marshall, A. (1893), 'Vote of Thanks', in 'Report of Goschen's Presidential Address to the British Economic Association' *Economic Journal* **3**(3) September, 387–90.

Marshall, A. (1895), *Principles of Economics*, third edition, London: Macmillan.

Marshall, A. (1897), 'The Old Generation of Economists and the New', in *Memorials of Alfred Marshall*, edited A.C. Pigou, London: Macmillan, 1925, pp. 295–311.

Marshall, A. (1898), *Principles of Economics*, fourth edition, London: Macmillan.

Marshall, A. (1907), 'Social Possibilities of Economic Chivalry', in *Memorials of Alfred Marshall*, edited A.C. Pigou, London: Macmillan, 1925, pp. 323–46.

Marshall, A. (1920), *Principles of Economics*, eighth edition, London: Macmillan.

Mill, J.S. (1843, 1896), *A System of Logic Ratiocinative and inductive, being a connected view of the Principles of Evidence and the Methods of Scientific Investigation*, London: Longmans, Green and Company.

Mill, J.S. (1844), 'On the Definition of Political Economy and on the Method of Investigation proper to it' in *Essays on some Unsettled Questions of Political Economy*, London: John W. Parker.

Pantaleoni M. (1898, 1957), *Pure Economics*, translated by T. Boston Bruce, reprinted New York: Augustus M. Kelley.

Parsons, T. (1931), 'Wants and Activities in Marshall', in *Alfred Marshall. Critical Assessments*, J.C. Wood (ed.), London: Croom Helm, Volume I pp. 197–208.

Schneewind, J.B. (1986), *Sidgwick's Ethics and Victorian Moral Philosophy*, Oxford: Clarendon Press.

Sidgwick, H. (1887), *The Principles of Political Economy*, second edition, London: Macmillan.

Whitaker, J.K., ed. (1975), *The Early Economic Writings of Alfred Marshall*, 2 volumes, London: Macmillan.

Whitaker, J.K., ed. (1996), *The Correspondence of Alfred Marshall. Economist*, 3 volumes, Cambridge: Cambridge University Press.

7. Kropotkin and Reclus: Geographers, Evolution and 'Mutual Aid'

Rob Knowles

The notion of 'mutual aid' is most often uncritically attributed to the Russian geographer of international standing, Peter Kropotkin.[1] The possible influences on his thought of his contemporary and close associate, also an internationally famed geographer, Elisée Reclus, are typically ignored (Fleming, 1979, p. 21). While it is most likely that Kropotkin did indeed formulate the notion of 'mutual aid' primarily on his own initiative, it was concurrently adopted by Reclus and integrated into his own evolutionary thinking in a similar manner to the way in which Kropotkin used it. It is therefore instructive to link Kropotkin and Reclus in this essay. This may prove especially fruitful as very little of Reclus's writings have been translated into English. The history of Kropotkin's evolutionary thinking and his perceptions of human nature is, however, the primary focus here and will be explained first, followed by a brief introduction to some of Reclus's evolutionary ideas. While Kropotkin wrote mostly about anarchist thought, Reclus concentrated his writing on geographical subjects.[2] His works, however, especially *L'Homme et la Terre* (Reclus, 1905), embodied many of his insights into a future society, and especially concerned humanity in the context of the earth as a whole. Kropotkin and Reclus were both communitarian anarchists and their ultimate visions of a future society were closely correlated.

Peter Kropotkin (1842–1921) was a seminal theorist of communitarian anarchism who published many works containing his critique of existing society as well as his views of a future society. He was not a utopian dreamer any more than was any other social theorist who put forward prescriptions for the way in which future society could or should function. Any such judgement is only a question of the perspective of the observer (Kropotkin, 1988, p. 83). As a Russian prince, he had received the best education Russia could provide and he was qualified as a geographer after university studies in St Petersburg in the late 1860s (Kropotkin, 1971, p. 224). Imprisoned in 1874 for his dissenting activities, he escaped after two years and pursued his socialist beliefs, finding himself profoundly attracted to communitarian anarchist ideas which he had first encountered in 1872 amongst socialists working in exile and amongst the watchmakers of the Jura mountains near the border between Switzerland and France (ibid., pp. 281–92, 391–8). In his writings he discussed at some length his economic ideas and pointed out to his critics that 'There is not one single principle of Political Economy that does not change its aspect if you look at it from our point of view' (Kropotkin, 1972, p. 193).

Eventually, after years of thought and activism, Kropotkin expressed his view that political economy:

> ...ought to occupy with respect to human societies a place in science similar to that held by physiology in relation to plants and animals...It should aim at *studying the needs of society and the various means, both hitherto used and available under the present state of scientific knowledge, for their satisfaction.* It should try to analyze how far the present means are expedient and satisfactory, economic or wasteful; and then, since the ultimate end of every science (as Bacon had already stated) is obviously prediction and practical application to the demands of life, it should concern itself with the discovery of means *for the satisfaction of these needs with the smallest possible waste of labor and with the greatest benefit to mankind in general* (Kropotkin, 1970c, p. 180, emphasis in original).

He was creating a bridge between 'modern science' and his particular view of the role of political economy. How was it then that a communitarian anarchist who denied the need for a state could confidently develop such a concept of political economy? What was the foundation on which he built that concept?

The answer begins by noting two basic premises. First, communitarian anarchist society would be comprised of social institutions, no different in principle from those which are relied upon by Institutionalist economists, although of course the socio-political context of today's Institutionalist economics and communitarian anarchism would be greatly different.[3] The leading Institutionalist economist Geoffrey Hodgson, for example, has alluded to the 'institutionalist' Walton Hamilton's definition of 'institutions' as 'a way of thought or action of some prevalence and permanence, which is embedded in the habits of a group or the customs of a people...Institutions fix the confines of and impose form upon the activities of human beings' (Hodgson, 1999, p. 143). Kropotkin's view of anarchist-communism was that 'customs and institutions are of absolute necessity for society, not only to solve economic difficulties, but also to maintain and develop social customs that bring men into contact with one another'. He believed that 'a certain moral level...' could be maintained in animal or human society through '*the practice of mutual aid...*', which functioned through '*the institution itself,* acting in such a way as to make social acts a state of habit and instinct'. For Kropotkin, each time such institutions 'issued from popular genius...' were allowed free rein, they yielded 'moral and intellectual improvement of the human race...' (Kropotkin, 1970a, pp. 137, 139, emphasis in original). Kropotkin's notion of 'mutual aid' will be explained in detail shortly, but for the moment it can be understood as the:

> ...conscience – be it only at the stage of an instinct – of human solidarity. It is the unconscious recognition of the force that is borrowed by each man from the practice of mutual aid; of the close dependency of every one's happiness upon the happiness of all; and of the sense of justice, or equity, which brings the individual to consider the rights of every other individual as equal to his own (Kropotkin, 1903, pp. xiii–xiv).[4]

Kropotkin's second basic premise, as for all communitarian anarchists, was that an ethic was prior to any consideration of the economy (Kropotkin, 1924, p. 8; Nettlau, 1996, p. xxii). The absence of either of these two premises would certainly turn any propositions for a future communitarian anarchist society into nothing more than a utopian dream. The primary purpose of this essay is to explain what it was about Kropotkin's understanding of human nature which enabled him to develop his ethic and to expand it into the foundation for social institutions within communitarian anarchist society. It will be seen that evolutionary scientific theory played a major part in this, but that his understanding of human nature relied on more than just scientific theory.

Here is the essence of Kropotkin's ethical thinking:

> [M]odern science has now worked out the elements of a philosophy of the universe, free of supernatural hypotheses and the metaphysical 'mythology of ideas', and at the same time so grand, so poetical and inspiring, and so expressive of freedom, that it certainly is capable of calling into existence the new forces. Man no longer needs to clothe his ideals of moral beauty, and of a society based on justice, with the garb of superstition: he does not have to wait for the Supreme Wisdom to remodel society. He can derive his ideas from Nature and he can draw the necessary strength from the study of its life (Kropotkin, 1924, p. 3).

Note the explicit rejection of any notions of 'superstition' here. Kropotkin, as most other anarchists, rejected the authority of not only the state but also the Church and its teachings, and all other 'supernatural hypotheses' (ibid., p. 119). His thinking therefore was not solely related to a preference for the explanatory power of science but it also involved the necessary rejection of all forms of authority from above, and especially those which produced metaphysical 'mythology'. Already there is a clue here to the direction of his view of human nature. It was possible for it to be authoritarian or to produce metaphysical mythologies but it was also possible for it to develop a free society of 'moral beauty'; 'a society based on justice...'. He asserted that 'No society is possible without certain principles of morality generally recognized...The fact is that moral principles are independent of religious beliefs: they are anterior to them' (Kropotkin, 1970b, p. 73). The question arises, then, of how did Kropotkin reconcile the conflicting tendencies within human nature. They had existed historically, and they existed as he wrote; yet he held a deep belief that they could be reconciled, or at least the authoritarian and supernatural elements could be overcome.

Adopting the scientific law of the *'indestructibility of energy'* he perceived the universe as 'a never-ending series of transformations of energy...' which meant that the 'birth of our planet, its evolution...' was nothing more than 'an infinitesimally small episode—a mere moment in the life of the stellar worlds' (Kropotkin, 1924, p. 3, emphasis in original). He applied the same genesis to 'organic life': 'the infinite variety of beings which now people and enliven our planet' had evolved from 'the simplest life-processes...'. It followed, for Kropotkin, that Nature had taught humanity two crucial lessons. The first was that of 'modesty' in the face of the infinite dimensions of the universe. The arrogance, or 'self-conceit', of thinking only as 'I' without the 'thou' was impossible. The second lesson was the power which humanity could wield 'if it skilfully utilizes the unlimited energies of Nature' (ibid., p. 4). Here, then, was scientific 'proof' of humanity having the power to work with Nature, but also humility concerning the way in which it must be approached. With just these two simple propositions in his hands, Kropotkin asserted that a new ethics, by which he meant 'the teaching of the fundamental principles of morality', was not only needed but was possible: 'if the study of Nature has yielded the elements of a philosophy which embraces the life of the Cosmos...it must be able to give us the rational origin and sources of the moral feelings...it must be able to show us where lie the forces that are able to elevate the moral feeling to an always greater height and purity' (ibid., p. 5). He had asked for and expected to receive a huge gift from 'Nature'.

In a list of the thinkers who had worked out various ethical systems, he understood that evolutionary ethics was primarily informed by 'Darwin, Spencer, and Guyau' (ibid., p. 7). There is not space here to examine in detail the way in which each of these thinkers contributed to Kropotkin's understanding of ethics, however it is important to review them briefly in order to explain the notion of 'mutual aid' which Kropotkin famously wrote about and promoted (Kropotkin, 1903). In formulating this notion Kropotkin had not exclusively leant upon the work of Darwin. In fact, in some ways, Darwin was peripheral to the way in which Kropotkin arrived at the idea. He acknowledged that the basic notion was not original to him (Kropotkin, 1924, p. 281)[5] although he noted that he had been thinking about how animal life and human beings associate in ways which help each other during his work and studies as a budding geographer, and as a Cossack officer, in eastern Siberia during the 1860s, and later in his studies into glacial deposits in Finland in 1871 (Kropotkin, 1971, p. 235; 1903, p. 9). It was while he was in Clairvaux prison in France between 1883 and 1886 that Kropotkin 'saw the necessity of completely revising the [Darwinian] formula itself and its application to human affairs'. He had come to hear of an

1880 lecture by the Russian zoologist, Professor Karl Kessler, and understood that he was hearing a suggestion of scientific corroboration of the observations he had made of his own accord. Kropotkin cited Kessler as stating that 'Mutual aid...is as much a law of nature as mutual struggle; but for the *progressive* evolution of the species the former is far more important than the latter' (Kropotkin, 1971, p. 498, emphasis in original). Kropotkin later discussed the notion with the secretary of the Royal Geographical Society, H.W. Bates, whom Kropotkin stated firmly supported his notion of mutual aid, but was unable to do so in writing because of Bates's untimely death (ibid., p. 499).

Kropotkin investigated Darwinian evolutionary theory and found in Darwin's *Descent of Man* (Darwin, 1888) support for the notion of the natural or organic existence of an instinct which was associative rather than only competitive, as implied by the 'struggle for existence'—a phrase which had been promoted by T.H. Huxley and believed by many to be, simplistically, the sum total of Darwinian theory (Kropotkin, 1924, pp. 284–7; MacRae, 1962, pp. 300–301). It takes only a cursory reading of Darwin's *Descent of Man* to see how Kropotkin found support for his notion of 'mutual aid'. Darwin had come to the following conclusions: '*Firstly*, the social instincts lead an animal to take pleasure in the society of its fellows, to feel a certain amount of sympathy with them, and to perform various services for them...*Secondly*, as soon as the mental faculties had become highly developed, images of all past actions and motives would be incessantly passing through the brain of each individual'. This would lead to a feeling of dissatisfaction with respect to the social instinct if it had momentarily yielded to another instinct. Hunger, for example, could cause this but it would be of short duration and 'not readily or vividly recalled'. For Darwin, '*Thirdly*, after the power of language had been acquired, and the wishes of the community could be expressed, the common opinion how each member ought to act for the public good, would naturally become in a paramount degree the guide to action...[and] *Lastly*, habit in the individual would ultimately play a very important part in guiding the conduct of each member; for the social instinct, together with sympathy, is, like any other instinct, greatly strengthened by habit, and so consequently would be obedience to the wishes and judgment of the community'. Interestingly, as part of this discussion on the social instinct and 'sympathy', Darwin cited J.S. Mill's reference, in his work *Utilitarianism*, to 'social feelings as a "powerful natural sentiment" ' (Darwin, 1888, pp. 98–9).[6] Darwin's view of the 'greatest happiness principle', which was inherent in Utilitarianism, was that it was 'more correct to speak of ...[it] as the standard, and not as the motive of conduct'. That principle might be 'a most important secondary guide and object; the social instinct, however, together with sympathy (which leads to our regarding the approbation and disapprobation of others), having served as the primary impulse and guide' (ibid., pp. 120–21). There was abundant material here for Kropotkin to work with in supporting his own theory of human nature (Kropotkin, 1903, pp.1–6; 1924, pp. 32–45). Essentially, Darwin had provided Kropotkin with two tenets: (1) 'the social instinct is the common source out of which all morality originates...', and (2) 'of the two instincts – the social and the individual – it is *the social instinct which is the stronger, the more persistent, and the more permanently present*. And he was unquestionably right' (Kropotkin, 1924, pp. 37, 43, emphasis in original).

Kropotkin also noted that the Scottish moral philosopher and political economist Adam Smith had used the notion of 'sympathy' in his writings on 'moral sentiments'. He applauded Smith's having 'explained morality on a purely natural basis, as an inherent quality of human nature and not as a revelation from above'. He noted Smith's notion of 'sympathy' as the 'chief motive force in the development of moral conceptions...' and his understanding of 'sympathy' as 'the feeling inherent in man as a social being'. Kropotkin discussed Smith's ideas on morality at some length (ibid., pp. 204–10). Darwin had also noted Smith's idea: 'Adam Smith formerly argued...that the basis of sympathy lies in our strong retentiveness of former states of pain or pleasure' (Darwin, 1888, p. 106). Kropotkin's reference to Smith, however, was more openly appreciative:

> In a fine work, *The Theory of Moral Sentiment*, left to slumber in silence by religious prejudice, and indeed but little known even among anti-religious thinkers, Adam Smith has laid his finger on the true origin of the moral sentiment. He does not seek it in mystic religious feelings; he finds it simply in the feeling of sympathy (Kropotkin, 1970d, p. 94).

Kropotkin described how Smith argued that the more one acts 'as your thought and imagination urge...', when driven by circumstances, or those surrounding you, or by the intensity of your thought or imagination, 'the more will moral sentiment grow in you, the more will it become habitual'. Kropotkin then added, somewhat polemically, 'This is what Adam Smith develops with a wealth of examples. He was young when he wrote this book which is far superior to the work of his old age upon political economy...[his] only mistake was not to have understood that this same feeling of sympathy in its habitual stage exists among animals as well as among men'. For Kropotkin, 'The feeling of solidarity is the leading characteristic of all animals living in society' (ibid., p. 95). Kropotkin's criticism of Smith in this respect appears unfair, of course, given that Kropotkin had the advantage of not only Darwin's work, but the earlier evolutionary thinking of Herbert Spencer upon which to draw for evolutionary and biological insights.

Kropotkin's view of Spencer's writings on ethics was ambivalent. He admired mostly, in 'two magazine articles' which Spencer published in 1890, the way in which 'for the first time he spoke of sociality and morality in animals'. Prior to that time, Spencer had only focused on the notion of the evolutionary 'struggle for existence' and, erringly, according to Kropotkin, he related it to 'utilitarian morality', or the 'greatest happiness principle'. Whilst Kropotkin gave Spencer's work serious discussion in his *Ethics*, his major concern, which he had expressed earlier in *Mutual Aid*, was that Spencer refused to admit the importance of mutual aid for 'Man' (Kropotkin, 1903, p. x). Kropotkin did, however, credit Spencer mostly with having established 'rules of conduct on a *scientific basis*' (Kropotkin, 1924, p. 291).

It was the French philosopher Mark Guyau (1854–88), little known now but well respected in his own time, to whom Kropotkin gave the most credit for ideas which related directly to his own notion of mutual aid. After first publishing a book which critically examined the 'moral teaching of Bentham, the Mills (father and son), Darwin, Spencer, and Bain', Guyau published in 1884 his seminal work, *A Sketch of Morality independent of Obligation and Sanction*. According to Kropotkin, 'this book went through eight editions in France and was translated into all the languages of Europe' (ibid., pp. 322–3). It is most instructive to quote Kropotkin's analysis of Guyau's philosophy here:

> The moral element in man needs...no coercion, no compulsory obligation, no sanction from above; it develops in us by virtue of the very need of man to live a full, intensive, productive life...Man is not content with ordinary, commonplace existence; he seeks the opportunity to extend its limits...We feel, especially at a certain age, that we have more powers than we need for our personal life, and we willingly give these powers to the service of others. From this consciousness of the superabundance of vital force, which strives to manifest itself in action, results that which we usually call self-sacrifice...The same applies to our sympathizing with the sorrows of others...Man possesses a 'moral fecundity' (Guyau, in Kropotkin, 1924, p. 323).

In sum, for Guyau, as Kropotkin noted, 'Life has two aspects...According to the one, it is nutrition and assimilation; according to the other, production and fecundity. The more it takes in, the more it needs to give out; that is its law'(ibid., p. 324). There was, for Guyau, a struggle in life and a '*joy of risk in thinking*', each of which urge 'man' into action: 'It is action alone which gives us confidence in ourselves, in others, and in the world' (ibid., p. 330, emphasis in original). The way in which morality was seen to be intrinsic to humanity, and would therefore not require 'sanction', was explained by Kropotkin in this way:

> First of all, we find within ourselves the approval of the moral act, because our moral feeling, the feeling of fraternity, has been developing in man from the remotest times through social life and through observation of nature. Then man finds similar approval in the semi-conscious inclinations, habits, and instincts, which, though still not clear, are deeply ingrained in the nature of man as a social being. The whole human race has been brought up under these influences for thousands and thousands of years...And when we seek the origin of these feelings, we find that they are implanted in man even deeper than his consciousness (Kropotkin, 1924, p. 330).

The appeal of Guyau's philosophy for Kropotkin, with respect to 'mutual aid', is obvious. As he later recalled, Kropotkin now had a closely supportive and active philosophical treatise which he could add to his crucible which already contained Darwinian and Spencerian evolutionary theory, the insights of Adam Smith and even J.S. Mill with respect to 'sympathy' or 'moral sentiment' as a natural phenomenon, the lecture of Kessler on mutual aid, and his own field investigations and thought, to produce his own mature, evolutionary notion of 'mutual aid'. He had built a substantial philosophical and 'scientific' edifice.

Kropotkin felt sufficiently confident in his analysis to be able to state that 'it would be easier for man to revert to walking on all fours, than to renounce his moral instincts, for these instincts had been developing in the animal world long before the appearance of man on the earth' (ibid., p. 173). While he obviously felt comfortable relating human morality directly to his notion of mutual aid, it is not altogether clear how he was able to do so, beyond simple assertion or adopting the work of others. He did, however, helpfully clarify the relationships between mutual aid, justice, and morality in a flowing argument which proceeded as follows: 'The importance of *sociality*, of *mutual aid*, in the evolution of the animal world and human history may be taken, I believe, as a positively established scientific truth, free of any hypothetical assumptions' (ibid., p. 30, emphasis in original). He has recent support in this respect from the American biologist, Stephen Jay Gould, whose article 'Kropotkin was no Crackpot' stated that 'I would hold that Kropotkin's basic argument is correct. Struggle does occur in many modes, and some lead to cooperation among members of a species as the best pathway to advantage for individuals' (Gould, 1988, p. 21).

Kropotkin then argued that 'We may also take next, as granted, that in proportion as mutual aid becomes an established custom in a human community, and so to say instinctive, it leads to a parallel development of the sense of *justice*, with its necessary accompaniment of the sense of *equity* and equalitarian self-restraint' (Kropotkin, 1924, p. 30). Here Kropotkin was closely following the ethical arguments of the early nineteenth-century communitarian anarchist, Pierre-Joseph Proudhon (see ibid., pp. 268–78).[7] For Kropotkin, 'Proudhon's merit lies in his indicating clearly the fundamental principle following from the heritage of the Great [French] Revolution—the *conception of equity*, and consequently of *justice*, and in showing that this conception has been always at the basis of social life, and consequently of all ethics...' (ibid., p. 269, emphasis in original). Proudhon referred to his insights as having an anthropological basis; his work was of course pre-Darwinian. Kropotkin continued:

> A certain degree of identification of the individual with the interests of the group to which he belongs has necessarily existed since the very beginning of social life, and it manifests itself even among the lowest animals. But in proportion as relations of equity and justice are solidly established in the human community, the ground is prepared for the further and more general development of more refined relations...when he so fully identifies his feelings with those of others that he is ready to sacrifice his powers for their benefit without expecting anything in return. These unselfish feel-

ings and habits, usually called by the somewhat inaccurate names of *altruism* and *self-sacrifice*, alone deserve, in my opinion, the name of morality...(ibid., p. 30, emphasis in original).

Kropotkin then drew the threads of his argument together in this way: '*Mutual Aid—Justice—Morality* are thus the consecutive steps of an ascending series, revealed to us by the study of the animal world and man. They constitute an *organic necessity* which carries in itself its own justification, confirmed by the whole of the evolution of the animal kingdom...Like the need of food, shelter, or sleep, these instincts are self-preservation instincts'. He acknowledged that they could be weakened in certain circumstances, but if they did not eventually rebound into a position of dominance then 'the group, the race, or the species dies out and disappears' (ibid., p. 31, emphasis in original). There was neither intellectual nor emotional space here for default. Kropotkin had integrated his notion of mutual aid so absolutely with 'justice' and 'morality' that the nexus could not be broken without decimation of the group, race, or species.

It is helpful to review here just a few examples of mutual aid in action in the natural world, as Kropotkin saw it. Then natural science can be set aside while examples of human interaction, both historically and in his own time, are examined. First, what was it that he perceived in nature which triggered his curiosity and then enthusiasm for this notion of mutual aid? In a mundane example, he looked at bees, and noted that although the colony exhibited 'sociability' in terms of cooperation, there were bees which were lazy, robbers, and often drunk in sugar refineries or on sugar plantations: 'We see thus that anti-social instincts continue to exist amidst the bees...; but natural selection continually must eliminate them, because in the long run the practice of solidarity proves much more advantageous to the species than the development of individual endowed with predatory inclinations' (Kropotkin, 1903, pp. 17–18). He described the sociability of many birds, including pelicans, cranes, birds of prey, and parrots. Pelicans, for example, were described as fishing in 'numerous bands, and after having chosen an appropriate bay, they form a wide half-circle in face of the shore, and narrow it by paddling towards the shore, catching all fish that happen to be enclosed in the circle' (ibid., p. 23). Many other examples were set out, from dogs and horses to mammals and sea life. Kropotkin provided a rich tapestry of natural evidence with which to convince his readers. He stated that 'Association is found in the animal world at all degrees of evolution...[and] in proportion as we ascend the scale of evolution, we see association growing more and more conscious' (ibid., p. 53). Further, he asserted that it was 'life in societies' which was 'the most powerful weapon in the struggle for life, taken in its widest sense'. Such life patterns enabled the most 'feeble' of natural life to resist or protect themselves from 'beasts of prey': 'it permits longevity; it enables the species to rear its progeny with the least waste of energy and to maintain its numbers albeit a very slow birth-rate; it enables the gregarious animals to migrate in search of new abodes'. In a link then to human beings, he further concluded, with support drawn from Darwin, that 'The highest vertebrates, and especially mankind, are the best proof of this assertion' (ibid., p. 57). Eventually, Kropotkin also concluded that mutual aid could eliminate competition: 'Happily enough, competition is not the rule either in the animal world or in mankind. It is limited among animals to exceptional periods, and natural selection finds better fields for its activity. Better conditions are created by the *elimination of competition* by means of mutual aid and mutual support'. He cited Darwin in support of this assertion as well (ibid., p. 74). The implications for political economy, with competition not being perceived as exclusively natural to human nature, was of course important for Kropotkin's communitarian anarchist approach to the economy.

Placing his philosophical musings and scientific theory aside, it is especially instructive to view Kropotkin's understanding of human nature in terms of concrete examples—those which he examined or recounted as illustrations of human nature in action. This is not a difficult task as, alongside his well-known commitment to evolutionary science, Kropotkin was a keen advocate of 'social investigation'.[8] For him, this was very much a part of his science:

> [S]ince man is part of nature, and since the life of his 'spirit', personal as well as social, is just as much a phenomenon of nature as is the growth of a flower or the evolution of social life amongst the ants and the bees, there is no cause for suddenly changing our method of investigation when we pass from the flower to man, or from a settlement of beavers to a human town (Kropotkin, 1970c, p. 152).

He always sought empirical evidence to support the theoretical premises he had adopted or developed and stated that his approach was 'an analysis of *tendencies of an evolution that is already going on in society*, and on *inductions* therefrom as to the future...' (ibid., p. 158). 'Social investigation' was a practice he had begun at a young age and in his mature years the most prominent example of his work was the exceptionally detailed material in his book *Fields, Factories and Workshops* (Kropotkin, 1907 [1899 English edn]). The purpose of that work was to explain, using empirical evidence, that it was possible, taking advantage of technology and new horticultural knowledge and techniques, to produce sufficient food, clothing and shelter for all, although this book had a special focus on agriculture and horticulture. It was a denial of the assumption of scarcity which underpinned bourgeois political economy and a reflection of Kropotkin's own perspective on the way in which political economy should be directed. When Kropotkin had been in Clairvaux prison, re-thinking 'Darwin's formula', he related his evolutionary thinking about mutual aid to investigations he began making for a series of articles which appeared in a French journal he edited and which were later published as a book titled *The Conquest of Bread* (Kropotkin, 1972 [1892 French edn]). Additional material appeared later in

Fields, Factories and Workshops. His focus was not only on the social and economic conditions of his time, he sought evidence from history as well: 'Sociability and need of mutual aid and support are such inherent parts of human nature that at no time of history can we discover men living in small isolated families, fighting each other for the means of subsistence' (Kropotkin, 1903, p. 153).

Kropotkin's examination of mutual aid among the 'savages' and the 'barbarians' in history can be skipped over here without any loss of understanding of his approach to human nature (ibid., chapters III and IV). The way in which he perceived medieval society did, however, hold meaning in terms of a lost world of co-operation, one which had been eventually overrun by state power. It was not nostalgia which caused him to examine this period, as some critics might suggest as being appropriate to a 'utopian' thinker. Kropotkin was a thoroughgoing 'scientist', and always had a forward view. He sought from history evidence to support his evolutionary insights. After discussing the sense of community which existed in village life, he turned to the 'guilds', or 'brotherhoods, friendships and *druzhestva, minne, artels* in Russia, *esnaifs* in Servia [sic] and Turkey, *amkari* in Georgia, and so on'. These co-operative institutions had been formed as a consequence of the 'growing diversity of occupations, crafts and arts...' and the 'growing commerce in distant lands'. Kropotkin described the formation of a guild for a major public enterprise: 'when a number of craftsmen – masons, carpenters, stone-cutters, etc. – came together for building, say, a cathedral, they all belonged to a city which had its political organization, and each of them belonged moreover to his own craft; but they were united besides by their common enterprise, which they knew better than anyone else, and they joined into a body united by closer, although temporary bonds; they founded a guild for the building of the cathedral' (ibid., p. 171). He cited from the statute of an early Danish guild, which set out 'the general brotherly feelings which must reign in the guild...' and the rules associated with 'self-jurisdiction' in the event of arguments between 'brothers' or between a brother and a stranger. The statute also stated the 'social duties' of the members. For example, in the event of the loss of a house, or a ship, or a similar substantial disaster, 'all brethren must come to his aid'. If he is sick, two brothers were required to stay by his bedside until he recovered—or if he died, they must bury him and then provide for his children if necessary. Often, the widow would become 'a sister of the guild'. All were equal within the guild. If a brother broke the oath or faith with his brethren within the guild, he was excluded. Guilds of similar structure and arrangements were formed by serfs, by freemen, or for special purposes such as fishing, hunting, or trading and 'dissolved' when the necessity for associative activity had passed. Kropotkin noted that, at the time he wrote, Russia was still 'covered with *artels*' (ibid., pp. 169–74). Interestingly, he pointed out that 'Adam Smith and his contemporaries knew well what they were condemning when they wrote against the State interference in trade...Unhappily, their followers, with their hopeless superficiality, flung medieval guilds and State interference into the same sack'. He lamented the loss of the guilds as freely associated institutions (ibid., p.197, n. 191).

In his own time, Kropotkin observed 'All these associations, societies, brotherhoods, alliances, institutes, and so on, which must now be counted by the ten thousand in Europe alone, and each of which represents an immense amount of voluntary, unambitious, and unpaid or underpaid work—what are they but so many manifestations, under an infinite variety of aspects, of the same ever-living tendency of man towards mutual aid and support?' (ibid., p. 282). He was fond of describing the National Lifeboat Association in England and the Red Cross in this context. They were powerful examples of mutual aid at work. He noted that 'every year more than a thousand ships are wrecked on the shores of England' and acknowledged that 'the State and men of science...' had established lighthouses, charts, signals, meteorological warnings and so on to diminish the danger. The fact remained, however, that there were still that many ships wrecked and 'several thousand human lives to be saved every year'. Kropotkin observed that 'a few men of good will' had invented a lifeboat which could withstand the rough weather and then sought public interest in supporting them; they 'do not turn to the Government'. He asserted that the men knew that 'they must have the cooperation, the enthusiasm, the local knowledge, and especially the self-sacrifice of the local sailors'. There also needed to be a 'feeling of solidarity, a spirit of sacrifice not to be bought with galloon' if the boats were to be launched in the middle of a storm, in darkness perhaps, or against a tide. The way Kropotkin perceived it, the Lifeboat Association was 'a perfectly spontaneous movement, sprung from agreement and individual initiative. Hundreds of local groups arose along the coast'. The associations were voluntary and they did not have a hierarchical organisation: 'The work is wholly conducted by volunteers organizing in committees and local groups; by mutual aid and agreement!' (Kropotkin, 1972, pp. 153–4). With irony, Kropotkin drew a sketch of the requirement for the services of the Red Cross:

> Imagine somebody saying fifty years ago: 'The State, capable as it is of massacring twenty thousand men in a day, and of wounding fifty thousand more, is incapable of helping its own victims; consequently, as long as war exists private initiative must intervene, and men of goodwill must organize internationally for this humane work! (ibid., p. 155).

He suggested that, if someone had made that proposal, 'To begin with, he would have been called a Utopian'. What did occur, however, was that 'Red Cross societies organized themselves freely, everywhere, in all countries, in thousands of localities'. Again, it was a spontaneously formed and voluntary organisation (ibid., pp. 155–6). What was it that caused such people to volunteer to go into a war zone and care for the wounded, often under fire? The answer was, for Kropotkin, that 'The moral sense is a natural faculty in us like the sense of smell or of touch' (Kropotkin, 1970d, p. 98).

A close friend of Kropotkin, as indicated, was the French communitarian anarchist and geographer of international repute, Elisée Reclus (1830–1905). Reclus and Kropotkin first met in Switzerland in 1877. Kropotkin was a recent arrival after his escape from the Russian prison. It was the tentative beginning of a long-term friendship and collaboration, especially based on mutual respect and largely common ways of viewing a future anarchist society (Kropotkin, 1971, pp. 423–4 ; Fleming, 1979, pp. 20–21, 132–7). Reclus related the story, similar to that which Kropotkin told, of the way in which the followers of Charles Darwin's evolutionary theory concentrated exclusively on the 'simplistic [*simpliste*] hypothesis' of the 'struggle for existence'. They ignored in Darwin's *Origin of Species* and his *Descent of Man* his discussion of the 'accord for existence', as Reclus expressed the notion. He noted that examples of mutual aid amongst animals cited in the works of naturalists are 'innumerable' (Reclus, 1905, Vol. 1, p. 139, my translation). What, then, was the notion of mutual aid for Reclus? In discussing the phenomenon of 'imitation' in animal life, he stated that it also extended to human groups. It occurred 'ordinarily' in an unconscious manner – 'like a sort of contagion' – but it also occurred consciously. Unconscious imitations were the most important, although conscious manifestations were also of consequence. For Reclus, because 'the practice of arts and sciences suppose the pre-existence and culture of the aptitude of imitation', there would be no 'social life nor any professional life' without the human 'instinct and talent to imitate'. He then observed that 'Imitation itself blends in a great many ways with mutual aid [*l'aide mutuelle*] – or more briefly, helping one another [*l'entr'aide*] – which existed in the past, which still exists in our days and which will be in all times the principal agent of the progress of man' (ibid., pp. 139–40, my translation).

For Reclus, 'the best proof' of the dominance of mutual aid was the 'fact that the most happy species' were not those which were best equipped for 'plunder and murder' but those with not very effective weapons and which 'mutual aid [amongst] themselves with earnestness: they are not the most ferocious, but the most affectionate'. In human society, then, Reclus asserted that 'At all times, society at birth tries to produce groupings which later become expanded to cities'. It followed that 'It is incontestable that mutual aid was the origin of the most powerful factors of progress' (ibid.). In correspondence to an English friend in 1884, Reclus set out his 'ideal' in terms of mutual aid:

> My ideal is that tree in Cafrerie, where thousands of birds are nestling, the 'republicans', happy and conscious of their force, looking without fright at the eagle who soars in the sky above the city. We have no need of a master: no will exterior from ours makes us remain in the same community, this is done by the conscience of our

solidarity with all. We are of use to our brothers and our brothers are useful to us (Reclus, 1927b, p. 289).[9]

Eventually Reclus saw 'mutual aid, in all its fullness' as the 'safeguard of the unfortunate and of the [human] race itself' (Reclus, 1905, Vol. 1, p. 319, my translation). It is clear from all Reclus's writings that the primary inspiration for his ideas was the Darwinian theory of evolution. Marie Fleming cites Reclus from correspondence in 1892 stating that 'In the history of the world all the armies of a Napoleon are not worth so much as a word of a Darwin, fruit of a life of work and thought' (Fleming, 1979, p. 151).

Reclus had a particular perspective on evolution which intrinsically also involved revolution, but not necessarily in a political form. He defined 'evolution' as 'the infinite movement of all which exists, the incessant transformation of the universe and all its parts since its eternal origins and through the infinity of ages'. He believed that there would not have been human 'progress' without revolutionary changes in human society, in thought or in action: 'In effect, evolution embraces the whole of human things and revolution must also embrace it'. He saw human progress as being 'solidary' and he included in the dimensions of progress 'social and political progress, moral and material, science, art or industry'. In sum, for Reclus, 'Evolutionists in all things, we are equally revolutionaries in all, knowing that history is nothing but the series of accomplishments, succeeding those of preparations...One can say then that evolution and revolution are two successive actions of the same phenomenon, evolution preceding revolution, which then precedes a new evolution, which is the mother of future revolutions' (Reclus, 1898, pp. 1–3, my translation).[10] In a reflection of the appreciation which Kropotkin later expressed for the way Reclus described the life of a river,[11] Reclus explained the interrelationship between evolution and revolution in this natural analogy:

> Like fallen debris barring a river, water accumulates little by little above the obstacle, and a lake forms through slow evolution; then suddenly an infiltration is produced in the barrier to the lower part of the river, and the fall of a stone would induce a cataclysm: the barrier would be violently carried away and the emptied lake would again become a river. In this way there would be a small earthly revolution (ibid., p. 3, my translation).

In explaining his own commitment to revolutionary change, Reclus suggested that 'If the revolution is always behind [in terms of time] evolution, the cause is the resistance of the [social] surroundings [*des milieux*]...Each transformation of matter, each realisation of an idea is, in the same period of change, contrary to the inertia of the surroundings [*milieu*], and the new phenomenon cannot accomplish itself except through an effort more violent or through a force more powerful than the resistance at its greatest strength'. Further, progress occurs through a continual change in points of departure for each individual and it is the same for a species. He asserted that 'the genealogical tree is, like the tree itself, a mixture of branches in which each one finds its force of life, not in the preceding branch, but in the original sap'. When the old societal formations become inadequate, 'life displaces itself by realising itself in a new form. A revolution is accomplished' (ibid.).[12] Evolutionists saw that there was nothing to be gained by calling for a revolution based only on a vague idea. It was necessary for evolutionists, who now had scientific insight into the way they wanted to see the next revolution realised, to work towards enunciating a goal or a 'compass' for the people. It was 'social science' which could not only teach 'the causes of servitude' but also the 'means of emancipation', which would help the people 'disengage themselves little by little from the chaos of conflicting opinions'. A revolutionary or emancipatory enlightenment therefore could be provided by evolutionists through their insights into 'social science' (Reclus, 1898, pp. 6–8, my translation).[13]

The basic tenets of Reclus's approach to a future society were drawn together into a whole in this way. His expression is clear and it is most instructive to cite his words as he wrote them:

> The society we imagine, and whose evolution we are studying in the present chaotic crowd of conflicting units, is a society in which work is going on, not by the behest of a whole hierarchy of chiefs and sub-chiefs, but by the comprehension of common interests and the natural working of mutual aid and sympathy...

He extended this appreciation of an evolving future society into the area of the family and 'social morals':

> In fact, the change we propose in society is precisely the change which is going on in the family itself, where the old idea of a ruling master, having the right, and even the duty, to chastise with the rod wife and children, is gradually abandoned, and where love, mutual respect, and permanent kindness are considered the only natural ties between all. And everywhere the same evolution is going on in social morals (Reclus, 1927a, pp. 346–7).

Inherent within this form of society was the notion of 'mutual aid' and 'sympathy'. It is with respect to these notions that Reclus and Kropotkin most closely merged their views on the functioning of communitarian anarchist society.

Perhaps, overall, Reclus can be most accurately seen as an evolutionary philosopher of anarchism, as well as an expert in 'social geography'. For Reclus, humanity was part of animality on the earth, and he was almost as equally embracing of the rest of the animal world as 'brothers' as he was human beings. It was not by coincidence or caprice that he was a vegetarian from early in his life. He believed that 'in many respects the domestication of animals, as we practise it today, exhibits a veritable moral back-sliding; for, far from having improved them, we have deformed, degraded, & corrupted them'. He attributed much of this consequence to 'our rôle of flesh-eaters'. He was concerned that not only was the 'corruption of species a great evil' but 'civilised science tends to their extermination' and he referred, among other instances, to the losses of bird life 'destroyed by European sportsmen in New Zealand and Australia, in Madagascar...' and the loss of whales from the temperate seas. Reclus sought a return to a closer and more respectful relationship between humanity and other life on earth (Reclus, 1933, pp. 9–10 ; 1927b, p. 294). Sounding mystical, but in profound accord with his essential beliefs, he stated:

> Let us long for the day when the doe of the forest shall come to meet us, to win our caresses by the look of her dark eyes, and the bird shall perch triumphantly on the shoulder of the loved woman, knowing himself beautiful, and demanding, he also, his part in the kiss of friendship! (Reclus, 1933, p. 16.)

Environmental issues, despite being treated as 'externalities' by today's hegemonic neoclassical paradigm of economic theory (Hodgson, 1999, p. 64), are increasingly, if slowly, forcing their way towards the core of economic considerations. Reclus's perception of humanity and the earth was holistic and resonates sympathetically with the ideas and work of many ecological thinkers today. As John Clark points out, Reclus's 'synthesis of anarchism and social geography makes him an important precursor of ecological anarchism and social ecology—a thinker from whom all who are interested in these currents have much to learn' (Clark, 1996, pp. 1–2, 5; cf. Olwig, 1980, pp. 40–41).[14]

Kropotkin and Reclus represent the most incisive evolutionary thinkers of their time with respect to insights into the 'accord for existence', as Reclus called 'solidarity' or 'sociability'. Kropotkin's work on the notion of 'mutual aid', which was adopted by Reclus, was seminal and has had an enduring influence on evolutionary thought, even if marginalised. The new vistas of evolutionary ideas which are opened up by the counter-balancing of a crude 'struggle for existence' interpretation of evolution by a notion of association and solidarity, for all animal life, including humanity, has the potential to induce fresh approaches to economic ideas. No matter how the future vision of society was seen by the communitarian anarchists, their scientific thinking and the breadth and depth of their perspective on human society should not be idly dismissed.

NOTES

1. The best biography of Kropotkin, despite its political focus, is Miller (1976). The popular biography (Woodcock & Avakumovic, 1970) is more appropriate for general reading than scholarly study. Kropotkin's memoirs (Kropotkin, 1971) contain useful biographical information but need to be read with the usual caution with respect to autobiographical works. Useful anthologies of Kropotkin's writings are Baldwin (ed.) (1970), (Miller (ed.) (1970),

Walter and Becker (eds) (1988), and Kropotkin (1988). The main works of Kropotkin in English are Kropotkin (1903, 1907, 1972).

2.   Reclus's monumental geographical work, *La Nouvelle Géographie Universelle* (Reclus, 1878–1894), was published in nineteen volumes. Its smaller precursor, *La Terre* (*The Earth*), was published in two volumes and has been translated into English (Reclus, 1877). Kropotkin noted that for the 'Universal Geography', Reclus was awarded the 'Royal Gold Medal' by the Royal Geographical Society and the work placed him 'in the foremost rank of modern geographers' (Kropotkin, 1927, pp. 339–41).

3.   For an example of the relevance of Kropotkin's evolutionary thought to Institutionalist economists, see Dugger (1984).

4.   Kropotkin's book *Mutual Aid* was a collection of his articles which were published in the journal *The Nineteenth Century* in September and November 1890, April 1891, January 1892, August and September 1894, and January and June 1896. The book was first published in London in 1902 (Miller, 1976, pp. 300, 319).

5.   Apart from acknowledging Darwin, Kropotkin stated that Francis Bacon was the first to point out that the social instinct is more powerful than the personal instinct. He also noted that Hugo Grotius reached the same conclusion, and that Spinoza mentioned mutual aid among animals. In his book, *Mutual Aid*, Kropotkin cited eight works of varying relevance, dated between 1872 and 1885, which pre-dated his own writings on the notion of 'mutual aid' (Kropotkin, 1903, pp. xii, 6, n. 1).

6.   Kropotkin also similarly discussed John Stuart Mill's writings. See Kropotkin (1924, pp. 240–41).

7.   For Proudhon's discussion of justice and *equité*, see Proudhon (1970, pp. 226–30, 242–3). It is notable that Proudhon (1809–65), in 1840, asserted the existence of a 'social instinct' in humanity: 'man is moved by an internal attraction towards his fellow, by a secret sympathy which causes him to love, congratulate, condole; so that, to resist this attraction, his will must struggle against his nature. But in these respects there is no decided difference between man and the animals…Certain species unite for hunting purposes, seek each other, call each other…to share their prey; in danger they aid, protect and warn each other…The social instinct, in man and beast, exists to a greater of less degree - its nature is the same' (Proudhon, 1970, p. 228). The Russian communitarian anarchist, Mikhail Bakunin (1814–76), in 1867, argued for the existence of an 'egoistic' and a 'social' instinct: 'The elements of what we call morality are already found in the animal world. In all the animal species, with no exception, but with a great difference in development, we find two opposed instincts: the instinct for preservation of the individual and the instinct for preservation of the species; or, speaking in human terms, *the egoistic and the social instincts*' (Maximoff [ed.], 1964, p. 146). Bakunin did have some knowledge of Darwin's evolutionary theory at this time. For an extended discussion of Bakunin's ethical ideas, see Knowles (2002).

8.   For Kropotkin's references to the late nineteenth century British 'social investigation' of Charles Booth, J. Thorold Rogers, and Arnold Toynbee, for example, see Kropotkin (1907, pp. 138–9). Kropotkin lived in exile in England from 1886 until he returned to Russia in 1917 (Miller, 1976, pp. 164, 234). Charles Booth's 'great social survey', *Life and Labour of the People of London*, was undertaken during the 1880s and 1890s. McBriar has noted that 'the Socialists were dependent on the work of social investigators—of Charles Booth above all'. Socialists interpreted Booth's (and others') findings as meaning that 'scientific investigation had tipped the balance decisively in favour of social causes of poverty being more important than individual failings' (McBriar, 1987, p. 90).

9.   Letter from Elisée Reclus to Richard Heath dated 6 June 1884.

10. This pamphlet was accessed via the Internet at http://melior.univ_montp3.fr/ra_forum/reclus/textes/evolution_et_ideal/reclus.html. Retrieved on 9 May 2001.

11. Kropotkin noted that 'It is especially in the description of rivers and their drainage areas that Elisée Reclus excelled' (Kropotkin, 1927, pp. 340–41).

12. In a pamphlet written in 1895, Reclus referred to the English, American, and French Revolutions in a similar context and asserted that 'without those revolutions society would have been at a standstill in industry, in science, art, social philosophy' (Reclus, 1927a, p. 350).

13. It did not follow that Reclus denied the possibility of violent revolution. To the contrary, he saw it as a real possibility. He had fought in and lived through the Paris Commune of 1871 and saw the blood flow on the streets from the actions of the reactionary forces. He also pursued a rational argument in favour of individual expropriation of property which properly belonged to the workers; that is, theft. Other prominent anarchists disagreed with Reclus's views and it was primarily against his argument that Kropotkin later wrote his pamphlet 'Anarchist Morality' (Reclus, 1898, pp.146-7; Fleming, 1979, pp. 197–9).

14. Clark's reference to 'social ecology' is to the persistent theoretical and practical work undertaken primarily, to date, by followers of the writings of the American ecologist Murray Bookchin, whose classic work was Bookchin (1972). For a brief comment on the basic tenets of 'social ecology' and an instructive overview of the principles and the literature of socialism or anarchism and ecology see, for example, Dobson (1995, pp. 62–3, 170–86).

REFERENCES

Baldwin, R.N. (ed.) (1970), *Kropotkin's Revolutionary Pamphlets: A Collection of Writings by Peter Kropotkin*, New York: Dover Publications.

Bookchin, M. (1972), *Post-Scarcity Anarchism*, Montreal: Black Rose Books.

Clark, J.P. (1996), Review of Marie Fleming, *The Geography of Freedom: The Odyssey of Elisée Reclus*, *Social Anarchism*, http://melior.univ-montp3.fr/ra_forum/reclus/textes/geography_of_freedom.html. Retrieved on 25 February 2002.

Darwin, C. (1888), *The Descent of Man and Selection in Relation to Sex,* London: John Murray.

Dobson, A. (1995), *Green Political Thought,* London: Routledge.

Dugger, W.M. (1984), 'Veblen and Kropotkin on Human Evolution', *Journal of Economic Issues,* **XVIII**, 971–85.

Fleming, M. (1979), *The Anarchist Way to Socialism: Elisée Reclus and Nineteenth Century European Anarchism,* London: Croom Helm.

Gould, S.J. (1988), 'Kropotkin was no Crackpot', *Natural History,* **97**, 12–21.

Hodgson, G.M. (1999), *Economics and Utopia: Why the Learning Economy is Not the End of History,* London: Routledge.

Knowles, R. (2002), ' "Human Light": the mystical religion of Mikhail Bakunin', *The European Legacy,* **7**, 7–24.

Kropotkin, P. (1903), *Mutual Aid: A Factor of Evolution,* London: William Heinemann.

Kropotkin, P. (1907), *Fields, Factories, and Workshops: or Industry Combined with Agriculture and Brain Work with Manual Work,* New York: G.P. Putnam's Sons.

Kropotkin, P. (1924), *Ethics: Origin and Development,* London: George G. Harrap & Co.

Kropotkin, P. (1927), 'Obituary: Elisée Reclus', in J. Ishill (ed.), *Elisée and Elie Reclus: In Memoriam,* New Jersey: Oriole Press.

Kropotkin, P. (1970a), 'Anarchism: Its Philosophy and Ideal', in R.N. Baldwin (ed.), *Kropotkin's Revolutionary Pamphlets: A Collection of Writings by Peter Kropotkin,* New York: Dover Publications.

Kropotkin, P. (1970b), 'Anarchist Communism: Its Basis and Principles', in R.N. Baldwin (ed.), op. cit.

Kropotkin, P. (1970c), 'Modern Science and Anarchism', in R.N. Baldwin (ed.), op. cit.

Kropotkin, P. (1970d), 'Anarchist Morality', in R.N. Baldwin (ed.), op. cit.

Kropotkin, P. (1971), *Memoirs of a Revolutionist,* New York: Dover Publications Inc.

Kropotkin, P. (1972), *The Conquest of Bread,* New York: New York University Press.

Kropotkin, P. (1988), 'Are We Good Enough?', in N. Walter and H. Becker (eds), *Act for Yourselves: Articles from "Freedom" 1886–1907 by Peter Kropotkin*, London: Freedom Press.

MacRae, D.G. (1962), 'Darwinism and the Social Sciences', in S.A. Barnett (ed.), *A Century of Darwin*, London: Mercury Books.

Maximoff, G.P. (ed.) (1964), *The Political Philosophy of Bakunin: Scientific Anarchism*, New York: The Free Press.

McBriar, A.M. (1987), *An Edwardian Mixed Doubles: the Bosanquets versus the Webbs. A Study in British Social Policy 1890–1929*, Oxford: Oxford University Press.

Miller, M.A. (ed.) (1970), *Selected Writings on Anarchism and Revolution*, Massachusetts: The M.I.T. Press.

Miller, M.A. (1976), *Kropotkin*, Chicago: University of Chicago Press.

Nettlau, M. (1996), *A Short History of Anarchism*, London: Freedom Press.

Olwig, K.R. (1980), 'Historical Geography and the society/nature "problematic": the perspective of J.F. Schouw, G.P. Marsh and E. Reclus', *Journal of Historical Geography*, **6**, 29–45.

Proudhon, P.-J. (1970), *What is Property? : An Inquiry into the Principle of Right and of Government*, New York: Dover Publications.

Reclus, E. (1877), *The Earth: A Descriptive History of the Phenomena of the Life of the Globe*, London: Bickers and Son.

Reclus, E. (1878–1894), *La Nouvelle Géographie Universelle*, Paris: Hachette.

Reclus, E. (1898), *L'Èvolution, la Rèvolution et l'idèal Anarchique*, Paris: P. V. Stock.

Reclus, E. (1905), *L'Homme et la Terre*, Paris: Librarie Universelle.

Reclus, E. (1927a), 'Anarchy', in J. Ishill (ed.), *Elisée and Elie Reclus: In Memoriam*, New Jersey: Oriole Press.

Reclus, E. (1927b), 'Extracts from Elisée Reclus' Letters', in J. Ishill (ed.), op.cit.

Reclus, E. (1933), *The Great Kinship*, New Jersey: The Oriole Press.

Walter, N. and H. Becker (eds.) (1988), *Act for Yourselves: Articles from "Freedom" 1886–1907 by Peter Kropotkin*, London: Freedom Press.

Woodcock, G. and I. Avakumovic (1970), *The Anarchist Prince: A Biographical Study of Peter Kropotkin*, New York: Kraus Reprint Co.

8. Sounding the Trumpet: T.A. Jackson on Darwin, Marx and Human Existence

Erin McLaughlin-Jenkins

In 1936, Thomas Alfred ('Tommy') Jackson, a working-class intellectual and socialist lecturer, wrote that 'Darwin's work demonstrated – though to this day few Darwinians realize it – that nature proceeded not in a mechanical way but in a revolutionary (i.e. a dialectical) way' (Jackson, 1936, p. 232). This statement from *Dialectics: The Logic of Marxism, and Its Critics, An Essay in Exploration* formed part of Jackson's caustic and witty indictment of the vulgar Marxism dominating the British Labour Party. The British Left had long relied on evolutionary theory as a prop for socialism, but the ambiguities in biological thought – created by the ongoing muddle of Darwinism and Lamarckism – had commingled with parallel confusion in socialist theory and practice. Marx and Darwin needed to be simultaneously disengaged from their misguided expositors, Jackson believed, because Scientific Socialism – derived from the theories of Marx and Darwin – had been increasingly usurped by evolutionary socialism—the quasi-Lamarckian ideology of the soft-bellied, compromising, reformist wing of the Labour Party, referred to contemptuously by Jackson as 'Spencerised Fabians' (Jackson, 1936, p. 230). Describing Darwin as a revolutionary signalled Jackson's intention to rescue Darwin's theories from vulgar Darwinians such as Herbert Spencer, while reminding Labour Party officials such as James Ramsay MacDonald that in adopting Spencerian 'biological sociology', they necessarily rejected the fundamental conclusions of Marx and Engels, namely dialectics (Jackson, 1936, pp. 102–4). In what is an impressive analysis of the theoretical problems undermining Marxism and Darwinism, Jackson strove to distinguish the originals from the fakes and to once again affirm the natural congruence between dialectical materialism and Darwin's version of evolution. This chapter explores Jackson's intellectual development, his attempt to rectify the theoretical confusion surrounding evolution, economics, and social development, and his commitment to working-class emancipation.

THE BECOMING PROCESS

T.A. Jackson (1879–1955) compositor, socialist agitator, journalist, and lecturer, was the son of a radical compositor and foreman. He was born in
Clerkenwell in 1879 and attended school until age 13. Jackson claimed that his
mother began to teach him to read at age three. Due to serious eyesight problems, he was forced to wear glasses, preventing him from participating in rough
games and sports.[1] Reading was his solace and his passion, and happily, the
family library contained works by Dickens, Shakespeare and Scott, along with
history books, an atlas, an encyclopedia and an illustrated family Bible (Jackson,
1953, pp. 13–15). Described in detail in his autobiography, *Solo Trumpet: Some
Memories of Socialist Agitation and Propaganda*, Jackson became disillusioned
with partisan politics in his early teen years, and he devoted himself to intellectual improvement as a means of developing a 'critically-scientific view'.[2] It
was a time when Darwinian texts had reached the used bookstores, and Jackson
found his imagination 'fired up' by writers like T.H. Huxley and John Tyndall
(Jackson, 1953, p. 42). At the same time, Jackson became critical of 'Christian
beliefs' because they demanded a passive endurance of suffering and provided
a 'bar to the acceptance of Socialism'. To 'burst through this barrier' was a
'necessary contribution towards Socialist advance' (Jackson, 1953, p. 96).

In pursuit of scientific knowledge, Jackson went to South Kensington Natural History Museum to study evolution. This led to the dissolution of 'the last
shreds' of his 'belief in the Supernatural' (Jackson, 1953, p. 42). Soon after,
having studied Robert Blatchford's mixed bag of evolutionism and socialism in
Merrie England (1893), Jackson was 'struck as by a thunderbolt' with the thought
that a society based on private property was necessarily an immoral one (Jackson,
1953, p. 49). This was Jackson's conversion moment, and he became a lifelong
advocate of his understanding of socialism and evolution. Jackson's exaltation
continued with a reading of that 'masterpiece of popularization', Friedrich
Engels's *Socialism: Utopian and Scientific* (1892) and of Engels's and Karl
Marx's *Communist Manifesto* (1848). The two components of his thinking –
evolutionism and socialism – were brought into a 'blazing revelation', as bits of
'miscellaneous information' fused into 'a completely inter-related Universe'
(Jackson, 1953, pp. 58–9).

These revelations nurtured Jackson's rejection of bourgeois society, and he
appropriated science as a counter-culture in support of collectivist goals. Like
the liberal-capitalist Darwinians who vied with the Anglican-Tory elite in 1860s
and 1870s for cultural authority, the generation of left-wing activists coming of
age in the late nineteenth and early twentieth centuries also drew upon science
as the arbiter of justice in a world dominated by repressive authorities and self-
serving dogmas. However, this contest was not between old money and new
money: it was a direct challenge to the capitalist system and its political and

religious infrastructure. Jackson's journey from secular and scientific ideas to the more radical ideologies of Robert Blatchford and Karl Marx typified the intellectual awakening of angry disillusioned proletarian intellectuals beginning in the 1880s. For example, Tom Bell, Tom Mann and Ben Tillett were pursuing similar intellectual and political paths as they converged on London to join the labour and socialist movements.[3] Across Great Britain, intelligent, discontented young workers eagerly read their secondhand copies of Darwin, Huxley, Tyndall and Spencer, but they soon became wary of the ideological agenda of the scientific naturalists. The Darwinians openly addressed questions concerning religion, capitalism, poverty, political freedom and philosophical reflections on ethics, morality and truth; but these issues were circumscribed by the theory of natural selection, which had become a biological rationale for class inequality. The power of science was as clear as its corollary: interpreting the natural world was vulnerable to the subjective manipulations of pro-capitalist apologists exemplified above all in the work of Herbert Spencer.[4] For the young discerning intellectual with an anti-establishment agenda, finding 'good' science – a science supporting collectivism and social equality – meant connecting with evolutionary socialists and scientific socialists.

At age twenty, in a state of untrained exaltation, Tommy Jackson met Jack Fitzgerald, an Irish bricklayer who taught classes in Marxist economics in his spare time. As fellow members of the Social Democratic Federation (SDF) and close associates thereafter, it was Fitzgerald who brought discipline and structure to Jackson's eclectic ideology and his materialist ethics. Jackson described Fitzgerald as 'very nearly the best-read man I have ever met', and Fitzgerald helped Jackson make his way through Marx's difficult *Capital* (Jackson, 1953, pp. 60, 64). As a reward for his sophisticated understanding of scientific Marxism, Fitzgerald gave Jackson secondhand copies of Henry Mansel's *Bampton Lectures* and Herbert Spencer's *First Principles* (Jackson, 1953, pp. 59–61). It was during these early years with the SDF that Jackson first took his turn at the stump, becoming one of the volunteer Sunday lecturers sounding the trumpet of Marxism and Darwinism.

'THE DARWINIAN BASIS OF MARXISM'

Tommy Jackson claimed that after reading George Henry Lewes's *Biographical History of Philosophy* (1857) during his teen years, he was transformed:

> As I worked through Lewes's *History* I gathered in my book-hunts all the works he named which came within reach…They were, I confess without shame, stiff going…I was…acquiring a grasp of the Universe, objective and subjective, as a unity in multiplicity in perpetual process of self-transformation. I was, though I would not have

known what you meant if you had told me so, preparing myself for Marx! (cited Macintyre and Morton, 1979, p. 6).[5]

As he describes it, each stage in his life led to the critical moment at which his world was transformed by Marxism. This hindsight recollection parallels the 'becoming process', or a 'real evolution', as defined by Marxists (Jackson, 1945, p. 20).[6] It is a dialectical approach to change and development, and it remained the guiding principle of Jackson's life from his conversion in the opening years of the twentieth century until his death in 1953. Grounded in 'Scientific Socialism' – a combination of Marxian and Darwinian theory – Jackson struggled to clarify and unify the theory and practice of the British Left while intellectually grappling with contemporary problems in culture and society.

Historians of British socialism are familiar with the importance of evolutionary thinking as a rationale for social change.[7] The pursuit of scientific ideas in the late nineteenth and early twentieth centuries varied considerably within the working sector, ranging from serious engagement with the philosophical and political meaning of science to science as recreation, career goal or self-improving hobby. As such, working-class interest in science paralleled larger trends in scientific culture at that time. Born in an age when scientific ideas were widely available through the cheap press, inexpensive books, free libraries and popular lectures, workers benefited from improved access to science. Additionally, secularists, radicals, republicans, socialists and labour advocates regularly popularized scientific ideas in lectures, pamphlets and periodicals as part of their social critique and propagandist efforts. Workers who were familiar with these groups were exposed to a variety of scientific topics and controversies, in particular, to those involving evolutionary theory and the social meaning of Darwinism.

Recognizing the importance of science as a cultural authority and opposing the sociobiology of middle-class scientific naturalists, the British Left aligned its interests in science with the advocacy of class struggle and emancipation. By the late nineteenth century, scientific ideas and language were regular features of socialist lectures, periodicals and pamphlets. Derived in part from Marx's inclusion of Darwinism in Scientific Socialism, this recourse to the natural sciences underscored socialist and communist theory well into the twentieth century:

> Everyone who studies human society seriously must soon reach the conclusion that such a state of affairs as we are facing cannot have arisen accidentally or by chance. It can have arisen only as an outcome of historical, political and economic events and forces. To study these events, and to trace out these inter-relations with their consequences, and so to discover the law of development of human society is, therefore, to proceed just as a scientist proceeds when in any field of nature – mechanics, physics, chemistry or biology – he studies that which has actually happened as a means of discovering the general laws of nature's working, and therewith how man can use these laws in the future (Jackson, 1945, p. 6).

However, evolutionism meant different things to different kinds of socialists, and lines were drawn between revolutionary and reformist factions. Scientific Socialists employed a dialectical model of change, emphasizing the inherent instability of nature and society and the revolutionary impact of disruptions. Moreover, while they acknowledged the importance of change at the individual level, they determined that the most significant modifications of nature and society take place at the group level—or rather, species and class (Jackson, 1936, pp. 124–6). These Marxist socialists cited Darwin as their main scientific authority because he generally took a non-progressive, ecological view of development and was concerned mainly with the relationship between varieties and species. With respect to their sociopolitical program, this faction agitated and educated on behalf of working-class emancipation through class struggle; however, even dedicated socialists such as Jackson promoted interim solutions such as individual education, co-operatives and trade unionism. There could be no compromise with capitalism, scientific or other, but preparation was part of the plan.

For the more moderate Labour socialists, revolution was less appealing than evolutionary socialism's depiction of the essential continuity of nature and society. Nature was in a constant state of gradual progress and society was moving slowly towards improved sociability: natural co-operation would inevitably replace individual natural selection (Macintyre, 1980, p. 49; McLaughlan-Jenkins, 2001b, pp. 455–7). This view was based in part on Darwinism but was weighted heavily in favour of Spencerian Lamarckism. It stressed individual development in the context of *social* evolution, and this emphasis informed the ethical mandate and reformist political goals of this faction (Jackson, 1936, pp. 120–6).[8] Their program included education, social reform and parliamentary action, all of which provided the means to prepare for and assist the evolutionary process while compromising with capitalism.[9] Tommy Jackson railed against the MacDonaldite reformists who, he believed, abused both Marx and Darwin with their non-dialectical notions of gradual and continuous progress, rejecting their erroneous sociobiology and reformist socialism by way of rescuing the revolutionary and dialectical meaning of pure Darwinism.[10]

Jackson claimed that evolutionary theory was a commonplace in his day but that it was rarely understood (Jackson, 1936, p. 212). In its general use, the theory meant simply that everything was in a state of flux. Beyond that, there was disagreement as to the nature of the flux and how change came about. The fundamental notion of struggle was a point of widespread agreement but, again, struggle of what kind and to what end? These ideas were of critical importance because biology was seen to be at the heart of social theory and class relations. Distinguishing non-dialectical evolutionism and its corollary, non-dialectical social theory, from dialectical evolutionism and social theory, Jackson counterpoised Darwin and Spencer, disruption and continuity, and revolution and reform.

For Jackson, vulgar Darwinism was embodied by Herbert Spencer, a reactionary, non-dialectical materialist, with no more than a superficial understanding
of nature, society, humanity and history. Spencer frequently served as a foil for
the revolutionary Left because his overt advocacy of individualism and his public criticism of socialism both encapsulated and promoted an anti-revolutionary
view. If we are to take Jackson as an indicator, this situation changed little
between 1880 and 1936, although criticisms had broadened to encompass not
merely Spencer's competitive sociobiology but also its repercussions for the
British Labour Party.

Herbert Spencer asserted that all change conforms to the laws that govern
the natural world (Spencer, 1891[1857], p. 10). These overarching natural laws
are inviolable and work gradually and imperceptibly to direct life towards ever-
increasing complexity. The law of organic progress is differentiation: the
'advance from homogeneity of structure to heterogeneity of structure'. As examples, Spencer cited the 'development of a seed into a tree, or an ovum into an
animal', in which differentiation produces the 'complex combination of tissues
and organs constituting the adult animal or plant' (Spencer, 1891[1857], pp. 9–
10). The direction of 'change is of necessity towards a balance of forces; and of
necessity can never cease until a balance of forces is reached' (Spencer, 1898,
p. 432). Furthermore, Spencer claimed that:

> In every species throughout all geologic time, there has been perpetually going on a
> rectification of the equilibrium, that has been perpetually disturbed by the alteration
> of surrounding circumstances; and every further heterogeneity has been the addition
> of a structural change entailed by a new equilibration, to the structural changes en-
> tailed by previous equilibrations (Spencer, 1898, p. 435).

Spencer concluded that there 'can be no other ultimate interpretation of the
matter, since change can have no other goal' (Spencer, 1898, p. 435).

This ultimate striving in nature for balance and heterogeneity was ably assisted by the competitive struggle for resources and survival as defined by the
theory of Natural Selection:

> Already it has been pointed out that the evolving of modified types by 'natural selec-
> tion or the preservation of favoured races in the struggle for life', must be a process
> of equilibration, since it results in the production of organisms that are in equilibrium
> with their environments; and at the outset of this chapter, something was done to-
> wards showing how this continual survival of the fittest, may be understood as the
> progressive establishment of a balance between inner and outer forces (Spencer, 1898,
> p. 457).

In Spencer's scheme, struggle in nature between greater and lesser organisms with respect to environmental and biological changes drove homogeneous
organizations to take on ever-increasing differentiation, resulting in complex,

heterogeneous structures. The result overall was equilibrium: change and struggle occur but the gradual accumulation of innovations that improve species never disturb the fundamental continuity of the natural order.

With respect to human society, Spencer concluded that the 'law of organic progress is the law of all progress', and he inferred a natural basis for capitalism from the law of differentiation and natural selection (Spencer, 1891 [1857], p. 10). The former highlighted the central role of individual development and the latter verified the natural basis of competition between individuals. For Spencer, the individual was the ultimate measure of society and the real object of history. He defined species, or society, as an 'aggregate of individuals' (Spencer, 1898, p. 428). The individual exists objectively within an abstract, artificial, functionally interdependent conglomerate of closely related individuals competing for quantitative advantage, producing limited change under the guiding hand of nature's law of equilibration. This process constitutes the 'history of all organisms':

> Whether it be in the development of the Earth, in the development of Life upon its surface, in the development of Society, of Government, of Manufactures, of Commerce, of Language, Literature, Science, Art...From the earliest traceable cosmical changes down to the latest results of civilization...(Spencer, 1891 [1857], p. 10).

Humanity had progressed slowly from its savage origins to its civilized present through the same process that governed all life. In tribal form, society existed in its 'first and lowest form' as a 'homogeneous aggregation of individuals having like powers and like functions' (Spencer, 1891 [1857], p. 19). Each individual had to perform the 'same drudgeries'. However, in the course of 'social evolution', increasing differentiation gradually led to specialization, or a sophisticated division of labour, within a complex, mutually dependent, civilized nation. The driving factors were the struggle for existence and survival of the fittest. Working as a balanced whole, civilization offered greater happiness and freedom in the pursuit of self-interest. Progress was the inevitable result.

From Jackson's perspective, Spencer missed the point, several of them, in fact. Continuity is not the issue; disruption is. Nature and society do not regulate instability; instability regulates nature and society. There is no equilibrium, only perpetual conflict. Spencer's description of the universe as progressive and balanced, driven by the laws of differentiation and natural selection, took a narrow view of conflict. According to Jackson, Spencer viewed struggle in the lesser sense of competition for resources, relevant mainly as an individual adjustment of the internal to the external. Conflict was subordinated to the overarching stability of the natural order. Consequently, temporary disruptions remain a vital part of the mechanism that fosters growth within a constantly adjusting equilibration of forces. Internal forces change and grow while the external forces guide and regulate. Nature influences but cannot be influenced and, therefore, changes in nature are quantitative rather than qualitative. Humanity is part of nature, just a quantitatively more complex animal, and so unable to effect changes in the larger structure or order of things (Jackson, 1936, p. 239). Evolution, from this perspective, simply provides a 'description' of the way the world has been filled up with diverse species, while the differences between species and varieties – as between ape and man – remain 'formal' and 'superficial' (Jackson, 1936, pp. 238–9).

Jackson agreed that development, competition for resources, and even continuity are discernable features of existence, but he rejected universal equilibrium as the defining feature of change in the natural world (Jackson, 1936, pp. 239–41). Setting aside the laws of differentiation and natural selection as effects rather than causes, Jackson offered dialectics as the fundamental law of change. Within any given situation, the seeds of conflict are always present and building to a point of crisis. At that point, the old structure becomes an obstacle that must be crashed through: something new is created. This change is not a mere adjustment but a real and objective change in structure (Jackson, 1936, pp. 236–8). Unity, or continuity, occurs for a time when the opposing forces form a synthesis; this is called unity in opposition. However, the seeds of future conflicts are contained within the synthesis and a new crisis point is inevitable. Conflict and disruption are eternal; equilibrium does not exist except on the surface. This assumes that change is not merely quantitative but qualitative. If the overarching law is dialectical transformation, then all structures and systems are part of a reciprocal, interdependent relationship: nature changes and nature is changed. There are no aspects of nature that are privileged in the sense of being beyond the law of dialectics. There is no natural order, only change. Stability is not punctuated by periods of temporary disruption; instability is punctuated by periods of temporary continuity, or at least an appearance of continuity.

According to Jackson, Darwin recognized the non-progressive and disruptive qualities of the natural world in ways compatible with the holistic views of dialectical materialists. Rejecting natural theology's fixity of species and Spencerian–Lamarckian linear ascent, Darwin's ecologically complex descriptions of random, interconnected changes in nature made for a bleak view of the negative consequences of evolution by natural selection that included extinction and regression. Crisis and conflict went beyond gaining simple advantage. But Jackson interpreted this as confirmation that nature has 'method in its madness', in that variation occurs regularly as 'an active opposition of the organism and its environment' (Jackson, 1936, p. 238). As opposed to Spencer or Lamarck, Darwin's theories suggested a truly profound and revolutionary re-thinking of the natural world:

> All of which proves, what? That the species is not a fixed archetype to which varieties 'conform' because they 'must' or 'ought'—but a regularly periodical persistence

in variation ... It is a definite variability of a periodical kind; though it is capable of indefinite extension and further variation in various ways, its variability remains definite and periodical and is governed not by the 'caprice' of the organism, but by the cumulative interaction between the living thing and the conditions in which it lives (Jackson, 1936, p. 238).

Jackson concluded that unadulterated Darwinism indicated an 'active interrelation' in the natural world that stresses both disruption and continuity, or stability and instability, as inter-related factors of change. It was this aspect of Darwin's work that was both 'dialectical and revolutionary' (Jackson, 1936, p. 238). Spencer, Jackson argued, missed this and instead interpreted evolutionary theory non-dialectically as simple development involving increase and decrease in a progressive movement towards greater complexity (Jackson, 1936, p. 212).

With respect to human development, an issue of primary importance in Jackson's critique of Spencer is the individual's relationship to society. For Jackson, society is real:

[Society is] all the individuals in the totality of their interrelation. To ask which is more important, the individual or society, is to ask which is more important, the inside or the outside of a windowpane (Jackson, 1950, p. 11).

As Marx stated: 'men make their circumstances as much as circumstances make men' (quoted Jackson, 1936, p. 189). According to Jackson, the individual cannot be isolated from the whole:

Thus to understand society...one must grasp the fact that society is something over and above the mere sum of the separate individuals who at any moment compose the society. This 'something other and beyond' is, firstly, the product of the *inter-relation* of the individuals into a 'whole' or 'totality.' Secondly, and more significantly, it is the developed and developing outcome of the *interaction* of the individuals, and the mutual modifications of the *activities* of all the individuals who compose (and have composed) human society...These activities...all grew out of and bottomed upon one prime fact, universally operative – the fact that *all* men, without exception, are at all times dependent upon *production* – upon those labour activities...which result in the conversion of Nature...(Jackson, 1945, p. 18).

Jackson viewed the relationship between the individual and society as an interactive one that included the real subject of history – men and women – as co-participants in the modification of real societies and actual nature (Jackson, 1936, p. 208). Spencer had it wrong, plain and simple.

One of the weaknesses of Jackson's conscription of Darwin to the revolutionary cause is especially evident when he shifts his analysis from the larger context of man and nature to the internal development of human society. This issue is complicated because Darwin's views in *Descent of Man and Selection in Relation to Sex* (1871) are generally compatible with Spencer's sociobiology, though less assured of infinite progress. Darwin's ecological struggle abounding with equal parts of stability and disruption was, once transferred to society, tamed and shorn of its dialectical gusto. Darwin, like Spencer, acknowledged an historical ascent from primitive to civilized, and he accepted the inevitability of class inequality as a permanent consequence of natural selection (Darwin, 1981 [1871], pp. 166–71). Humanity – biologically, historically and socially – is subject to the same laws that regulate animals and plants (and these could operate at the group level—see *Descent of Man*, chapters 3 and 4). Humans are essentially sophisticated animals; the difference is quantitative, not qualitative. Jackson responded to this anomalous congruence between Darwin and Spencer with uncritical silence. Darwin was crucial to the establishment of a natural basis for Marxism, so undermining his credibility was counterproductive. Prudently, Jackson drew upon Darwin for biological demonstrations of dialectics and turned to Marx for social science. Besides, there was always Herbert Spencer to serve as a foil; he was expendable.

Jackson agreed with Spencer on some issues but only in a very general sense: all things are in flux and the processes of development in nature and society are governed by the same laws. However, for Jackson, the 'essential' law that directed change and linked nature to society was dialectics, not the 'accidental' fact of increasing complexity or natural selection (Jackson, 1936, pp. 194–8). This is another way of saying cause and effect, and Jackson subordinated Spencer's laws to the law of dialectics, thereby reducing them to effects or 'accidents'. The outcome of this was to create an equivalency between man and nature as mutable actors in an interdependent unity in opposition. This leads to one of the central assumptions of dialectics: human beings are active participants in a reciprocal relationship with nature, thereby distinguishing us from the passive animal and plant kingdoms. While he acknowledged that we are on some levels merely a biological being, Jackson asserted that we are also much more than that (Jackson, 1936, p. 212).

Jackson rejected Spencer's – and so Darwin's – reduction of humans to mere quantitative superiority, insisting that humans were qualitatively distinct from animals. He claimed that once humans began creating their own subsistence, they entered a dialectical relationship with nature: nature changes man and man changes nature. The transformation of nature into shelter, food and commodities indicates an active, equal relationship with nature that takes the form of unity in opposition (Jackson, 1936, pp. 189, 208–9). Humankind was no longer a passive recipient of nature's bounty and dearth. Although Spencer acknowledged that once the social phase of human history began, evolution worked on the intellect rather than physiological development, Jackson insisted that this was a narrow view that failed to grasp the dialectical meaning of the transformation (cf. Spencer, 1898, pp. 468–9). The revolutionary significance was that cause and effect – nature and human activity – interact and juxtapose, regulated by the one overarching law: dialectics. Humanity's active role in this relation-ship differs from animal behavior in real, qualitative ways while simultaneously subordinating nature to the same universal laws of change at work in human history.

Having established that humans transcend biology in that there is an equal and dialectical relationship between nature and humanity, history became the record of humanity's productive activities. Beginning with the premise that human needs and desires 'compel action', the provision of subsistence is desig-nated as the main stage on which nature and humanity interact in socialized production. This is Marx's materialist conception of history, and it contends that the various historical forms of socialized production constitute the real rather than abstract development of humanity, and that in each case this in-volves interaction with and transformation of nature. Furthermore, this interrelation proceeds dialectically in that each system carries seeds of antago-nism that reach a crisis point and erupt into opposition. This is followed by a synthesis as the two opposing systems dissolve into unity. Of course, the new unity carries the seeds of further antagonism, and the process continues until all groups have their needs met in a classless society. Darwin had provided a natu-ral basis for social transformations, and then Marx's materialistic reconstruction of Hegelianism defined the social basis for the transformation of nature. Aligned with dialectical materialism, these transformations are revolutionary, not in-cremental.

Consequently, Jackson rejected Spencer's non-dialectical version of histori-cal development. In Spencer's view, the transition from primitive communities to civilization represents one example of the linear, cumulative ascent from simple to complex social arrangements driven by individuals struggling to sur-vive in opposition to other individuals. Each manifestation of social transformation is analogous to a tree developing from seed to sprout to young tree and finally, to a mature tree with broad branches. No real qualitative change has appeared, only a more complex version of the original seed. In this way, the transitions through primitive society, ancient societies, feudalism and capital-ism demonstrate growth more than fundamental change, and this quantitatively progressive movement is as much guided by the hand of nature as is organic development.

Jackson likened Spencer's historical account to the building of a house that, as it is outgrown, is simply replaced with a new and bigger house. As develop-ment demands, the house must be improved and all live consensually from house to house to house. This omits the crucial element of class struggle in society that, for Jackson, is the source of social transformation. Jackson coun-tered this with the analogy of a chicken. When still an embryo, the eggshell is a safe, warm environment; however, once grown to chick, the shell becomes an obstacle that must be broken out of and discarded. A complete change, or revolution, is needed. Society outgrows its shell and does not build a bigger shell; it crashes through the old and transforms. The 'act of birth' is 'revolutionary' (Jackson, 1945, p. 60). The transition from primitive to feudal to capitalistic is not merely a quantitative improvement: it results in a whole new species of society. Moreover, systemic change does not end with capitalism, as Spencer believed: capitalism's inherent instability leaves it open to the dialectical process and, inevitably, revolution. Jackson rejected all versions of reformist 'home improvement' rhetoric and the capitalistic compromises of the Labour Party, pointing instead to the obstacles engendered by the bourgeois eggshell.

WORKING-CLASS EMANCIPATION: MIND AND BODY

For Jackson, as for Marx, theory had to lead back to the real object of history: the flesh-and-blood Toms, Dicks and Harrys of the world (Jackson, 1936, p. 98). But, what is it that Jackson hoped to secure for ordinary Britons: economic equality, or more than that? In response to critics who charged that Marxism was rigidly determined by economic considerations, Jackson acknowledged that 'man does not live by bread alone' and that workers also needed 'food for their fancy, their sympathy, their power of creative imagination' (Jackson, 1950, p. 116). He believed that 'no class feels so hungry for these things as does the wage-worker class' (Jackson, 1950, p. 17). Art and science survive transitions in society, and 'the classless, socialist and communist society of the future will make culture and its appreciation within the grasp of all' (Jackson, 1950, pp. 17–18). Encouraging the enjoyment of classic fiction was cited by Jackson as one example of the 'genuineness of Communist concerns for the preservation of mankind's cultural heritage.' In fact, Jackson asserted that a 'cultivated imagination' is an indispensable 'precedent for revolutionary class-struggle' (Jackson, 1950, p. 18). Contrary to critics of communism, the goal of Marxism was not 'to perpetuate the proletariat or its need to struggle' but to 'abolish both' through the reintegration of humanity (Jackson, 1950, p. 19). Freedom was the objective and that included intellectual as well as economic equality:

> Freedom does not consist simply in the absence of external constraints. It consists in the possession of power sufficient to overcome all obstacles to self-development and self-determination (Jackson, 1968 [1940], p. xxiii).

Human beings are conditioned by their 'concrete relationship to nature' – meaning productive relations – and by the 'scope, character, and quality of their physical powers'—i.e., ability to act within given circumstances (Jackson, 1936, p. 208). The greater the opportunity for activity and equality, the more will each man and woman share in Britain's cultural heritage. Jackson had abiding respect for the 'militant, self-reliant resistance to oppression' shown by the British proletariat, and he believed that British workers were 'potentially capable' of 'overcoming all tyrannies left upon earth' (Jackson, 1968 [1940], p. xxiii). It was this faith and respect that sustained Jackson in his relentless pursuit of working-class emancipation in the broad sense in which he sought it and which led him into endless conflicts with the British Labour Party, whose conservative members numbered among the critics of Marxism.

In 1901, Jackson's apprenticeship at the printing works was completed but he did not come 'out of his time' as an employed compositor. Being in the middle of a dispute with his employer and having earned a reputation as a socialist agitator, he was fired and soon blacklisted. He tried his hand at a number of odd jobs to support his wife and child, but the Jackson family struggled against poverty. It was a struggle that likely cost him the life of his first child, Eleanor Michel Jackson, who may have died from malnutrition.[11] There was little choice but to charge a fee for his lectures. Jackson, who had been a shy speaker from the beginning, committed himself to earning what he could as a public speaker (Jackson, 1953, pp. 87–91). This began his lifelong career as an agitator and propagandist for working-class emancipation, socialism and communism.

Jackson was affiliated at different points in his adult life with the Independent Labour Party (I.L.P.), the Scottish Labour Party (S.L.P.), the Socialist Party of Great Britain (S.P.G.B.), and the Communist Party; in the last two cases, he was an executive and founding member. His lecturing duties took him to nearly every corner of Great Britain and Wales, and he was considered to be one of the most impressive speakers on the socialist circuit (Macintyre and Morton, 1979, p. 21). Between 1900 and 1920, he lectured weekdays and weekends, squeezing in classes and debates where possible (Jackson, 1953, pp. 78, 90–91). Though a popular speaker, his views on Marxism and Darwinism sometimes got him into trouble. The South Wales I.L.P. complained that he was too atheistic, and the Leeds Secularist Society complained that he 'habitually waved the Red Flag over the Freethought platform' (Macintyre and Morton, 1979, p. 9). By 1919, Jackson had turned freelance, lecturing mainly in Leeds, but he 'allowed himself to be conscripted into the S.L.P.', taking part in a high-profile public debate over socialism (Macintyre and Morton, 1979, p. 11). This pattern of lecturing for a variety of worthy groups continued with Jackson even after he helped to found the Communist Party in 1920, and his independent, non-sectarian policies led to several confrontations with the Party between 1929 and 1932, resulting in his removal from the executive (Macintyre and Morton, 1979, p. 22).[12]

In 1919, Jackson was hired by the National Council of Labour Colleges as a full-time lecturer in their northeast district. This made Jackson not only a socialist lecturer of the stump variety but also an educator in the classroom:

If the ex-S.L.P. theorists were more influential within the Communist Party itself, Jackson's efforts with the wider circles of the labour college movement were equally significant. Each year the Plebs League, the Central Labour College in London and regional labour colleges all over the country trained some twenty thousand activists in the principles of historical materialism, economics, geography and Marxist philosophy. And even after the Communist Party fell out with the leadership of the labour college movement, Jackson continued to teach and argue within its ranks right up to the Second World War (Macintyre and Morton, 1979, p. 20).

After joining the Communist Party in 1920, his duties as an educator expanded. Between 1924 and 1929, Jackson was responsible for the Communist Party's education and propaganda programme, and from 1944 to 1949 he was employed by the Party's education department as lecturer in Communist Theory.[13] So much the teacher, Jackson even took on the task unintentionally, as when during the 1930s, he moved to Three Bridges, Sussex with his second wife Lydia in part to complete several writing projects. Having made contact with local unionists and the staff of the co-operative stores soon after his arrival, he was quickly elected to the management and education committees of the Crawley Co-operative. Subsequently, he was prevailed upon to give lectures to this small, railway community.[14] In a pamphlet co-written for the fiftieth anniversary of the Crawley and Ifield Co-operative Society, he spoke respectfully of the co-operative movement and particularly of the efforts of this community to have 'done so much…by patient plodding' (Denman and Jackson, 1938, p. 3). Wherever Jackson stopped, he joined up for the cause.

Another vital contribution Jackson made to working-class emancipation and the Communist Party was as editor of several newspapers. Beginning in 1921, Jackson was called upon to edit *The Communist*, the Party's first newspaper. *The Communist* was succeeded by the *Worker's Weekly* in 1926, which Jackson also edited. Over the next few years, until his conflict with the Party and his subsequent move to Sussex, Jackson edited the *Sunday Worker*, the *Worker*, and *Worker's Life*, and in later years, he contributed articles to the *Daily Worker*, the Party's official newspaper after 1929. Many of Jackson's articles on literature were re-printed in 1950 from the *Daily Worker* as *Old Friends to Keep*.

In addition to these achievements, Jackson's eclectic interests led him to write on a variety of cultural and political topics. A lover of classic literature, a considerable theorist, and an insightful historian, Jackson's work remains some of the most overlooked gems of twentieth-century Marxist writing. In addition to his tough-minded, historically situated autobiography, *Solo Trumpet*, Jackson wrote a history of the struggle for Irish independence in *Ireland Her Own* (1946). He analysed one of his favourite authors in *Charles Dickens: Progress of a Radical* (1937), critiquing both his work and Dickens's social views. Jackson published two collections of articles and lectures in addition to the compilation of literary articles in *Old Friends*. These were *Trials of British Freedom* (1937), an optimistic and friendly collection of articles from the *Sunday Worker* that extrapolated common themes from the history of British radicalism, and *Socialism: What? Why? How?* (1945), a sample of his lectures given to working people across Great Britain. Jackson jumped wholeheartedly into debates concerning evolutionary socialism and Scientific Socialism, lecturing and writing on Darwinism and economics as part of a Marxist explanation for human existence and in refutation of the Spencerized Fabianism of the Labour Party. A dedicated writer, lecturer and educator throughout his life, Jackson's achievements were honoured by the British Communist Party in celebration of his centenary.[15] In the commemorative pamphlet, Jackson was described as a 'leading representative of his generation of working-class theoreticians', whose work 'compares favourably with much contemporary Marxist theory' (Macintyre and Morton, 1979, pp. 24–5). An intellectual and theorist of exceptional merit, Tommy Jackson provides historians with a broadened understanding of the sociopolitical importance of Darwinism and an entirely new perspective on Charles Darwin as a misunderstood revolutionary.

NOTES

1. Jackson (1953), pp. 13–14, 39–40. Jackson's mother was concerned that the glasses would be broken if he played rough games.
2. Jackson, (1953), p. 42. It is interesting to note that this movement from political disillusionment to scientific inquiry conforms to basic patterns in working-class intellectual autobiography despite differences in geographical or temporal location, education, or income. See David Vincent (1981), and Gretchen Galbraith, (1997).
3. For more on this, see Erin McLaughlin-Jenkins (2001a), and John Laurent (1988).
4. Spencer's highly publicized biological defence of individualism and capitalism, along with his occasional attacks on socialism, made him a favourite target for the British Left. For more on this, see McLaughlin-Jenkins, 'Common Knowledge', chapter 6.
5. This pamphlet celebrates Jackson's centenary. The introduction is co-written but following this are individually authored sections. Vivien Morton, who wrote the first section, was Jackson's daughter, and she concentrated on biographical details for the most part.
6. I would like to thank the Fryer Library at the University of Queensland for making this material available to me.
7. See for example, James Hinton (1983); Stuart Macintyre (1980); and Mark Pittenger (1993).
8. See also Hinton (1983), p. 62. Hinton points out that the ethical dimension of labour socialism appealed to non-conformist traditions in Lancashire and Yorkshire, making the Independent Labour Party popular in this region.
9. The Lamarckian side of evolutionary socialism can be detected in the appeal to create co-operative environments that could assist the evolution of society towards socialist ethics. The emphasis on socialist schools for children is one example.
10. James Ramsay MacDonald was a frequent target of Jackson's scorn. See *Dialectics*, pp. 13–14, in which Jackson laments MacDonald's 'owlish stupidity', p. 102, in which he refers to MacDonald's 'smug self-gratification', and p. 116, in which he lists the many politically expedient religious masks MacDonald wore to appease various constituencies. See also Jackson (1953), pp. 81–3. (It is perhaps fair to add though, that MacDonald was a theorist in his own right, even if not everyone on the Left saw things quite the way that he did—especially after his expulsion from the Labour Party in 1931 after forming government with the Conservatives.)

11.   Bellamy and Saville, (eds) (1972–2000). The Jackson entry was compiled by John Saville and Vivien Morton, and it appears in volume IV, pp. 99–108. The citation can be found on p. 101.
12.   Afterwards, Tommy was removed from his position on the executive and was assigned exclusively educational and editorial duties.
13.   Bellamy and Saville (eds) (1972–2000), pp. 103, 106.
14.   Bellamy and Saville (eds) (1972–2000), p. 106.
15.   Macintyre and Morton (1979).

REFERENCES

Bellamy, J.M. and J. Saville (eds) (1972–2000), *Dictionary of Labour Biography*, 10 vols, London: Macmillan.

Darwin, C. (1981) [1871], *The Descent of Man and Selection in Relation to Sex*, Princeton, N.J.: Princeton University Press.

Denman, W.J. and T.A. Jackson (1938), *Fifty Years: Being the Story of the Crawley and Ifield Co-operative Society Limited*, Reading, U.K.: C.W.S. Printing Works.

Galbraith, G. (1997), *Reading Lives: Reconstructing Childhood, Books, and Schools in Britain, 1870–1920*, New York: St Martin's Press.

Hinton, J. (1983), *Labour and Socialism, A History of the British Labour Movement, 1867–1974*, Sussex: Wheatsheaf Books.

Jackson, T.A. (1936), *Dialectics: The Logic of Marxism, and Its Critics, An Essay in Exploration*, London: Lawrence and Wishart.

Jackson, T.A. (1945), *Socialism: What? Why? How?*, London: Communist Party.

Jackson, T.A. (1950), *Old Friends to Keep*, London: Lawrence and Wishart.

Jackson, T.A. (1953), *Solo Trumpet: Some Memories of Socialist Agitation and Propaganda*, London: Lawrence and Wishart.

Jackson, T.A. (1968) [1940], *Trials of British Freedom*, New York: Burt Franklin.

Laurent, J. (ed.) (1988), *Tom Mann, Social and Economic Writings*, Nottingham: Spokesman.

Macintyre, S. (1980), *A Proletarian Science: Marxism in Britain, 1917–1933*, Cambridge: Cambridge University Press.

Macintyre, S. and V. Morton (1979), *T.A. Jackson: A Centenary Appreciation*, pamphlet #73 of *Our History*, London: The History Group of the Communist Party.

McLaughlin-Jenkins, E. (2001a), *Common Knowledge: The Victorian Working Class and the Low Road to Science*, Ph.D. diss., York University, Toronto, Canada.

McLaughlin-Jenkins, E. (2001b), 'Common Knowledge: Science and the Late Victorian Working Class Press', *History of Science*, **xxxix**, 445–65.

Pittenger, M. (1993), *American Socialists and Evolutionary Thought 1870–1920*, Madison, Wisconsin: University of Wisconsin Press.

Spencer, H. (1891) [1857], 'Progress: Its Law and Cause', in *idem*, *Essays: Scientific, Political, and Speculative*, London: Williams and Norgate, pp. 8–62.

Spencer, H. (1898), *Principles of Biology*, 2 vols, New York: Appleton and Company.

Vincent, D. (1981), *Bread, Knowledge and Freedom: A Study in Nineteenth-Century Autobiography*, London: Europa.

9. Kenneth Boulding: Man of Images

Richard Joseph

Kenneth Boulding died on 18 March 1993 in Boulder, Colorado, aged eighty-three. He was a remarkable scholar who pursued interests that ranged over many disciplines. In a lifetime of scholarship he had written numerous books and hundreds of articles. He contributed to pioneering work in 'Keynesian economics, comparative economic systems, evolutionary economics, system theory, organization theory, ecology, conflict and peace studies and philosophy of the social sciences' (Khalil, 1994, p. 161).

The breadth of Boulding's work is indeed enormous. In fact, a bibliography of his published works runs to book length itself (Wilson and Dunahay, 1985). Appreciating the scope of his work is further made difficult by Boulding's view that everything is connected to everything else. As a founder of general systems theory, Boulding pursued a consistent theme of identifying patterns in a complex and seemingly random world. This search for pattern led Boulding in many directions: ecology, economics, biology, philosophy, and peace and conflict studies, to name but a few (Mott, 2000). This chapter on Boulding must therefore necessarily be selective in that it will discuss two important themes to which Boulding made a significant contribution: information and knowledge in economic processes; and societal evolution.

First, is the issue of information and knowledge in economic processes and systems. Why is this important? The widespread publicity given to the notion that we are living in an information age, has, in recent years, necessitated a deeper understanding of information and knowledge itself. Unfortunately, in the light of much of what is written about information today, we 'reach a stage under the impulse of advanced communication where there is simultaneously advancing knowledge and declining knowing' (Carey, 1978, p. 853). Partly contributing to this 'declining knowing' has been the rise and dominance of orthodox economics with its strict assumptions about information and the importance of competitive equilibrium. Boulding challenges these assumptions. His views on information and knowledge, especially as they relate to economic processes, present us with a theme that is very useful for understanding the economics of information. Boulding did not see the information age as beginning with the computer: it had its origins long before that (Boulding, 1984, p. vii).

Second, accompanying the malaise of 'declining knowing' is the sense that we do not know where we are heading, in other words, the direction of societal evolution. This is not a new issue of course. There is much concern today about the moral direction of societal evolution and in this regard, Boulding presents us with valuable insights. I will concentrate here on Boulding's views on evolution, mostly biological and societal evolution, the latter in which economic development is a key element. As a result we will get a picture of Boulding's image of economic man as part of this. It is hard to deny the central importance of knowledge and evolution as part of his thinking. Boulding once said that he had 'devoted his academic life to two questions: First, what does it mean to say that things have gone from bad to better rather than from bad to worse? Second, how do we get to better?' (Wright, 1988, p. 295).

Finally, in order to discuss these two points, it will be necessary to briefly distil some of Boulding's central beliefs. These have shaped his image of how he sees the world and they will provide us with an insight into his thinking.

This chapter, then, is divided into four parts. In Part 1 I will attempt to outline the essence of Boulding's beliefs that impinge directly on his image of information and knowledge. Part 2 deals with Boulding's contribution to the understanding of information and knowledge in economics. Part 3 covers Boulding's thoughts on evolutionary processes and the position of man in these processes. Part 4 is the conclusion. A theme that runs through Boulding's work is his deep religious conviction—he was a Quaker. This theme manifests itself both in the position he gives to information in economics and in his wider cosmology. It also influences his approach to evolution.

BOULDING'S PHILOSOPHY

British author, G.K. Chesterton[1] (1911, p. 15), wrote many years ago 'But there are some people, nevertheless – and I am one of them – who think that the most important thing about a man is still his view of the universe. We think that for a landlady considering a lodger, it is important to know his income, but still more important to know his philosophy'. Taking Chesterton's advice, I will attempt to distil some elements of Boulding's philosophy of relevance to this chapter. Boulding was a 'marginal man', according to his biographer, Cynthia Kerman (1976, p. 20):

> He was an intellectual in a non-intellectual segment of the population. He was set apart in school by his stuttering. He was from a community, Liverpool, which repre-

sented to many in England the dregs of society...Economically, socially and physically he had to break through barriers in order to become what he knew he could become.

Boulding was born in 1910 and grew up in poverty-stricken Liverpool, England. Despite a pronounced stutter, his early academic potential was recognized and through a number of scholarships, he went to study at Oxford. Originally studying chemistry, he moved into politics, economics and philosophy. Although educated at Oxford (he completed a Bachelor of Arts degree in 1931 and a Masters degree in 1939), his background prevented him from being fully accepted by the English 'establishment'. A scholarship opportunity to study at the University of Chicago (1932–4) presented him with an international perspective that was to shape his career forever (Pfaff, 1976). Boulding moved to the U.S. in 1937 and this move proved to be permanent. Apart from a period of a year at the League of Nations (1941), Boulding held academic positions at a number of universities in the U.S.—the most notable being the University of Michigan (from 1949) and the University of Colorado (from 1967). He never undertook a Ph.D.

Boulding was a stimulator of ideas and to some extent iconoclastic without being revolutionary (Kerman, 1976, p. 19). He has been described as a heretic. Boulding had little time for Marx's materialism.[2] For example, on this point, economist Robert Solo has commented that Boulding 'is a caste of mind that cannot comprehend the power and value of Marx's truth' (Solo, 1984, p. 464). Boulding's (1978, p. 21) remarks in *Ecodynamics* corroborate Solo's point:

> Darwin's unfortunate metaphor of the 'struggle for existence' is a very poor description of the immense complexity of ecological interaction and the enormous number of strategies for survival in an evolutionary process. Hegelian contradiction and the thesis-antithesis-synthesis pattern is again a poor metaphor to describe the complexity of evolutionary systems. The simple rhetoric of class struggle and revolution, therefore, must be regarded as an essentially minor element in the ongoing process of human development and societal evolution, although, it is sometimes important as a special case under particular circumstances. The evolutionary vision, however, must be seen quite clearly as an alternative to Marxism as a general theory. The general idea of an overall theory of social and historical dynamic processes owes a great deal to Marx, but his particular theories were quite inadequate to describe the complexities of reality and must be relegated to the position of a rather unusual special case.

The contribution by Boulding as a stimulator of ideas is particularly evident in his work on economics. From an early career that saw him make a significant 'conventional' contribution to economics (his 1941 book, *Economic Analysis*, became a standard text for students), with time he adopted a position that was very critical of orthodox economics. As Kerman (1976, p. 20) observed, Boulding had at times described economics as 'the theory of the no-person group' and econometrics as 'the attempt to find the celestial mechanics of a nonexistent universe'. Solo, interestingly enough, hardly sees Boulding as a heretic: 'He dwells well within the academic city of economics, and indeed has contributed substantially to its creation' (Solo, 1984, p. 463).[3]

Boulding had deep religious convictions—he had a Methodist-Quaker background and this manifested itself partly in his strong pacifist stance and his work on peace and conflict resolution. I suspect that his Christian religious belief shaped his work to its core. There seem to be two dimensions to this. First, there is a central belief in the value of the human person. As Kerman (1976, p. 23) notes, it is a deep respect for an individual's integrity and the potential that is in each human being that gives Boulding meaning to why knowledge is important. In an insightful remark, Kerman comments:

> ...Boulding has a secret suspicion that prophets often come in disguise. God moves in unexpected ways and the people who do not fit the expected mold are sometimes those who hold the future in their hands (p. 23).

Such a belief gives rise to the remark from Bolding that 'Humble honest ignorance is one of the finest flowers of the human spirit' (Kerman, 1976, p. 20). Knowledge is then important for the individual for self-fulfilment but needs to be directed in a value-laden way. The unexpected is part of the divine force acting in the world. This recognition of humility, underpinned by the limits of man's knowledge, no doubt permitted his religious convictions to give a sense of meaning to uncertainty and the problem of the optimality of information in economics.

Second, the importance of knowledge forms a central part of his view on the broader evolution of society. For Boulding, human society is not unconnected from the natural world but is very much a part of it. The Christian values of non-violence, benevolence and love form part of Boulding's goals for society of which knowledge plays a central developmental role. As Kerman (1976, p. 22) notes about Boulding's philosophy:

> Essential for both foundation and goal are the growth, development, and utilization of knowledge, for only as we have realistic images of what exists and what is possible – only as we develop ideas and try them out – can we have the technology to progress, the information on which to base justice, and the experience to move from where we are to where we want to be.

As such, for Boulding, a sense of direction and the process of achieving this is vitally important: '[O]ne learns only from failure, success only confirms existing images' (Pfaff, 1976, p. 10). The foundations of this direction and process have mixed origins. Wright (1988), in his book, *Three Scientists and their Gods*, typifies Boulding as straddling the ideas of both Adam Smith and Teilhard de Chardin[4] (a Jesuit scholar and mystic who had a grand schema of the unity of the world through evolution). From Smith, Boulding saw the analytical side of evolution—the importance of dynamic processes, specialization and the division of labour in allowing the growth of complexity. From Teilhard de Chardin, Boulding was able to see the religious significance of evolution, even though he did not go along with all that that philosopher had to say. Boulding was not a reductionist in the sense that he believed that all evolutionary processes can be described in terms of physics and chemistry: 'Any attempt to reduce the complex properties of biological organisms or of nervous systems or of human brains to simple physical and chemical systems is foolish' (Boulding, 1978, p. 20). Neither was he a determinist. Rather, it would seem as though Boulding preferred the word 'potential' to describe the direction of evolution (Wright, 1998, p. 292). In this, God plays a central but subtle role. For Boulding, the task for human beings is to align themselves with this potential as best they can. Biological evolution and social evolution are certainly not one and the same thing but there are commonalities. Information, knowledge and for that matter information technologies (a manifestation of this knowledge) are central to this commonality and hence the evolving complexity in society. Man is able to learn in this process in a way that can lead to realizing his greater 'potential'.

BOULDING ON INFORMATION, KNOWLEDGE AND EVOLUTION

Boulding places central importance on information and knowledge in explaining biological and social evolution. Since economic development is an outcome of this social evolution, it consequently has a central role in his reformulation of economics. Boulding is an avid user of metaphors to explain his views and he draws widely from the natural sciences, not only biology. There seems to be some debate as to just how 'evolutionary' Boulding's thinking actually was. For example, Khalil (1996) argues that Boulding is essentially concerned with development: 'While Boulding claimed to offer an evolutionary account of economic change, he has mainly presented an ecological account of transformation of artifacts.' Despite the importance of this debate, I feel Boulding's views somehow transcend the specific relevance of evolutionary biology to economics. In a sense, for Boulding, evolutionary biology provides a springboard for a more encompassing role awarded to knowledge.

The more encompassing role that Boulding ascribes to knowledge in the evolutionary process can be appreciated by understanding the importance of pattern in his thinking about evolution. Boulding (1978, pp. 9–10) says in *Ecodynamics*, his great synthesising work, that:

> The book is about evolution, the pattern that can be perceived in the structure of the universe in space in time...It is one of the principal contentions of this work that

evolution itself evolves. That is, it is not a single pattern but a succession of patterns, this succession itself having a pattern of its own.

Boulding is not particularly bound by the accepted tenets of Darwinian thinking about evolution and develops his own ideas. For example, he extends the notion of genetic evolution by redefining it in terms of knowledge or information structure:

> It is a powerful and accurate metaphor to see the whole evolutionary process from the beginning of the universe as a process in the increase of knowledge or the information structure. My Oxford philosophy tutor, who had the curious habit of crawling under the table while giving his tutorials, commented in a high British voice coming from underneath the table on a paper I had given on evolution, 'It is all very well to talk about evolution, Mr Boulding, but what evolves, what evolves, what evolves?' After forty years I have at least a glimmering of the answer. What evolves is something very much like knowledge (Boulding, 1978, p. 33).

Likewise, the notion of an 'environment', something which is important in evolutionary thinking, has no place in a world view in which the universe must be seen as a total system of interacting parts:

> There is no such thing as an 'environment', if by this we mean a surrounding system that is independent of what goes on inside it. Particularly, there is no sense at this stage of evolution on earth in talking about 'the environment' as if it were nature without the human race (Boulding, 1978, p. 31).

Solo (1984, p. 469) has commented that Boulding fundamentally revised the Darwinian image of evolution, shifting the central question '...from the mutation, selection and survival of species occupying niches in systems to what determines the survival, perhaps development or evolution, of systems. To that question, neither Boulding nor anyone else has an answer'. It is perhaps instructive to quote at length how Boulding argued this shift:

> The phrase 'the survival of the fittest'...is singularly empty of meaning, because if we ask 'What are the fittest fit for?' the answer, of course, is 'to survive'. so all this tells us is the survival of the surviving, which we knew anyway. A more accurate metaphor would be the survival of the fitting, the fitting being what fits into a niche in an ecosystem. There are innumerable niches, and hence innumerable strategies for survival...There are niches for the predator and niches for prey; there are niches for the strong and niches for the weak; there are niches for the selfish and niches for the altruistic. The principle of natural selection tells nothing about what will survive, or what qualities or properties give survival value.
> Another very unfortunate metaphor of Darwin's was 'the struggle for existence'. Struggle, either in the sense of organized effort to overcome difficulties or in the sense of organized conflict, is very rare in the biosphere. Populations interact, some decline to extinction, and some expand. In an ice age the tundra advances on the forest, but in no sense is there a 'struggle' between them...even in the predator–prey

relationship, there is catching and eating rather than fighting...It is the lion and the tiger that face extinction today, not the rabbit (Boulding, cited in Solo, 1984, p. 469).

Working backwards in the evolutionary process, Boulding was puzzled by the need to explain atomic explosions, architecture or the present distribution of living systems (Boulding, 1968, p. 141). These could not be explained by simple reference to a natural system: 'It is absurd to suppose we can think of nature as a system apart from knowledge, for it is knowledge that is increasingly determining the course of nature' (p. 141). In this regard, Teilhard de Chardin's notion of the 'noosphere' – a web of knowledge that envelops the surface of the planet – forms a central organizing idea distinct from the biosphere. For Boulding, biological, physical and other evolutionary processes increasingly need to be referred to it (the noosphere). Part of the noosphere included an unconscious element like the genome or the genosphere and part 'exists in human beings mainly in the form of drives that organize the learning process' (Boulding, 1978, p. 109). It is instructive to note that Boulding (1978, pp. 122–3) argued that there are two different genetic processes at work in the world:

> It is important to recognize that there are two different genetic processes at work in the world. The first of these may be called 'biogenetics'. It is the process whereby the know-how by which biological organisms are made is encoded in the DNA and the genes. Change in the biogenetic structure takes place through mutation in its own patterns in the genes. These are not produced by any learning process of the organism, as Lamarck thought, though the total biogenetic structure (the genosphere) is changed continually by the selective process that goes on in the populations of phenotypes which it produces...Besides the biogenetic structure, however, there is also what might be called the 'noogenetic structure' within the nervous systems of organisms, which is transmitted to offspring by a learning process. We find traces of this even in pre-human organisms, even perhaps in worms, and especially in the higher mammals and birds. Presumably the learned knowledge is represented by some kind of acquired brain structure, which is not produced by the biogenetic structure, though the biogenetic structure does produce the potential for it...Here we do have something like a Lamarckian genetic process. It is a different kind of process, however, from pure biogentics, which is clearly not Lamarckian...Once we get to the human races noogenetics dominates biogenetics to a remarkable extent...The processes by which each generation of human beings learns from the last are far more important than the process by which biological genes are inherited.

The element that really distinguishes things is knowledge, something that has become increasingly important since the advent of man. Knowledge is both a central and a rather vexatious idea for Boulding. In fact, his entire life's work was based on it—he was primarily concerned with expanding the 'knowledge of knowledge'. The neo-classical economists' neglect of knowledge, of course, provided him with the entrée to critique orthodox economics—something we will return to below. Knowledge, Boulding admits, is very difficult to define or quantify. In *Beyond Economics*, Boulding (1968, p. 142), in an instructive paragraph, summarizes some of his thinking:

> It [knowledge] is clearly related to information, which we can now measure; and an economist especially is tempted to regard knowledge as a kind of capital structure, corresponding to information as an income flow. Knowledge, that is to say, is some kind of improbable structure or stock made up essentially of patterns—that is, improbable arrangements, and the more improbable the arrangements, we might suppose, the more knowledge there is...The idea of knowledge as an improbable structure is still a good place to start. Knowledge, however, has a dimension that goes beyond that of mere information or probability. This is the dimension of significance which is very hard to reduce to quantitative form. Two knowledge structures might be equally improbable but one might be much more significant than the other.

The words 'improbable' and 'significance' in the above paragraph are two of the most instructive for appreciating Boulding's ideas: information (exhibiting improbability) is intimately linked to knowledge (manifesting significance) in his evolutionary model: '...the universe is not just composed of matter and energy, but that the evolutionary process in it is a process fundamentally in information and related concepts, with matter and energy being mainly significant as coders of information. The same information can be coded in many different ways, in structures of matter and energy' (Boulding, 1984, p. vii). However, the information processes in the world do not always lead to knowledge: 'In many respects, information is the enemy of knowledge. Knowledge is often gained by the orderly loss of information and by restructuring it, filtering it. Piling information on information merely produces noise' (Boulding, 1984, p. ix).

KNOW-HOW; KNOW-WHAT; AND KNOW-WHETHER

For Boulding there are three informational processes at work in evolution: know-how; know-what; and know-whether. Each process allows for an increase in complexity with the key being that the transition from know-how to know-what allows for the creation of further know-how. To explain know-how, Boulding (1984, p. vii) uses the analogy of the fertilized egg:

> When we look at biological evolution, we have to go beyond the Bell Telephone concept [improbability] into what can be called know-how, which is what the divided cell or fertilized egg has. Two fertilized eggs can have the same amount of information in terms of bits, but one knows how to make a hippopotamus and the other knows how to make a giraffe. It is clear that know-how goes beyond the simple information concept, although it is very hard to identify it and to quantify.

With regard to know-what, Boulding (1984, pp. vii–viii) makes the transition from biological systems to social structures, at the same time maintaining the information metaphor as an integrative theme:

> With the development of the human race (and perhaps a little earlier), a new structure emerges, which we can call know-what. This consists of the structures of the nervous system which presumably map into some kind of images of the 'mind', which also map into structure in the 'real world', whatever that is. Know-what is very different from know-how. The fertilized egg certainly has the know-how to make whatever organism it knows how to make, but it is very doubtful that it knows what it is doing. The remarkable thing about know-what is that it creates know-how, as we see with the fantastic burgeoning of human artifacts under the influence of a science-based technology. Science, fundamentally, deals with know-what and this enormously increases know-how.

Boulding (1968, p. vii) extends his hierarchy further into know-whether:

> One can even go beyond know-what into know-whether. This involves the evaluative structure of the human mind which enables us to make decisions and choices among different images of the future. Human behaviour cannot be explained without this further development in the hierarchy that starts with simple information. This actually goes back a long way in evolution. Even the amoeba knows whether to absorb a piece of grit or a piece of food.

The key to Boulding's view as to what makes this significant is the metaphor of 'the image'. Boulding (1966, p. 1) has referred to the image as 'the cognitive content of the human mind' and does not equate it exactly to knowledge itself. It is through the metaphor of the image, which was the theme of perhaps his most read book, *The Image* (Boulding, 1956), that man makes his entry into the knowledge process. It is man's ability to articulate an image and in particular his ability to realize an image of the future that makes the big difference:

> Necessity governed the solar system, at least until the advent of political astronomy; chance governed the biological systems until the advent of man. But with the coming of man into the world, a new kind of system developed because of the appearance of knowledge on a scale and complexity far beyond what had been achieved previously. The movements of man cannot be reduced to necessity. They cannot, for instance, be described by any system of differential equations. They cannot be accounted for by chance, for they do not have the characteristics of a random walk. They must be accounted for by the introduction of knowledge, that is, of images of the world in which the image of the world is related also to a value function or some principle of ordering. One exists and moves about because of freedom—that is, because of an image of the world and an image of a role structure which involves consistency with other people's role structures (Boulding, 1968, p. 142).

What we see from the above paragraph is a glimpse of Boulding's own image of the 'knowledge of knowledge'. Man is free and the evolutionary potential that has given him an ability to articulate an image of the future has set social evolution apart from biological evolution, through the introduction of knowledge. Social evolution is characterized not only by the rise in complexity but by economic development. For Boulding, economic development is characterized by both printing and organizing (Boulding, 1966, p. 5). The printing process he likens to the gene that is able to make a copy of itself or to the mass production of commodities. For Boulding, printing, even three-dimensional printing, is like rote learning and is unable by itself to organize an evolutionary or developmental process. Organizing, on the other hand, 'is the kind of process, for instance, by which the coded information contained in the gene is able to organize a phenotype such as a man. This is the way in which a blueprint organizes the construction of a building. This is the way in which an idea creates an organization, or an image of the future governs an individual life' (Boulding, 1966, p. 5). The key to development, which is a knowledge process, is learning. It is through learning that man has been able to build more complex machinery ('frozen knowledge' as Boulding calls it) and more imaginative ways of organizing knowledge. This, of course, gives rise to improvements in productivity. Boulding's view is not purely machine driven since development depends on the systemic nature of knowledge. It is precisely for this reason that some countries and their institutions are better able to organize for learning and others less so (Boulding, 1964). It would seem as though Boulding saw his own academic work following the organizing and pattern-recognition process he describes for development:

> Whatever originality this book may possess is a matter of building rather than of brickmaking; most of the bricks were made by others and my main task has been to fit them together into a reasonably coherent structure (Kerman, 1976, p. 17).

In sum, Khalil's (1996) claim that Boulding's work is more developmental than evolutionary carries some weight. There is no unit of evolution identified and this unit is not distinctly set apart from its environment, as one might expect if biological evolutionary models were followed exactly. However, in his defence, Boulding is not constrained by Darwinian models of evolution. Boulding is primarily concerned with the integration of different systems operating at different levels rather than a quest for unity: 'The theory of economic development is part of the general problem of evolutionary change, and its poor condition reflects the general poverty of the theory of dynamic systems' (Boulding, 1966, pp. 4–5). The pattern presented by knowledge is Boulding's way of explaining developmental processes and hence, making a contribution to understanding evolutionary processes in general.

BOULDING ON ECONOMIC MAN

Economics is certainly that field of study upon which Boulding believed his views ought to have a major impact. Unfortunately the mainstream economics profession seems to have ignored his calls for rethinking economics. In this section I will outline his views on key issues in the economics of knowledge, and specifically, as they relate to man in the economic process.

Boulding's views on the challenges that knowledge presents to economics can be summarized in part from his 1965 Richard T. Ely Lecture to the American Economic Association (Boulding, 1966). In this lecture he argued that economics has tended to neglect 'the commodity aspects of knowledge'. This has occurred in the theory of the market, the theory of development and the theory of decision-making. First, with regard to competitive markets, the cost of gaining knowledge about prices is not costless. For Boulding, the economists' assumption of 'perfect knowledge' is untenable. The epistemological problem also is not solved for imperfect markets since those participating in the market cannot tell the future. Second, in developmental theory, the omission of knowledge from the traditional factors of land, labour and capital ignores the key elements instigating change. Boulding refers here to the dual developmental processes of printing and organizing discussed above. Third, in the theory of decision-making, Boulding stresses the importance of learning. Preferences can be learned and the making of decisions always involves a choice of different images of the future. Boulding had written at one stage that 'Once we admit that utility of betterment functions are learned, neo-classical economics, especially welfare economics, falls apart at an alarming rate' (Katona, 1976, p. 27). For Boulding, knowledge and learning shape economic processes and the misrepresentation of man in economics has been a major flaw.

The key to Boulding's view of economic man, and indeed economics in general, lies in his notion of the image. In *The Image*, Boulding (1956, p. 82) argued that economists were not really interested in the behaviour of men, but rather of commodities: 'He [the economist] is aware, of course, at the back of his mind, that prices, outputs, etc., are in fact the result of human decisions. He likes to reduce these decisions, however, to a form as abstract and manageable as possible. Commodities are simple-minded creatures'. For Boulding, the behaviour of man, rather than the behaviour of commodities, is the key to understanding economics. The key to understanding the behaviour of man is his complex image structure that is shaped by information, messages and learning. Of course, including man in the picture this way has come at a cost and orthodox economics has traditionally been reluctant to relinquish the benefits it sees from developing more simple-minded but generalized and predictive formulations. Compounding this is orthodox economics' reluctance to come to terms with the peculiar commodity characteristics of knowledge itself.

The importance of man's images in economics broadens the scope and potentiality of economics enormously. For example, Boulding indentifies some ten characteristics of 'the image' in man with the following adjectives: spatial; temporal; relational; personal; value; affectional or emotional; conscious; unconscious and subconscious; certain or uncertain; and public. Little wonder that with such complexity at all levels, the behaviour of economic man is very difficult to predict. All these images are closely related to knowledge and potential. Grasping that potential is what man, and for that matter, life, is all about:

> The slightly chilling remark that man may be an unsuccessful experiment in curiosity veers a little too close to the cold winds of reality for comfort. One wonders, sometimes, whether the occasional appearance of new stars in the firmament does not represent certain unanticipated consequences of the discovery of atomic energy by intelligent beings (Boulding, 1956, p. 169).

Over and above all this is the condition of man in terms of the fact that he must live with uncertainty and the unexpected. In this regard, Boulding emphasises faith as very important as an 'organizer':

> We put philosophy into the back of the filing cabinet and shut it tight and return to the cheerful and ordinary business of life 'believing where we cannot prove'. From the abyss of reason we turn again to clutch at the slender rope of faith. Faith, yes, but what faith? To this question, of course, the theory of the image gives no answer. We can only say that there are elements in the image that are capable of organizing the life and activity of the individual. It is these organizing elements that constitute faith: the faith of the experimental scientist in his method; the faith of the believer in his God; the faith of the crusader in his cause; the faith of the soldier in his nation; or perhaps only in his buddies. All these are organizing images. Their origins are obscure and their consequences are profound. Where a faith is discovered that has this organizing power, it is likely to grow and to prosper. In our present state of knowledge, however, we must confess that the sources of organizing power are mysterious. Faiths are the genes of society. Their operation is as potent and as mysterious as that of the gene in biology (Boulding, 1956, p. 172).

CONCLUSION

In concluding, I will return to G.K. Chesterton (1911, pp. 58–9), this time to a remark of his about evolution:

> Evolution is either an innocent scientific description of how certain earthly things came about; or if it is anything more than this, it is an attack upon thought itself... You cannot think if you are not separate from the subject of thought. Descartes said, 'I think, therefore I am.' The philosophic evolutionist reverses and negatives the epigram. He says, 'I am not; therefore I cannot think.'

Boulding's view of evolution addresses both of Chesterton's points. It is an account of how things came about, but it also does not exclude man as mysteriously outside the biological system. What Boulding does is to incorporate man, a thinking and learning man, into the process.

As I have attempted to portray in this chapter, Boulding's philosophy, his Christian faith, stands out as an organizing image. I suspect this faith has shaped his image to a very great extent. Boulding's emphasis on information and knowledge in economics is very insightful and makes a significant contribution to how we might organize an economics of information. However, over and above that, Boulding has presented an integrated view of understanding physical, biological and societal evolution through the common link of knowledge. In the process, he has maintained a keen sense of value, justice and fairness in his image. It is in this sense that Boulding has shaped a realistic image of the future from past experiences. It is in this sense that the message of evolution that he has received and understood is given meaning. It is an image worth passing on.[5]

NOTES

1. I have no specific reason for using English writer G.K. Chesterton (1874–1936) to make this point here. Chesterton, a Catholic apologist, was a well-known writer in Boulding's youth and while I have no proof of a connection, I see no reason to believe that Boulding did not read Chesterton. I have no knowledge as to whether Boulding was influenced by Chesterton and I suspect they would disagree on numerous points—one of the more important being the value of seeing evolution as a process of constant change. Chesterton did, however, write about philosophical aspects of evolution and in this regard I feel justified in using him. I am referring in particular to Chesterton's 1925 book *The Everlasting Man* (cf. Footnote 12 in John Laurent's Chapter on Darwin in this volume). Given the fact that both Chesterton and Boulding held strong Christian beliefs, it would be an interesting exercise to compare how they dealt with evolution. In any event, focussing on Boulding's philosophy seems legitimate especially in view of his comments about the 'image'.

2. Solo (1984, p. 464) has commented that 'Except for a few pages in *The Organizational Revolution*, he [Boulding, 1953] has never, I think, attempted a critique of Marxist thought'. Interestingly, Chesterton may have had some insight into this though I have no way of knowing if it applied to Boulding: 'The Christian is free to believe that there is a considerable amount of settled order and inevitable development in the universe. But the materialist is not allowed to admit into his spotless machine the slightest speck of spiritualism or miracle...The Christian admits that the universe is manifold and even miscellaneous, just as the sane man knows that he has a touch of the madman...The materialist is sure that history has been simply and solely a chain of causation...Materialists and madmen never have doubts' (Chesterton, 1915, pp. 39–40). A further remark by Boulding on his views of Marxist thought can be found in a 'later article' appended to the second printing of *A Reconstruction of Economics* (1965). This article by Boulding was titled 'The Theory of Income Distribution: The Fruits of Progress and the Dynamics of Distribution'.

3. The issue of how radical Boulding sees himself in interesting. For example, in the Preface to the 1965 second printing of his book, *A Reconstruction of Economics* (1950), he observes that '...my point of view is evidently much more radical that I thought'. Likewise, Boulding (1963, p. 38), in his review of Machlup's (1962) book, *The Production and Distribution of Knowledge in the United States*, writes that 'The very concept of a knowledge industry contains enough dynamite to blast traditional economics into orbit'.

4. Wright (1988) provides an excellent commentary on the influence on Boulding of Adam Smith's 1776 work *An Inquiry into the Nature and Causes of the Wealth of Nations* and Pierre Teilhard de Chardin's 1959 work, *The Phenomenon of Man*. Boulding (1978, p. 109) makes specific reference in *Ecodynamics* to Teilhard de Chardin (1959) which he describes as outstanding (p. 361). Likewise, Boulding (1981, p. 154) refers to Teilhard de Chardin in *Evolutionary Economics*.
5. On this point of passing on images, I am indebted to Donald Lamberton for his considerable help in directing me towards some of the less well-known articles and reviews by Boulding which have shaped my thinking for this chapter.

REFERENCES

Boulding, K.E. (1941), *Economic Analysis*, New York: Harper and Brothers.

Boulding, K.E. (1950), *A Reconstruction of Economics*, New York: John Wiley and Sons, Inc. and London: Chapman and Hall Ltd.

Boulding, K.E. (1953), *The Organizational Revolution*, New York: Harper and Brothers.

Boulding, K.E. (1956), *The Image: Knowledge in Life and Society*, Ann Arbor: University of Michigan Press.

Boulding, K.E. (1963), 'The Knowledge Industry', *Challenge*, May, 36–8.

Boulding, K.E. (1964), *The Meaning of the Twentieth Century: The Great Transition*, London: George Allen and Unwin.

Boulding, K.E. (1965), *A Reconstruction of Economics*, Second Printing, New York: Science Editions, Inc.

Boulding, K.E. (1966), 'The Economics of Knowledge and the Knowledge of Economics', *American Economic Review*, LVI (2), May, 1–13, reprinted in D.M. Lamberton (ed.) (1996), *The Economics of Communication and Information*, Cheltenham, U.K. and Brookfield, U.S.A.: Edward Elgar, pp. 411–23.

Boulding, K.E. (1968), *Beyond Economics: Essays on Society, Religion and Ethics*, Ann Arbor: The University of Michigan Press.

Boulding, K.E. (1978), *Ecodynamics: A New Theory of Societal Evolution*, Beverly Hills, USA and London, U.K.: Sage.

Boulding, K.E. (1981), *Evolutionary Economics*, Beverly Hills, U.S.A. and London, U.K.: Sage.

Boulding, K.E. (1984), 'Foreword: A Note on Information, Knowledge and Production', in M. Jussawalla and H. Ebenfield (eds), *Communication and Information Economics: New Perspectives*, Amsterdam: North-Holland, pp. vii–ix.

Carey, J.W. (1978), 'A Plea for the University Tradition', *Journalism Quarterly*, 55 (4), 846–8.

Chesterton, G.K. (1911), *Heretics*, Sixth Edition, London: John Lane.

Chesterton, G.K. (1915), *Orthodoxy*, Fifth Edition, London: John Lane.

Chesterton, G.K. (1925), *The Everlasting Man*, reprinted in G.K. Chesterton (1986), *G.K. Chesterton Collected Works Vol. II*, San Francisco: Ignatius Press.

Katona, G. (1976), 'Economics as a behavioural science', in M. Pfaff (ed.), *Frontiers in Social Thought: Essays in Honor of Kenneth E. Boulding*, Amsterdam: North-Holland, pp. 27–36.

Kerman, C.E. (1976), 'Three facets of Boulding', in M. Pfaff (ed.), *Frontiers in Social Thought: Essays in Honor of Kenneth E. Boulding*, Amsterdam: North-Holland, pp. 13–24.

Khalil, E.L. (1994), 'Kenneth E. Boulding, 1910–1993', *Journal of Economic Methodology*, 1 (1), 161–6.

Khalil, E.L. (1996), 'Kenneth Boulding: Ecodynamicist or evolutionary economist?', *Journal of Post Keynesian Economics*, 19 (1), 83 [Available on Proquest]. Accessed 29 August 2001.

Machlup, F. (1962), *The Production and Distribution of Knowledge in the United States*, Princeton: Princeton University Press.

Mott, T. (2000), 'Kenneth Boulding, 1910–1993', *The Economic Journal*, 110 (464), F430–F444.

Pfaff, M. (1976), 'A personal dedication', in M. Pfaff (ed.), *Frontiers in Social Thought: Essays in Honor of Kenneth E. Boulding*, Amsterdam: North-Holland, pp. 3–11.

Solo, R. (1984), 'Solo on Boulding', in Henry W. Spiegel and Warren J. Samuels (eds), *Contemporary Economists in Perspective*, Greenwich, Connecticut and London: JAI Press Inc., pp. 461–71.

Teilhard de Chardin, P. (1959), *The Phenomenon of Man*, New York: Harper and Row.

Wilson, V.L. and S. Dunahay (1985), *Bibliography of Published works by Kenneth E. Boulding*, Boulder, CO: Colorado Associated University Press.

Wright, R. (1988), *Three Scientists and their Gods: Looking for Meaning in an Age of Information*, New York: Times Books.

10. Fritz Machlup: 'How One Thing Led to Another'

Donald Lamberton

I met Fritz Machlup once only, at a session of the December 1982 annual meeting of the American Economic Association in New York. It was a highly appropriate occasion for his presence. Meheroo Jussawalla had organized a session on information/communication economics and development,[1] under the chairmanship of Kenneth Boulding, Machlup's friend and long-time colleague. After a skiing holiday in December, Machlup died on 30 January 1983. Kenneth Boulding is reported to have said that 'Machlup had what he called the anti-Midas touch—even if he were to touch gold, he would turn it to life' (Miller, 1983, p. xi).

Geoffrey Hodgson has referred to Machlup as 'the prominent neoclassical theorist' (Hodgson, 1999, p. 110), presumably on the grounds that Machlup had admitted that 'the neoclassical theory of the firm is really a theory of market prices and costs, and is consequently not about firms at all' (ibid.). Hodgson also noted that Machlup had provided an '[e]arly analysis of the growing importance of the knowledge sector' (ibid., p. 283). I shall endeavour to show that these comments suggest failure to discern the importance not only of those statistical inquiries but also of what Machlup had to say about theories of the firm—the implications of his pioneering efforts to come to grips with the knowledge dimensions of the economy, the role of the theories of the participants in decision processes, the triggering of what began as a trickle but turned into a flood of non-profit maximization theorizing, and a defence of the economist's way of thinking that was to evolve into a proposal for a comprehensive information science. I prefer another categorization: 'a many sided person' rather than a 'neoclassical theorist'.[2] A dedicated neoclassical theorist would not have conceptualized and written *The Production and Distribution of Knowledge in the United States* (1962), with its central concept of the knowledge industry, described by Boulding as containing 'enough dynamite to blast traditional economics into orbit' (Boulding, 1963, p. 36). The 'many sides' included student, businessman, academic teacher and researcher, passionate defender of academic freedom, semantic disciplinarian, innovator, visionary, and even would-be unionist! But I am running ahead too quickly and must turn back to the earlier stages of the story of 'how one thing led to another'.

NOTABLE ÉMIGRÉS

The Intellectual Migration Europe and America, 1930–1960 (Fleming and Bailyn, 1969) sought to answer the question of what difference was made in the major fields of the natural sciences, the social sciences, and the humanities by this exodus from Europe. Included was a list of 300 notable émigrés. Most readers have undoubtedly been struck by the familiarity of many of these names of people of great intellectual and creative power in almost every area of the arts and sciences, e.g., Hannah Arendt, Béla Bartok, Bruno Bettelheim, Ernst Cassirer, Marc Chagall, Karl Deutsch, Albert Einstein, Walter Gropius, Otto Klemperer, Paul Lazarsfeld, Kurt Lewin, Karl Polanyi, Leo Szilard, Edward Teller, John von Neumann.

Fritz Machlup was amongst the handful of economists which included Fellner, Gershenkron, Haberler, Jacob Marschak, Modigliani, Stolper, and von Mises. He came to the U.S. in 1933. The difference Machlup made in economics can be traced in his prolific publication. A recent study (Scherer, 2000) focussed on the emigration of German-speaking economists after 1933 and their publications. Based on a Social Sciences Citation Index count for the years 1960–64, Machlup was placed fourth amongst émigré economists after Amitai Etzioni, Joseph Schumpeter, and Richard Musgrave and before Albert Hirschman, Abraham Wald, and Otto Eckstein. Scherer concludes that this group had high productivity and its members were recognized by election to honorific positions.[3] Scherer's analysis confirmed the judgement of Paul Samuelson that 'The triumphant rise of American economics after 1940 was enormously accelerated by importation of scholars from Hitlerian Europe' (Samuelson, 1988, p. 319).

The superbly crafted entry in the *New Encyclopedia of the Social Sciences Biographical Supplement* (Chipman, 1979) tells us the story from his birth in Austria on 15 December 1902 to the 1970s. In 1920 he enrolled at the University of Vienna, completing his dissertation on the gold exchange standard under von Mises in 1923. While a graduate student he had been a partner in a cardboard manufacturing firm and this business experience continued after his dissertation work. He became a member of the council of a cartel of Austrian cardboard producers. He was an office bearer of the Austrian Economic Society and associated with Hayek, Haberler, and Morgenstern.

Machlup's academic career was thus well under way, with a focus on currency and finance, methodology and philosophy of science. The combination of deteriorating conditions in Austria and the offer of a Rockefeller fellowship for 1933–4 led to his visiting a number of universities in the United States: Columbia, Harvard, Chicago, and Stanford. This period brought new and exciting contacts: Taussig, Schumpeter, Chamberlin, E.S. Mason, Viner, Frank Knight, Stigler, and Friedman, and after some leave to liquidate business interests in Austria, a visit to Cambridge and London added Keynes, Joan Robinson, Kahn, Sraffa and Hicks. His first real academic appointment – as Professor of Economics at the University of Buffalo – took effect in February 1936.

To Machlup's early books,[4] e.g., his dissertation and *The Stock Market, Credit and Capital Formation* (1931; English ed., 1940), were added:

International Trade and the National Income Multiplier (1943)
The Economics of Sellers' Competition: Model Analysis of Sellers' Conduct (1952)
The Political Economy of Monopoly: Business, Labor, and Government Policies (1952)
An Economic Review of the Patent System (1958)
The Production and Distribution of Knowledge in the United States (1962)
Essays in Economic Semantics (1963)
A History of Thought on Economic Integration (1977)
Methodology of Economics and Other Social Sciences (1978)
*Information Through the Printed Word: The Dissemination of Scholarly, Scientific, and
    Intellectual Knowledge* (1978–80)
*Knowledge: Its Creation, Distribution, and Economic Significance. Vol. I: Knowledge
    and Knowledge Production* (1981); *Vol. II: The Branches of Learning* (1982); *Vol. III:
    The Economics of Information and Human Capital* (1984)
The Study of Information: Interdisciplinary Messages (with Una Mansfield) (1983).

'HOW ONE THING LED TO ANOTHER'

Here we can glimpse more easily than in the mass of articles the progression towards the dominating motif in Machlup's later career. He described 'how one thing led to another':

> It was not a sudden flash, a brainstorm out of the blue; nor was it an idea suggested by conversation or by reading a particular book or article. Instead, it was a case of intellectual chain reactions, taking place gradually over a period of twenty-five years. It was a case of 'how one thing led to another.' Each link is plausible, but the beginning and the end are so unlike each other that no one could have foreseen this evolution (Machlup, 1980, p. xv).

A starting point, if one can be identified, was the 1933 discussions at Harvard on monopoly and competition. Machlup wrote first on pure theory but then turned to the institutions restricting competition. The patent system came into this category. But could the R & D encouraged by patent protection be separated from R & D not so induced? Therefore, R & D had to become a central matter and one that linked with education, which was a precondition for quality research. So too did efforts to create and disseminate scientific and technological knowledge. All these called for trained personnel, and so education of all kinds was drawn into the scope of inquiry. It was a small step to books journals, magazines and newspapers; and another small step from information through the printed word to the electronic media of communication, radio and television broadcasting. This took in artistic creation and communication and the roles of telegraph, telephone and the postal services.

Reflecting contemporary events, information services and information machines were added. Rapid growth rates could be observed and so the idea of measuring the share of all these activities captured in the knowledge industries as a percentage of GNP emerged. While the chain was 'long and tangled' (Machlup, 1980, xvii) the separate linkages came about readily enough. He would have found the Internet and the Human Genome Project exciting further links.

We had been given an early view of the territory Machlup felt needed attention by economists. As President-elect of the American Economic Association, he had chosen the theme Knowledge Production and Innovation for the 78th Annual Meeting in New York in 1965. Although he acknowledged the help of friends, Machlup crafted the program he thought was needed to achieve thematic unity, reflecting the structure of the knowledge industries portrayed in his 1962 book but projected in terms of their relationships with the whole economy and its domestic, international and developmental dimensions. Technological change and innovation dominated, with attention given to economic theory, comparative studies, econometric models, the legal framework, and policy approaches (see *American Economic Review*, LVI(2), May 1966, iii–vii).

The unity and broad scope of this program suggest that the final four volumes on *Knowledge* (1980–84) were in no sense a new venture but a culmination of the long years of effort to articulate the role of knowledge in the economy and society.[5] Their importance to our contemporary world has been captured neatly: 'Knowledge [not only] provides the new raw material for prosperity. It is a major instrument, to some even a weapon, in the rivalry between social classes, countries and trading blocks' (Eijsvoogel, 1990, p. 1).

It has been suggested that embarking on an 8-volume second edition of the dynamite-laden 1962 *The Production and Distribution of Knowledge in the United States* was 'the most ambitious project of his life' (Chipman, 1979, pp. 489–90) and that the scope of the plan of those volumes was 'possibly the richest of his pedagogical-research products' (Perlman 1991, p. viii). '[T]he initial phase of Machlup's thinking about the nature of learning and economic knowledge' could be found in the original edition of *Economic Semantics*

(Perlman, 1991, p. xx).[6] The plan was for much more than a second edition and involved a great effort in the telling of what proved to be an unfinished story. Volumes I–III kept close to the general title but *The Study of Information: Interdisciplinary Messages,* published after his death, conveys a vision of 'a third culture', to paraphrase C.P. Snow. Machlup chose to address only that part of 'the entire universe of learning...characterized by the keyword *information*' (Machlup and Mansfield, 1983, p. 3). To this end, he persuaded thirty-nine information scientists to write their interdisciplinary messages so that he could 'see the stir of the great Babel, and not feel the crowd' (Miller, 1983, p. x).

Six more volumes would have surely provided more answers, many of which are needed urgently. There is now greater awareness of information economics in both its destructive implications for neoclassical, mainstream economic thought (Stiglitz, 1999, 2000, 2002) and its positive contributions to analysis of modern economic conditions. There is, however, an unfortunate divide. Perhaps because it has been somewhat easier to link the analysis of incomplete and imperfect information with old modes of thought, what I call the asymmetry school of information economics is developing separately from work more directly based on Machlup's knowledge-industry approach. It will be a great loss if the present impetus peters out and bridges are not built between those two academic territories. The theoretical and empirical challenges are enormous and are compounded by tribal and disciplinary conflicts. Machlup pointed the way to a relevant, humane and evolutionary economics. The thematic unity of his American Economic Association meeting program carried through to his chapters 10, 'A New Classification' and 11, 'A Sample Bibliography', in *Knowledge,* Vol. III. Here there is a balanced program accommodating both information asymmetry thinking and the role of knowledge in society, which extends to information as a resource and commodity, information as perception of pattern, and information as a constitutive force in society (Braman, 1989). 'R & D' is not the only kind of information. Perhaps it is indicative of two cultures within information economics that even the voluminous list of references that accompanies the latest Nobel Lecture (Stiglitz, 2002) does not touch on the work of Machlup. To repeat, information economics has to be linked and intertwined with evolutionary economics, and this requires Machlup's 'breadth and depth' (see Dreyer, 1978), which can be traced from the AEA program through to *Knowledge,* Vol. IV.

It may help with this reconciliation to ask whether Machlup did appreciate those destructive consequences for the most central of traditional economic concepts—competitive equilibrium. I suggest he did. Consider his superb essay on the 'Optimum utilization of knowledge'. The essential difficulty he saw with the notion of optimum utilization of knowledge lay in 'the absence of specifications concerning its utilization by whom, for whom, for what, for how much, and (most critically) *what* knowledge' (Machlup, 1982a, p. 10). He added that '[k]nowledge is not a pile of homogeneous material, but a complex structure of heterogeneous thoughts, each available at zero marginal cost but usable only together with resources available only at positive, and often very high cost'. We could, he argued, take cost effective action, trying to act intelligently, taking full account of pertinent knowledge to hand or available at reasonable cost. But to be Pareto-efficient was a very different matter, inviting 'speculations that may again widen the focus to include choices among alternative actions on different fronts, actions for which different batches of knowledge are used: in this case, we may easily slip again into the sea of undecidability' (ibid.).[7]

THEORIES OF THE FIRM

Now we return to the conundrum posed by Geoffrey Hodgson at the beginning of this chapter. A permissible preliminary answer is to say simply that Machlup was not deserving of the epithet 'neoclassical'. Other reactions could be that (a), Machlup did have some business experience to draw upon (as late as *Knowledge*, Vol. III, we find him drawing on that experience of cardboard mill management [1984, fn. 55, pp. 192–3]); and (b), that the famous polemic against Richard Lester impacted on empirical investigation and curbed the uncritical use of information obtained from questionaires (see Chipman, 1979, p. 487). But these do not seem to me to get to the heart of the matter.

Hodgson emphasizes that the neoclassical theory of the firm is really a theory of market prices and costs, and is consqently not about firms at all. This is fully consistent with Machlup's paper. However, Machlup's statement is worded carefully:

> The model of the firm [as used in traditional price theory] is not, as so many writers believe, designed to serve to explain and predict the behavior of real firms; instead it is designed to explain and predict changes in observed prices...as effects of particular changes in conditions...In this causal connection, the firm is only a theoretical link...(Machlup, 1967, p. 399).

Without engaging in a detailed exercise in the history of economic thought, it is useful to note some of the points made by Machlup in that paper and in his earlier paper that had covered some of the same ground:

- [E]mpirical research on business policies cannot assure useful results if it employs the methods of mailed questionnaires, if it is confined to direct questions without carefully devised checks, and if it aims at testing too broad and formal principles rather than more narrowly defined hypotheses (Machlup, 1946, p. 190).

- The marginalist solution of price determination under conditions of heavy competition is not seriously contested (Machlup, 1967, p. 394).

- Many of the proponents of a more realistic theory of the firm are quite aware of the fact that the managerial extension and enrichment of the concept of the firm was not needed except where firms in the industry were large and few, and not under the pressure of competition (Machlup, 1967, p. 401).

Machlup distinguished carefully between clearly known and imperfect information. He doubted anything could be imperfect about, e.g., a tax change, and pointed out that the analysis was not intended to extend to the firm's '*complete environment*' (Machlup, 1967, p. 415).

Non-profit maximization theories have proliferated since those times and their implications are probably greatest for the least competitive circumstances. Given Machlup's concession that oligopoly and monopoly left scope for such theorizing, he might well have directed his attention more directly to the implications of the information production and handling functions of such firms. With this might have gone further development of the matter of the participants' own theories and their decision making. This is a link that Machlup does not appear to have examined, and it has become central to a mixed bag of initiatives: organizational obsolescence (Arrow, 1974); lock-in (Arthur, 1994); cognitive dissonance (Akerlof, 1970). There would appear to have been growing recognition that there are basic issues of organizational efficiency, especially of those non-competitive firms whose existence Machlup recognized, and these have loomed more importantly with the very knowledge growth trends Machlup measured and the associated structural changes and policy interventions. He took note of Hayek's 'rule-guided action' and 'rule-guided perception' (Machlup, 1977a, p. 49) but then he perhaps relied upon his idea that the market mechanism is 'the largest and most effective information system in existence' (Machlup, 1979, p. 113). In so doing, Machlup was in line with Hayek's reasoning which always tended to be cast in terms of market information rather than scientific and technological knowledge. Machlup's work on knowledge has certainly aided research into knowledge management, although a great deal of management writing still belongs to the storing and shipping tradition, with too little consideration of the meaning dimensions. It has lost sight of the fact that '[c]reative processing of substance to turn raw data into useful knowledge remains a monopoly of our flesh and blood minds' (Oettinger, 2001, p. 12).

HUMAN NATURE AND EVOLUTIONARY ECONOMICS

It would be far too ambitious of me to attempt to follow in the footsteps of Vernon Venable, whose book, *Human Nature: The Marxian View* (1946) set out 'what Karl Marx…and Frederick Engels, conceived within the framework of their theories of nature and society as a whole, to be the nature of the human being, the determinants of man's development and transformation, the springs of human motivation, and the scientific methods to be followed both for under-standing human nature and for changing it' (Venable, 1946, p. x). My objective is a much more limited one: to focus on Machlup's thinking about man's distin-guishing capability.

It would seem that no one has a generally accepted explanation of how the human brain converts electrical and chemical discharges into consciousness. Scholars like Ian Tattersall invoke an innovation theory, and reason that the invention of language is 'the best current bet' as to what that innovation was (Tattersall and Matternes, 2000, p. 44).[8] Language communicates ideas and experiences from one person to another:

> [I]t is fundamental to the thought process itself. It involves categorizing and naming objects and sensations in the outer and inner worlds and making associations be-tween resulting mental symbols. It is, in effect, impossible for us to conceive of thought (as we are familiar with it) in the absence of language, and it is the ability to form mental symbols that is the fount of our creativity, for only once we create such symbols can we recombine them and ask such questions as 'What if...?' (Tattersall and Matternes, 2000, p. 44).

Our culture, the accumulated knowledge of which it is comprised, is then the distinguishing characteristic of man (Cavalli-Sforza, 2000); and '[l]anguage is central to our conception of what it means to be human' (Bever, 1983, p. 297). I suggest that Machlup has done economics a major service by making knowl-edge central to economics.

How do Machlup's ideas relate to evolutionary economics and the study of human nature? If 'Capitalism is restless because knowledge is restless', as Metcalfe (forthcoming) argues, then surely Machlup's invention of the knowl-edge industry concept, his careful delineation of its dimensions, his succinct analysis of some of its implications for economic theory, and his later efforts to explore the links between economics and other disciplines engaged in the study of information, establish his credentials in respect of evolutionary economics. As Boulding has argued: 'The plain fact is that knowledge or something equiva-lent to it in the form of improbable structures is the only thing that can grow or evolve, and the concept is quite crucial in any evolutionary theory' (Boulding, 1963, p. 25).

NOTES

1. Papers from this session, and another organized by Helene Ebenfield on the economics of information, under the chairmanship of Leonid Hurwicz, were published in Jussawalla and Ebenfield (1984).
2. Theodore Schultz (1984) was content to say 'Machlup is every inch an economist'.

3.   In Machlup's case, President of the American Economic Association and six honorary doc-
      torates—three in Europe and three in the United States (King, 1983, p. 28).
4.   My first contact with his writing was his two *Economica* papers (1939–40) on 'The theory of
      foreign exchanges' – judged by Chipman to be 'seminal' – to which I was introduced in
      undergraduate economics at the University of Sydney.
5.   This breadth of view influenced my own efforts to shape the notion of information econom-
      ics, e.g., *The Economics of Information and Knowledge* (1971), *The Information Revolution*
      (1974), my 1974 University of Queensland Inaugural Lecture entitled 'Who Owns the Unex-
      pected? A Perspective on the Nation's Information Industry', *The Economics of Communication
      and Information* (1996) and subsequent publications. Other formative influences go back to
      the writings of, and encouragement from, G.L.S. Shackle and P.W.S. Andrews, as is apparent
      in my *The Theory of Profit* (1965), where I had earlier begun to address the information and
      organization theme.
6.   This collection of Machlup's papers was presented to him by some of his students to mark his
      sixtieth birthday and was published in 1963. It included his important paper, 'Marginal analy-
      sis and empirical research' from the *American Economic Review,* which relates to his views
      on theories of the firm.
7.   See Lamberton (1999), 'Information: Pieces, batches or flows?', in Dow and Earl (eds), Vol.
      I ; Lamberton (forthcoming a), 'Intellectual property, "entangled particles" and hi-tech poli-
      cies', in H. Bloch (ed.), *Growth and Development in the Global Economy.*
8.   See Lamberton (ed.) (forthcoming b), *The Economics of Language.*

REFERENCES

Akerlof, G.A. (1970), The market for 'lemons': Quality uncertainty and the market proc-
    ess, *Quarterly Journal of Economics,* **LXXXIV**, 488–500.
American Economic Review (1966), **LVI** (2).
Arrow, K.J. (1974), *The Limits of Organization,* New York: Norton.
Arthur, W.B. (1994), *Increasing Returns and Path Dependence in the Economy,* Ann
    Arbor, MI: University of Michigan Press.
Bever, T.G. (1983), Linguistics and its relations to other disciplines, in F. Machlup and
    U. Mansfield (eds), *The Study of Information: Interdisciplinary Messages,* New York:
    Wiley, pp. 297–317.
Boulding, K.E. (1963), 'The knowledge industry'. Review of Fritz Machlup, *The Pro-
    duction and Distribution of Knowledge in the United States, Challenge,* **11**, pp. 36–8.
Braman, S. (1989), 'Defining information: An approach for policymakers', reprinted in
    D.M. Lamberton (ed.), *The Economics of Communication and Information,* Chelten-
    ham, U.K.: Edward Elgar, pp. 3–12.
Cavalli-Sforza, L.L. (2000), *Genes, People and Languages,* London: Penguin Books.
Chipman, J.S. (1979), 'Machlup, Fritz', New York: Free Press *New Encyclopedia of the
    Social Sciences: Biographical Supplement.*
Dreyer, J.S. (1978), *Breadth and Depth in Economics Fritz Machlup – The Man and his
    Ideas,* Lexington, MA: Lexington Books.
Eijsvoogel, J. (1990), 'Introduction', in J. Groen et al.(eds), *The Discipline of Curiosity:
    Science in the World,* Amsterdam: Elsevier, 1–7.
Fleming, D. and B. Bailyn (1969), *The Intellectual Migration: Europe and America,
    1930–1960,* Cambridge, MA: Belknap Press of Harvard University Press.
Hodgson, G.M. (1999), *Economics & Utopia: Why the Learning Economy is Not the
    End of History,* London: Routledge.
Jussawalla, M. and H. Ebenfield (eds) (1984), *Communication and Information Eco-
    nomics: New Perspectives,* Amsterdam: North-Holland.

King, D.W. (1983), 'Professor Fritz Machlup 1903–1983', *Bulletin of the American Society for Information Science,* **9**, 28–9.

Lamberton, D.M. (1965), *The Theory of Profit,* Oxford: Blackwell.

Lamberton, D.M. (ed.) (1971), *Economics of Information and Knowledge,* Harmondsworth, U.K.: Penguin Books.

Lamberton, D.M. (ed.) (1974), *The Information Revolution, Annals,* **412**, American Academy of Political and Social Science.

Lamberton, D.M. (1975), *Who Owns the Unexpected? A Perspective on the Nation's Information Industry,* Brisbane: University of Queensland Press.

Lamberton, D.M. (ed.) (1996), *The Economics of Communication and Information,* Cheltenham, U.K.: Edward Elgar.

Lamberton, D.M. (1999), 'Information: Pieces, batches or flows?', in S.C. Dow and P.E. Earl (eds), *Economic Organization and Economic Knowledge: Essays in Honour of Brian J.Loasby,* Vol. I, Cheltenham, U.K.: Edward Elgar, pp. 209–24.

Lamberton, D.M. (forthcoming a), 'Intellectual property, "entangled particles" and hitech policies', in H. Bloch (ed.), *Growth and Development in the Global Economy,* Cheltenham, U.K.: Edward Elgar.

Lamberton, D.M. (ed.) (forthcoming b), *The Economics of Language,* Cheltenham, U.K.: Edward Elgar.

Machlup, F. (English ed. 1940; first published 1931), *The Stock Market, Credit and Capital Formation,* London: Hodge.

Machlup, F. (1943), *International Trade and the National Income Multiplier,* Philadelphia: Blakiston.

Machlup, F. (1946), Marginal analysis and empirical research, *American Economic Review,* **XXXVI,** reprinted in F. Machlup, *Economic Semantics,* Second Edition, New Brunswick, N.J.: Transaction Publishers, 1991, pp. 147–90.

Machlup, F. (1952), *The Economics of Sellers' Competition: Model Analysis of Sellers' Conduct,* Baltimore: Johns Hopkins University Press.

Machlup, F. (1952), *The Political Economy of Monopoly: Business, Labor, and Government Policies,* Baltimore: Johns Hopkins University Press.

Machlup, F. (1958), *An Economic Review of the Patent System,* Washington, D.C.: Government Printing Office.

Machlup, F. (1962), *The Production and Distribution of Knowledge,* Princeton, N.J.: Princeton University Press.

Machlup, F. (1967), 'Theories of the Firm: Marginalist, Behavioral, Managerial', *American Economic Review,* **LVII,** 1–33, reprinted in F. Machlup *Methodology of Economics and Other Social Sciences,* New York: Academic Press, 1978, pp. 391–423.

Machlup, F. (1977a), 'Hayek's contribution to economics', in F. Machlup (ed.), (1977), *Essays on Hayek,* London: Routledge & Kegan Paul.

Machlup, F. (1977b), *A History of Thought on Economic Integration,* London: Macmillan.

Machlup, F. (1978–80), *Information Through the Printed Word: The Dissemination of Scholarly, Scientific, and Intellectual Knowledge,* 3 Vols: 1. *Book Publishing;* 2. *Journals;* 3. *Libraries,* New York: Praeger.

Machlup, F. (1979), 'An economist's reflections on an Institute for the Advanced Study of Information Science', *Journal of the American Society for Information Science,* **30**, 111–13.

Machlup, F. (1980), *Knowledge: Its Creation, Distribution, and Economic Significance,* Vol.I, *Knowledge and Knowledge Production,* Princeton, N.J.: Princeton University Press.

Machlup, F. (1982a), 'Optimum utilization of knowledge', *Knowledge, Information, and Decisions: Society,* **20**, 8–10.

Machlup, F. (1982b), *Knowledge: Its Creation, Distribution, and Economic Significance,* Vol. II, *The Branches of Learning,* Princeton, N.J.: Princeton University Press.

Machlup, F. (1984), *Knowledge: Its Creation, Distribution, and Economic Significance,* Vol. III, *The Economics of Information and Human Capital,* Princeton, N.J.: Princeton University Press.

Machlup, F. and U. Mansfield (eds), (1983), *The Study of Information: Interdisciplinary Messages,* New York: Wiley.

Metcalfe, J.S. (forthcoming), 'Institutions and Progress', in H. Bloch (ed.) (forthcoming), *Growth and Development in the Global Economy,* Cheltenham, U.K.: Edward Elgar.

Miller, G.A. (1983), Foreword, in F. Machlup and U. Mansfield (eds), *The Study of Information: Interdisciplinary messages,* New York: Wiley.

Oettinger, A.G. (2001), 'Knowledge innovation: The endless adventure', *Bulletin of the American Society for Information Science and Technology,* **27**, 10–15.

Perlman, M. (1991), Introduction, in Fritz Machlup, *Economic Semantics,* Second Edition, New Brunswick, N.J.: Transaction Publishers, pp. vii–xxi.

Samuelson, P.A. (1988), 'The passing of the guard in economics', *Eastern Economic Journal,* **14**, 319–29.

Scherer, F.M. (2000), 'The emigration of German-speaking economists after 1933', *Journal of Economic Literature,* **XXXVIII**, 614–26.

Schultz, T.W. (1984), Foreword, in Machlup, *Knowledge: Its Creation, Distribution, and Economic Significance,* Vol. III, *The Economics of Information and Human Capital,* Princeton, N.J.: Princeton University Press, p. xvii.

Stiglitz, J.E. (1999), *Public policy for a knowledge economy: Remarks at the Department for Trade and Industry and Center for Economic Policy Research,* London: World Bank.

Stiglitz, J.E. (2000), 'The contributions of the economics of information to Twentieth Century economics', *Quarterly Journal of Economics,* **115**, 1441–78.

Stiglitz, J.E. (2002), *Information and the Change in the Paradigm in Economics,* Nobel Lecture, Columbia Business School.

Tattersall, I and J.H. Matternes (2000), 'Once we were not alone', *Scientific American,* **282**, 38–44.

Venable, V. (1946), *Human Nature: The Marxian View,* London: Dennis Dobson.

11. Toward an Evolutionary Theory of *Homo œconomicus*: The Concept of Universal Nomadism

Jason Potts

Nomina si pereunt, perit et cognitio rerum.[1]
Linnæus, *Journey in Västergötland*

Our nature lies in movement, complete calm is death.
Pascal, *Pensées*

UNIVERSAL NOMADISM

The purpose of this chapter is to explore a possible connection between evolutionary psychology and evolutionary microeconomics in relation to the theory of the mind of the agent. The connection is universal nomadism.

A defining axiom of evolutionary microeconomics in the growth of knowledge tradition (in the manner for example of Friedrich von Hayek, George Shackle, Brian Loasby, and Ulrich Witt) is that the economic agent has a *mind*. Agents have minds by definition because they construct, carry, adapt and use *knowledge*. The evolutionary microeconomic agent lives cognitively in an environment of knowledge. However, it is clear to most researchers in this tradition that, sooner or later, some explicit statements will be required about the nature of the mind that is able to do this. I shall argue here that a plausible candidate exists in the form of the model of the mind developed in evolutionary psychology.

Evolutionary psychologists argue that the human mind is a product of Darwinian evolution just as much as any other adapted trait. The mind, they say, is a complex and massively modular system of subroutines, or 'modules', each of which is an adaptation to a recurrent problem in the ancestral environment (see, e.g., Barkow et al., 1992; Pinker, 1994; Plotkin, 1997). The ancestral environment was, primarily, the African savannah. They argue that the reason humans can effortlessly do some rather technically difficult things (e.g., perception in three dimensions, face recognition, or monitoring reciprocal exchanges), but find other problems of similar order much more difficult (e.g., triangulating light gradients, extracting patterns from data arrays and solutions from extensive-form games), is because we have evolved powerful cognitive modules for some of life's problems but not for others. Evolutionary psychologists conceive of the mind as a deep and rich suite of problem-solving routines, and then further suggest that these pre-configured routines are the basis of 'instinctual behaviour'. These adapted cognitive modules, as instincts, can then be said to be, as Popper (1985, 1999) and Dennett (1995) propose, instances of *biological knowledge*.

The overarching thing evolutionary psychology says about the mind is that, contra 2,000 years of thinking otherwise, the mind is not a blank slate, it is not a *tabula rasa* upon which can be written anything and everything. But rather than arguing that metaphor, evolutionary psychologists favour a different one. Humans, they almost say, all run the same operating system and come equipped with many of the same programs. Individuals may learn to do different things with these, and perhaps run different languages or compile data differently, but, essentially, all human minds share a great many similar, and fantastically complex, processing capabilities. The human mind is said to be a loosely coupled and massively parallel system of modules. In theory, each module is adapted to a specific problem in the ancestral environment. Among other things, this begs some reconsideration of basic notions of human rationality (see Plotkin, 1995).

It was of course Descartes who taught us how to axiomatically demarcate humans from other animals with the criterion of the cogito: 'Humans have rationality with which they reason and think, whereas animals have no such powers because they are driven by instinct.' Ergo, the superiority of humans over animals follows from the absence of instinct in rational human action. But in evolutionary psychology, precisely the opposite is said to be true; and to the extent that humans do have superior intelligence and rationality over other species, it is because we have *more* instincts than they, not fewer. Our abilities to interact socially and form complex coalitions, our ability to communicate ideas, indeed the very abilities that make an economic system possible, are adaptations of the mind. In 1994, Leda Cosmides and John Tooby aired this view in the *American Economic Review* in an article provocatively titled 'better than rational'. Predictably enough, they were politely ignored.

The reason that economists of orthodox stripe ought not to find these sorts of revelations about the nature of human rationality anything but curious, of course, is that economic theory is well insulated from the cognitive sciences because its microeconomic agent is rational in the Cartesian sense, whereby it is able to learn all things and process all information. *Homo œconomicus* – whether the Benthamite utility maximizer or the Baysian agent with rational expectations,

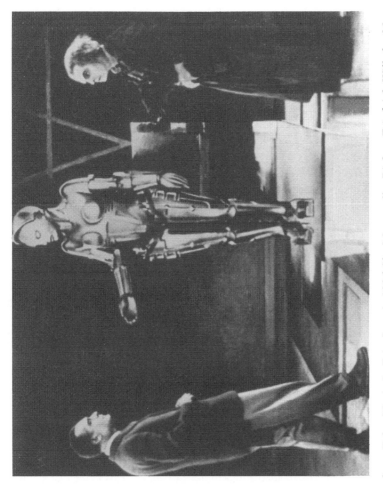

Figure 11.1 The cyborg False-Maria in Fritz Lang's 1926 film Metropolis. Rights: Friedrich-Wilhelm-Murnau Striftung. Distribution: Transit Film GmbH.

or a finite state automata, or anything in between, demon or cyborg (Mirowski 2002) – does not actually have a mind. And so it is immaterial whether or not the mind of *Homo sapiens* is adapted or not. Computationally, *Homo œconomicus* is a Turing machine (Velupillai, 1995) and nothing could be more rational than that. But what Cosmides and Tooby were really saying is that a Turing machine would never be arrived at through any evolutionary process.[2] The sort of rationality attributed to *Homo œconomicus* is not the sort of rationality that *Homo sapiens* has evolved. In any event, they were ignored and not much more was ever said about the matter.

Jack Vromen (2001), however, recently pointed out that evolutionary psychology is relevant wherever there is an explicit conception of economic agents with minds, such as in the Austrian and Behavioural schools and in evolutionary economics in the growth of knowledge tradition (Loasby, 1999; Potts, 2000). If the evolutionary economic agent has a mind, then a way of theorizing about this is to begin with the adapted mind of *Homo sapiens* and consider any general economic problems that may have shaped the mind.

I shall argue here that we may connect the adapted mind of *Homo sapiens* to the evolutionary rationality of *Homo œconomicus* with the overarching economic problem of the complexity of the distribution of resources in the ancestral environment. Humans evolved in a complex environment of semi-desert and savannah, where resources were only semi-stable in space and time. The solution was to be *nomadic*. For hundreds of thousands of years, a major force of selection over the human (and pre-human) population, body and mind, was adaptation to climatic variation and shifting and migrating resources. *Universal nomadism* is the idea that this Nomadic behaviour may have levered itself into a new domain of language and ideas, an abstract space where knowledge itself is the resource that must be constantly tracked and settled. Universal nomadism is proposed as a theory of evolutionary microeconomic behaviour in a complex knowledge environment.

There are major differences between an economic problem consisting of the allocation of scarce but known resources and an economic problem of the mapping and tracking of uncertain and shifting resources. To say that knowledge is given is to abstract from the second definition of the problem. But where knowledge is not given, where knowledge must be discovered, then to live in such a world is to live with the second sort of economic problem, and indeed the very problem that gave rise to adaptations of nomadism. It seems to me that a closer examination of the adapted nature of the human mind may shed some light upon how economic agents live in an evolving knowledge environment, where they must continually track the market evolution of the sorts of jobs they might have, or the commodities they might want, and so forth.

I shall argue here that the connection between evolutionary psychology and evolutionary economics is the universal economic problem of complexity in the resource environment. The argument is, in essence, that the very mechanisms adapted to solve the problem in the physical world, i.e., nomadism, were capitalized as the beginnings of a growth of knowledge process in which knowledge itself is the complex and shifting resource. We proceed as follows. In Section 2, 'Once were nomads', we consider the nature of nomadism in relation to environmental complexity. In Section 3, 'Nomadic space maps' we examine the adaptations that emerged about knowledge of the environment, and, specifically, in relation to the nature of language and of maps. Section 4, 'The nomadic instinct', considers how we might interpret the nomadic instinct computationally, as a set of rules, and Section 5, 'Nomadism, novelty, and competition', considers some implications for the endogenous generation of novelty in an economic system. In the concluding section, I discuss in broader context the implications of universal nomadism for an evolutionary theory of the economic agent.

ONCE WERE NOMADS[3]

We begin with the context of hominid evolution at a time some four million years ago, when the earth's climate became much colder and drier as a result of a massive glaciation of the polar caps. The climactic shift transformed much of Africa from high canopy rain forest to mosaic savannah and arid semi-desert. This dramatic change in the environment had a watershed effect on the hominid line from which we are descendant. We (in the anthropological sense) came out of the trees because the trees began to disappear. The hominid species evolved from a brachiating forest ape to a walker on the plains (*Australopithecus*) by adaptation of the pelvis to allow an upright posture, and of the foot with sprung arches adapted to walking. (Apes have flat feet, and so lack the four-point contact rhythm that powers the human gait.) The *Homo sapiens* line emerged several million years later, again precipitated by further climatic change (the second great ice-age), with the 'rapid' expansion of the neocortex and increase in brain size.

The upright walking posture and large brain are both regarded as adaptations to a semi-desert environment with seasonal variation in resources that is also only semi-stable from one year to the next. The ancestral human environment demanded mobility, and demanded it over a great range of environments. The adaptations of peripatetic mobility into the body plan achieved this very effectively, and are part of what makes the human species a great generalist, able to live in many different environments. Of course, other flora and fauna were also affected in the same way, which is to say that mobility is an arms-race, and so the scavenging, hunting and gathering of shifting and migrating resources called for one of two strategies. Either, to occupy and protect a particular place and simply wait for resources to come by, which would necessitate adaptations for when resources did not show (for example, the strategy of plants with seed pods that can lie dormant for many years). Or, to simply go to where the resources are and to follow them where they go.

The hominid line adopted the second strategy, that of itinerant tribal movement in the ongoing search for ever-shifting resources in the semi-desert and savannah environment. The physical adaptations to this environment were then augmented by cognitive and behavioural adaptations, and it is the latter in relation to the problem of a complex distribution of resources that I shall call the *instinct of nomadism*.

Nomadism, then, is both a physical and behavioural adaptation to an environment in which the economic problem is that resources are unevenly distributed over both space and time. Rains, for example, may or may not come, and so vegetation and migratory herbivores may or may not follow, and so forth. Nomadism is a strategy for survival: if resources are plentiful, stay, if they are not, go in search of where they are. Nomadism is a conditional search strategy for resources backed by the physical and cognitive architecture to do so. For a species capable of staying in one place only so long as the environment was benevolent, nomadism was an adaptation to an environment that was just as often not. The human mind, in this thesis, evolved in an environment where the economic problem played out over a temporally and spatially unstable resource environment. The human mind, then, has certain physical and cognitive adaptations to a tribal and nomadic lifestyle due to the selection pressures of hundreds of thousands of years of scavenging, hunting and gathering. And this force of selection was, in essence, environmental complexity in the distribution of resources.

The empirical assumptions to support this thesis are plausible. The complexity of the ancestral environment is mostly a function of the complex savannah habitat (see Diamond, 1997). Archæological evidence points strongly to sustained social groupings into familial and tribal populations, and this evidence is consistent worldwide. There is also strong evidence from both biological and cultural anthropology for sustained and predominant nomadic behaviour among hominids. Given this, I suggest it is reasonable as a first approximation and broadly consistent with evolutionary psychology to propose that the human mind will have adapted to these selection pressures. This is the primary nature of the mind module I hypothesize as the *instinct* of nomadism.

I am arguing that the mind harbours a module, or system of modules, that carries the cognitive adaptations to a nomadic lifestyle. The implication is that if it does indeed exist – for I am only hypothesizing its existence here, I have as yet no demonstratable proof – then, according to the theory, it should still be with us today. And by further implication, *Homo œconomicus* should be equipped with it as well. If it exists, then we should be able to detect it somehow. The question, then, is Where is it?

An obvious suggestion is that this primordial aspect of human behaviour is, perhaps, discernable today in the popular romanticism of the travels of middle-class youth or in the itinerant cultures of the dispossessed: Gypsies, Aboriginals, Eskimos, desert tribes, and the like. But that is not what I mean; nomadism is not an ostensible behaviour, but, rather, a way of thinking. The nomadic instinct is not a lifestyle choice *per se*, but an evolutionary adaptation stamped into the cognitive architecture of all human minds by the selection pressures our ancestors faced in a semi-desert and savannah environment.

The ancestral environment was complex and only semi-stable. Without the ability to control the dynamics of resources, the adaptations of nomadism (of which more soon, but in essence triggers and strategies for search behaviour, including language to map the already searched physical space) were a viable solution that made possible the survival and reproduction of the species in an environment where resources were only semi-stable over time and space. At all locations, periods of plenty were interspersed with periods of want. Nomadism was, as a reformulation of the theory advanced by Chatwin (1987), how we solved the economic problem. We adapted to a complex distribution of resources by becoming complex in our geographical behaviour. The theory of universal nomadism is, in essence, that we now carry those solutions as biological knowledge, and this is significant for the way in which we carry economic knowledge.

However, all such selection pressures changed dramatically as settled patterns of agriculture began to displace hunting and gathering (and pastoralism, to a degree) with the concentration of the human population into large urban forms. This first arose some ten thousand years ago in Mesopotamia and has since spread throughout the world (see Diamond, 1997). This is where the modern economic problem – of the allocation of scarce but known resources – first arises. The growth of knowledge associated with the domestication of certain animals and plants transformed human societies into a new form in which particular resources were now accumulated in a single place. With different resources accumulated in different places, trade between these groups of agents sustained the populations of each (Sahlins, 1972). A social economy emerged as settlement and commerce displaced and marginalized the nomadic lifestyle everywhere. A political economy did not arrive until much later.

The adaptations of nomadism were forged over a period of many hundreds of thousands of years by the selection pressures set up by a complex and semi-stable distribution of resources. During this period, our ancestors lived predominantly in small nomadic tribes. The fact that we are dealing with geological time here, and the attendant difficulties this presents for the fine detail of evidence of camps and settlements, negates a strong assertion about tribal nomadism as the predominant condition of the hominid line from which we descend. But, in the absence of counter-evidence, of which there is nothing that is substantial, it seems, let us suppose that tribal nomadism was the predominant circumstance of hominids along the line of *Australopithecus* to *Homo sapiens* to *Homo œconomicus*.

Homo œconomicus arrived only very recently in human evolutionary history, to coincide with the shift by *Homo sapiens* to settled patterns of societies and to be the representative of the new economic problem, namely, that of the allocation of a societal product. Now, the fact of the matter is that little or no significant change has occurred in the human genome in the 500 or so generations since these technical and societal changes occurred. The implication is that the 'stone-age mind of modern man' is still, I suggest, very much that of a nomad.

One of the major points that evolutionary psychology makes is that, although our knowledge-based economies are entirely modern, our minds are not (see Vromen, 2001). Yet, if the theory of universal nomadism is correct, these very stone-age minds are precisely what has carried and developed the knowledge our modern economies are made of.

This is obviously problematic. How can a nomadic mind generate the vast knowledge and coordination of settled economies? How can a biological organism, with the same genome it had when it was a tribal and nomadic species, so dramatically switch to live in a settled economic environment that would seem to deny, by construction, every aspect of the nomadic impulse?

One possible interpretation is of nomadism as entrepreneurship (see for example, Marchesnay, 2000). However, a problem with this line of thinking is that, in order to be consistent with evolutionary psychology, we would have to argue that *all* economic agents have this property. But the fact is that not all economic agents are entrepreneurs; only some of them are.[4] If we are all evolutionarily adapted as nomads, then why are we are all not continually wrought by uncontrollable wanderlust? If the nomadic way of life is now marginalized toward extinction, what of the nomadic instincts in each of us? If we are all nomads, then, as the strong form of this theory would seem to have it, why are we not all entrepreneurs?

Three complementary hypotheses can be suggested here. The first two hypotheses are variations upon the theme of changes in selection pressure. First, if we think of nomadism as a constellation of behavioural mechanisms, which is a view I would encourage, then it is reasonable to suppose that, like other human traits (such as height, pigmentation, aggressiveness, susceptibility to disease, and suchlike), there will be variation in the strength of the trait within the population. For the sake of argument, suppose there are two behavioural types: 'strong nomadism' and 'weak nomadism'. The supply of resources in any one location in an arid steppe would have been uncertain from year to year. But movement also has its costs, and so we would expect that the distribution of these two types of behaviour would find some equilibrium in the population. Perhaps there is an optimal nomadism—behavioural equilibrium, whereupon shifting environmental conditions would shift the balance. The domestication of certain plants and animals, and the resultant change in the pattern of resources would, therefore, represent a change in the selection environment that would then shift the equilibrium to allow weak nomadism to increase as a proportion of behavioural types in the population. And that is why there are so few nomads.

Yet, even if there were no significant variation in the strength of the instinct in the population, it could well be argued that nomadism is an instinct triggered by environmental changes (associated perhaps with resource depletion, and similar in kind to, say, the photoperiodicity triggers of bird migration). Control over resources in the environment is precisely control over these triggers. In the absence of these triggers – which is to say by the sustained success in producing resources – the instinct simply lies dormant. And so it could be the case that we are not nomads because the environmental pressures required to induce this mechanism are not presently great enough. So this, alternatively, is why there are so few nomads.

Both hypotheses support the argument that the human species once were nomads, but differ as to whether changes in the environment brought about by control over the environment have either:

(1)   lowered the frequency of the strong nomadic instinct in the population; or

(2)   effectively rendered dormant the nomadic instinct in the human population to the extent that the triggering effect of the environmental conditions has weakened.

According to these theories of where the nomads have gone, either the frequency of the trait has diminished, or its triggering mechanism has weakened. And there are surely experimental tests that could be devised to sort between these, were we confident that these are the only options. However, I suggest a third possibility: The nomadic instinct has neither weakened nor become dormant, but rather has remained constant and perhaps even strengthened by a shift in the *space* over which it acts. Furthermore, it would seem this shift in the operational space of nomadism also coincides with the vast growth in human knowledge and wealth that has occurred over past millennia.

The theory of universal nomadism is the theory that the shift in the economic problem, from the tracking of a complex distribution of resources, to the allocation of a finite social product, coincided with a shift in the space over which the nomadic instinct operates. Specifically, the shift in the space of the nomadic instinct was precisely the arrival of the sort of cognitive architecture that could produce an economic system around a growth of knowledge process.

There is the third possibility: That *Homo sapiens* once were nomads and that we still are nomads; but what has changed is the space over which we are nomadic. Our ancestors were nomadic in complex physical space, and now we are nomads in a complex abstract space. I am specifically referring here to an evolutionary conception of *Homo œconomicus* living in a knowledge environment that is itself evolving. This is the idea of universal nomadism: a generalized solution to the economic problem of complex and semi-stable resources, first played out over physical resources (the adapted mind of *Homo sapiens*), and now playing out over knowledge resources (evolutionary *Homo œconomicus*). In other words, there are two distinct economic problems: (1) the allocation of scarce resources; and (2) the coordination of the discovery of new resources. Universal nomadism is entirely about the latter.

The point is that *Homo sapiens* and *œconomicus* have both long lived simultaneously in the two worlds of physical things and abstract ideas. The nomadic instinct evolved as an adaptation to complex variation in the ancestral physical environment, but *Homo sapiens*, eponymously, has never lived exclusively in a physical environment. *Homo sapiens* is the wise man who makes tools and gives names to things and thereby lives also in a space of ideas. This is the basis of the co-evolution of the growth of knowledge and the growth of economic systems in consequence of the nomadic behaviour (a physical and cognitive adaptation) shifting to a social space of communicated knowledge. The growth of knowledge can be conceptualized in evolutionary agent-based terms if we suppose the agent is adapted to live in complex shifting environments, be they physical or abstract. Nomadism, although generally conceived as a behaviour in physical space as a kind of complex migration, is argued here to be much more general.

Nomadism is a *behavioural strategy in a space*. Humans live in two forms of space: physical and abstract. Modern evolutionary theory (in biology, psychology, epistemology and complex systems theory) tells us that these are both complex environments. The underlying structural equation in universal nomadism is that these two spaces are related by the common economic problem they present. Universal nomadism proposes that the behavioural mechanisms for dealing with a complex physical environment, as the instinct of nomadism, have since adapted to a complex knowledge environment by the equivalence of the underlying economic problem of an unstable distribution of resources in a space. The theory of universal nomadism states that the nomadic instinct, originally shaped by the complex dynamics of the physical environment, is now largely operative over the space of ideas.

And this, I suggest, is where all the nomads have gone. As ancient nomads were restless in physical space, modern nomads are restless in the space of ideas, driven to wander and search for the connections between ideas to make a knowledge resource that might form some kind of settlement as a technology.

But, like the complex savannah, the space of ideas is only ever semi-stable due to the shifting landscape of other ideas, which then triggers the search anew for further ideas. As ideas and minds began to interact, the nomadic instinct shifted its domain to explore the resources of this new space of resources.

Now, if this is a plausible conception of equivalence of problem domains (see Hirschfeld and Gelman, 1994), and workable as a concept that overarches both, then we may use it to construct a theory of the origins of novelty in economic systems. In essence, the co-opted nomadic instinct becomes interpreted as the novelty-generating mechanism that drives the growth of knowledge and the wealth of nations and, happily, is a property of all individual agents. In this view, evolutionary economics would be conceived as the study of an evolving economic system, and economic systems evolve because knowledge evolves. Knowledge evolves because it is carried by adaptations in the human mind (problem solving modules) and mental environment (such as language) to live socially in complex environments. By this thesis, then, the principle expression of the nomadic instinct is made by those who wander about the semi-arid but sometimes bountiful space of ideas. All agents, then, are potentially entrepreneurial, if by entrepreneurship we mean nomadic behaviour in the economic realm of useful knowledge.

Yet again, however, we seemingly must choose between a conception of this evolutionary behaviour as a distribution over a population, or as a differential behaviour latent in every member of the population. In the first instance, we might define a subpopulation of artists, engineers, academics, entrepreneurs and others who specialize in creativity and problem-solving, as distinct from the mass population who (merely) use the output of this process. There are many inherent problems in defining such classifications, but in principle at least, it would be possible to measure the size of the populations and test for the significance of changes in the population size. Perhaps the motive to search the space of ideas is a variable manifest in the relative population sizes of those who colonize knowledge and those who explore it.

There is another way to frame the matter. We might simply assume that there exists a heterogeneous population in terms of the strength of the triggers, such that all are potentially nomadic in the space of ideas, but some are more easily given to search than others. This could, conceivably, be analyzed with a replicator dynamics model of search rules with variable environmental stability parameters. Or it could be framed in terms of the stability of a mental paradigm and factors that lead to search for a new one.

Both are consistent with the thesis of universal nomadism. However, we should be careful to note that universal nomadism is not a metaphorical statement, a way of theorizing about an advanced knowledge-based society as if it were somehow 'like' the behaviour of ancestral nomads. That in itself would be rather specious. Instead, the argument is that some nomadic instinct exists in all humans as an adaptation and that this instinct is innately operative over both physical and abstract spaces. Specifically, the hypothesis is that the nomadic instinct did evolve exclusively with reference to a physical space but that about 40,000 years ago, or at whatever time period is to be associated with the emergence of language in anatomically modern humans, the nomadic instinct extended to an idea space, which in turn interacted with physical space, and so on, to add a whole new level of complexity to the system of agents. The motive instincts driving search in physical space are, I hypothesize, the same instincts applied to the space of ideas and the seat of the mental behaviours that are more often known as imagination and problem-solving.

NOMADIC SPACE MAPS

Nomadism is behaviour in a space. What, then, is the relation between the behaviour and the space? In a physical space, nomadic behaviour is not generally a random walk, which does of course occur in nature (as with ants and bees), but this is not generally called nomadic. Nor is nomadism a precise cycle with return to the original point, as with much animal migration (although see Pronk [1993] for discussion of migration as nomadism). Random walks and migratory cycles are not nomadism, I suggest, because they are adaptations to a stochastic or periodic environment, not a complex one. Nomadism is an adaptation to complexity.

Nomadism is a complex behaviour adapted under the pressures of a complex environment, and so human nomadism *qua* animal behaviour is perhaps like the kind of foraging that bees or ants do, but without the absolute fixity of the hive or nest and with the mechanism of language—both of which make it very different to this kind of behaviour. The point is that nomadism does not reduce to search algorithms alone, but to the memory store of areas searched and knowledge gathered as well. In any event, nomadic behaviour is greatly facilitated by the construction of maps of environmental space. These are nomadic space maps. A map of a space enables behaviour in that space to be other than random.

Humans, as cognitive social creature with language, are constantly engaged in the individual and social construction of maps of their environment. These maps go by many names including technologies, languages, paradigms, representations, and so forth. But, rather than conceptualizing these in terms of what they represent, the theory of universal nomadism points towards the logic of the actual cognitive modules involved. The question is: What is the geometric nature of the space in which maps are cognitively constructed?

There are many possible spaces we could assign to the maps of agent environments, but two candidates are obvious: (1) The space may be Euclidean, in the form of maps of orderings that, we might suppose, is an adaptation from visual processing. Or (2), the space may be Graphical, in the form of maps of associations that might be an adaptation from language processing. If nomadism demands maps, what sort of maps does the mind supply, fields or lattices (Potts, 2000, chapter 2)? This manner of thinking is of course making a highly stylized distinction between enormously complex mind modules, about which little is known. But the point I am arguing here is that the way in which language works and the way in which vision work are computationally different because they deal with problems in different spaces. Visual processing is largely about adding depth and field to a two-dimensional data array and using all sorts of cues associated with light gradients and metric relationships and so forth to achieve this. Visual processing is all about fields. But language processing is much more about associations. A map of associations between named objects is a language. I would propose, then, that language maps provide a natural context and complexity for nomadism to emerge as a behavioural solution.

The maps of knowledge that connect the economic agent to the economic system must be both coherent and adaptable. Both of these properties are also essential to all languages that are supported cognitively. I suggest, then, that the nomadic instinct is more closely related to language processing than to visual processing, to the extent that these are the major processing components of the mind, for the simple reason that language processing enables a communicable networked memory store that can be itself adapted by each generation. Evidence of this hypothesis is in the form of the near-universal prevalence of *totemic geography* among extant nomadic peoples (see Chatwin, 1987). It follows that maps of idea space are, perhaps, primed to be networks as well.

The function of language is often conflated with the demands of social communication, with the pay-offs from successful social communication being the selection mechanisms driving language. The problem with this theory is that this does not necessarily select for a spoken language *per se*. A symbolic language of gestures and displays, as prevalent throughout the animal kingdom, is sufficient for primitive social communication and does not require radical adaptation of the throat and larynx to achieve this (e.g. Corballis, 2002). Some theorists argue that a spoken language is a more efficient way of achieving this same goal and, therefore, this is why humans have spoken language. This may or may not be the case, but, in any event, a theory of sufficiency honed into efficiency is a rather weak foundation for the origin and nature of human language.

The theory of universal nomadism argues that a spoken language was selected for because it is a technology adapted to map-making—that is to say, because language is a *necessary* condition for the construction of maps in which *features of the environment are mapped by naming them*, thus translating a physical space into an idea space by overlaying it with a subject-object structure. The adapted capacity for spoken language was the basis for the emergence of economic systems in terms of the growth of knowledge. Furthermore, the invention of different kinds of language – such as symbolic, harmonic, written – open new spaces for further adaptation as the differences between languages come to drive this same evolutionary process.

Knowledge of the physical environment is a map of a threaded network of journeys. The organization of knowledge is the creation of a map. This instinct, I suggest, was then co-opted by the substitution of a physical space for an idea-space. Both require maps, and the maps are the organization of knowledge. However, the possibility of translation hinges upon the map being a networked map, which first required that a Euclidean visual map be translated into a networked language map of objects and connections. In such a system, the subjective perception of objects in the environment then appears as elements of a map. This subjective ontology of the object is generally true as it extends to abstract things.

THE NOMADIC INSTINCT

Successful nomadic species that map and record their environment will require a large brain adapted to a language that builds concepts and ideas. The adaptations requisite for a successful physical nomadic lifestyle thus provide the sufficient conditions for nomadic behaviour in the space of ideas.

The concept of a nomadic instinct is quite obviously a theoretical construct. However, I also envisage it as a kind of mind-module, or mental organ, composed of a suite of behavioural rules. Perhaps its physical location will bear some relation to the cortical regions associated with language processing and the prefrontal lobes associated with thought and planning. Or, and assuming that it is indeed a singular and spatially localized system, it may be somewhere completely different. Whatever its format, my primary conjecture concerning its existence is based upon an argument from its plausibility as an adaptation to a persistent environmental economic problem faced over hundreds of thousands of years, namely, the unstable distribution of resources in space and time in the ancestral environment. Hominids adapted to this environment, according to the thesis presented here, with the instinct of nomadism. Nomadism, therefore, is a solution to a problem, and, hypothetically, a module in the cognitive architecture of all humans.

The nomadic instinct, then, would have the following features:

(1)   A set of triggers, including one that is a function of declining utility of settlement (a trigger threshold as a function of cumulative time in one place). Triggers are generally perceptions of problems in the environment. Analysis of these triggers is therefore equivalently analysis of *perceptions of problems*. Emotion may have some role here.[5]

(2)   Search heuristics guided by a map. The map may relate to either visual processing (a Euclidean map) or to language processing (a network map). Either way, the search heuristics operate over a space by constructing objects in the space as a map.

(3)   A halting (choice) function that signals when to stop searching further. Emotion may also be important here too.

Several inferences can be made. First, although the module evolved in the context of a mapping of a physical space, the fact that this was greatly enhanced by the records of others over this same space indicates that it is primarily a language mapping of a space by identifying features as objects and constructing connections between these objects. A Euclidean physical space is reconstructed as a network space that could be represented as 'poems' or 'songs' or some such, as the language-based proto-mechanisms for the cultural transmission of knowledge. For this reason, the nomadic instinct is hypothesized to be more closely associated with language than spatial visual processing, and it is this feature which enables it to be co-opted to more abstract spaces, such as a space of ideas.

Second, the maps in both cases record networks of 'ancestral' journeys and so describe the geometry (geography or organization) of the space. Language does not precede this, but instead is the raw product of this process. As we discover and recognize new things or concepts, we give them names, and so call them into existence in our minds. Reality and language are constructed simultaneously, and so knowledge is said to be emergent. In this view, the economic agent does not possess knowledge as a stock of capital and nor is knowledge simply the space of all possibilities and common understandings. The evolutionary economic agent is not outside of knowledge in this way, but rather is actively engaged in the exploration, construction and testing of knowledge.

Third, the mechanisms of the instinct are not equivalent to a set of search heuristics, but incorporate mechanisms that trigger when to search and when to stop searching, as well as mechanisms to record the results of the search. Evolutionary psychology is a branch of cognitive science, which is an approach to a theory of the mind that draws much inspiration from the concept of the computer (Mirowski, 2002). This is why switches, halting functions, memory store and access appear so prominently in this theory of the mind. However, in evolutionary psychology the main questions concern how such information processing modules could have evolved. That is why instinct is not the solution to an optimal search problem, but rather refers to the computational nature of life in an environment with a semi-stable resource distribution. Search heuristics are part of this mechanism, but it is the whole system of adaptations that are involved in the efficacious behaviour of an agent in a complex environment.

The theory of universal nomadism may contribute to a 'pre-revelation analysis' (see Witt, 1997) of the mechanisms that produce the raw materials of knowledge. If so, one may use evolutionary economics to analyze the effect of novelty generated in this endogenous manner upon a population of agents and agencies under various assumptions. New ideas enter the economic system as a result of actions in an idea-space driven by an innate restlessness of the agents in that space. The nomadic instinct is distributed over the population of all humans and is facilitated by the construction of maps, as a language that describes the organization of the elements of that space.

Testable implications follow. Because the instinct for creative search is, according to the theory, evenly distributed over the population, we should not expect to see an uneven generation of novelty at the level of individual agents when controlled for context. But, because creativity is greatly facilitated by the construction of maps that describe the organization of knowledge then, ergo, where we do observe a strong output of ideas feeding the growth of knowledge, we should also expect to see well-developed maps of that knowledge. We should not, therefore, expect to see sustained flows of novel ideas into the growth of knowledge where that knowledge is only poorly mapped. Evidence of such would refute the strong form of the thesis of universal nomadism. This may help to explain empirical reports of the overwhelming importance of prior experience in the both the development and adoption of novel technology (see Freeman and Soete, 1997).

NOMADISM, NOVELTY, AND COMPETITION

As such, universal nomadism suggests a possible way of interpreting the mechanisms that govern the generation of new ideas, as the variation that drives the economic process (see, e.g., Metcalfe et al., 2001), in terms of selection pressures due to environmental complexity shaping evolutionary adaptive behaviours. Novelty is due to an instinctual behaviour in idea space, as a kind of restlessness (declining utility, decaying preference) with existing ideas as they are variously diffused and exploited.

It is standard practice in economic analysis of growth processes, irrespective of whether they are capital driven, technology driven, or knowledge driven, to assume that novelty arrives randomly into the economic system. This is a perfectly defensible position, as the economics concern is all about the choice processes involved as novelty is adopted and diffused through the economic system. Now, although stories are sometimes told of where the novelty comes from, rarely do these have any bearing on the economic model. In general, no significant feedback between the economic system and the generation of novel generic ideas is presumed in the modern growth-theory literature. The quality of the 'random exogenous shock' approach is its convenience and analytical tractability, two features of obvious value. But, it does tend to ignore the possibility of feedback between the existing situation and the arrival of new ideas, and, in consequence, few sensible things have ever been said about the way that incentive structures affect the growth of knowledge.

Universal nomadism, on the other hand, makes a specific inference: The motivation to introduce novelty is only weakly related to price incentives and more strongly related to maps of possible journeys. I suggest that the origin of ideas in the economic system, like the origins of novelty, are explicable at least in part as a story about the construction of maps of the environment and nomadic behaviour in the presence of these maps. Relative prices still provide local incentives, but it is maps of possible journeys that provide the global incentives. If that is the case, then novelty generation through basic research, often thought to be an economically rather high risk strategy, may be better understood as an enterprise of mapping knowledge. If so, then the proper measure of basic research is increased variety through high-level mapping. This is not a market mechanism in terms of relative prices, but it is a market process of the mapping of knowledge (Potts, 2001).

The theory of universal nomadism weakens the relation between stability analysis and static equilibria by positing the eventual inherent disutility with *any* equilibrium in technical, structural and organizational form. So, in order to proceed from an equilibrium to a steady-state conception it would sooner or later have to be shown why the nomadic instinct had somehow been re-directed away, and, so, why there was no competition by the introduction of novelty. This is equivalent to arguing that, from the evolutionary perspective, the notion of a competitive equilibrium is a contradiction in terms.

In the first place, processes of technical innovation are themselves a form of selection (as competition) in the same sense that a migratory journey is a form of competition. Migratory species, in general, are much less aggressive than sedentary species because the migration itself is the selection process. Territory is the outcome of the migration. Sedentary species, instead, must compete locally for territory and access to resources, and are thus more aggressive in displays and actions. For established knowledge and technology, competition is much more severe, and of the market and price type, than the behaviour of those that journey along the roads of knowledge.

In other words, competitive selection is something that occurs most strongly in stable environments. Price competition, typically, is strongest in stable knowledge environments. In a volatile or turbulent environment (of knowledge, or of changing climate and habitat) collaboration and co-operation are far more likely to be prevalent. Furthermore, a symbiotic and co-evolutionary relationship invariably develops as collaboration makes possible the very basis for rivalry and competition: witness, for example, industrial districts in their early phases. Eventually, stable technological environments will induce price competition or market exclusion behaviour. This itself may be an effective trigger for nomads to leave and search anew. Nomadic species engage in rivalry, but they are not by nature adversarial. A kind of indifference relation between settling and protecting a territory and wandering in search of new territory would seem to be germinal to any analytical definition of nomadism.

Can we offer universal nomadism as a theory of the entry of novelty into economic systems? An account of the origin of novelty is not just desirable, but is strictly necessary for any evolutionary framework in order to generate the variation upon which the mechanism of selection acts. There are several ways to supply variation. By far the easiest, as discussed above, is to build it directly into the model, as random variation in some metrical property of the units of selection, and to account for this theoretically by making it exogenous. For example, high-energy radiation from the sun may randomly change DNA. Or quantum fluctuations in neural circuits may randomly rewire cognitive modules. Sometimes it is even coupled directly to the selection mechanism, as with random changes in the environment brought about by climatic fluctuations. And so forth, so long as some selective property exhibits variation it does not really matter how or why this occurs. This way of defining variation is the technique most beloved of modellers, because it enables them to define variation as a sample set drawn from different distributions, as control variables, and to use stochastic techniques to explore the parameters of the system. And that has often proven very useful for theoretical development. There is, of course, a great variety of exogenous shocks that can hit an economic system; and if we add in the notion that humans just naturally are creative, then, surely, it is perfectly reasonable to simply assume that novelty arrives randomly into the economic system. This is one solution to the problem of articulating the mechanism of variation. Yet, there are two difficulties.

First, it overlooks the possibility of systematic effects issuing from our evolutionary inheritance from our ancestral environment in which, as I have emphasized, we also faced ongoing economic problems of knowledge. It is clear by dint of our continued existence that we did solve these problems somehow. And, if the selection pressures were strong enough, those solutions should still be with us in the form of adaptations carried in our genes. This is precisely what underpins the theory of universal nomadism.

Second, it is not even obvious what this variation would refer to. Should we be content with explanations of the arrival of new commodities into a market, or should analysis ultimately rest upon the arrival of new ideas in the mind? The latter is typically seen to be the province of psychology or some such discipline, and so many economic theorists are content with the idea that at time t

there are *n* commodities and at time *t*+1 there are *n*+1. This is of course a modeling expedient rather than an analytical proposition. It tells us nothing about the origins of new knowledge, and to the extent that it forces an *ex ante* specification of all possible things that could happen, it does place the theorist in an all too privileged position vis-à-vis the possibilities of novelty.

We avoid both problems by locating the origin of novelty in the search through mental maps of the environment. The essence of universal nomadism is the existence of a cognitive module (in concert with physical and behavioural adaptations) that enabled ancestral humans to adapt to an environment in which *resources* were not so much scarce as they were semi-stable; sometimes bountiful, sometimes scarce, sometimes non-existent, but always uncertain. It is a story about the human mind, the dynamics of resources and the growth of knowledge. Universal nomadism is the theory that humans are cognitively adapted to live socially in a complex environment. These adaptations make possible the growth of knowledge and thus economic evolution.

CONCLUSION

In the evolutionary view of the mind as a 'crowded zoo of evolved, domain specific programs', the underlying point is that the mind is modular. Modularity in mind, as Herbert Simon explained with the concept of bounded rationality (Simon, 1959), simply means agents *use* abstraction in the navigation of their environment, an abstraction that takes the form of subroutines being triggered by an input conditional on computing an output or enlisting other related programs to the task. One of these modules, I have suggested, is the instinct of nomadism. And its significance is that, as the concept of universal nomadism, it ranges between the individual (the seat of the nomadic instinct) and the social (the level at which the map of the space exists), and so connects the agent and the environment as a mechanism in the growth of knowledge.

Maps represent the organization of knowledge. The economic, social, cultural and institutional forces that enter into the construction of the map will, by the effect this has on the generation of new ideas, feed back into the same process. The main implication for the microeconomic agent is that it is not an isolated unit that can be understood when removed from its context in a structure of knowledge. It is, in this sense, much more accurate to conceive of a population of agents, which evolve as a population woven into a web of knowledge. The agent is the smallest behavioural unit, but it cannot be meaningfully isolated from its nature as a locus of connections. The point is that the evolutionary economic agent is quite different from the neoclassical *Homo œconomicus* because evolutionary behaviour is not about choice, but rather refers to a process of adaptation between a component and the system in which it is embedded.

The behaviour that accompanies a teleology of muddling through, which is to say of first and foremost concerning the discovery of suitable solutions to problems through a capacity to be open-ended and flexible in the face of contingency before then settling to refine the solution, is the prime element in evolutionary economic behaviour. Evolutionary behaviour is problem-solving behaviour. And the point I have argued is that we might hope to base a theory of evolutionary economic behaviour upon what is known about the physical, cognitive and social evolution of the human species. By implication, evolutionary economics will need to be much more closely integrated into other domains of evolutionary theory about the nature of the human mind.

But this also implies that we must be clear about the reason we require a more substantially articulated theory of the evolutionary economic agent. Contemporary evolutionary economic literature seems to harbour two rather different conceptions of the nature of evolutionary economic theory. The first, and seemingly most common approach to evolutionary economics, is to hew as closely as possible to existing theoretical economic conceptions and attach the evolutionary aspect of one's work to its subject matter. In this way, evolutionary economics is understood to be the branch of economics that deals with technological and institutional change, industrial dynamics and the statistical side of economic dynamics, all using whatever tools are sharpest and convenient (Nelson and Winter, 1982). These approaches tend to be model-focused, pragmatic, and equivocal about whether or not the underlying theoretical explanations are consistent with evolutionary theory. This is evolutionary economics in the sense of being an economic analysis of subject matter that is evolving. The theory of the evolutionary economic agent has little direct contact with this approach, and universal nomadism has no real significance here.

The other approach is to view evolutionary economics as a genuinely new theoretical framework. In this view, the economic subject matter, the economy, *is* itself an evolutionary process, in the specific sense of an emergent growth-of-knowledge process (Loasby, 1999; Potts, 2000). Those who view evolutionary economics this way tend to be united about a theory of processes as well as sharing degrees of reservation about the appropriateness of equilibrium-based methods of analysis (Kirman, 1992). They often engage in criticism and in analytical reconstruction of frameworks and concepts. It is here, and only here, that we can sensibly ask questions about the nature of the evolutionary economic agent and, consequently, it is here that I hope this chapter may make some contribution toward an evolutionary theory of the economic agent that is consistent with both evolutionary psychology and a conception of evolutionary economics as analysis of the growth-of-knowledge process.

ACKNOWLEDGEMENTS

This chapter originally began as inquiry into 'machines that choose' and the role of triggering and halting mechanisms conceived as a theory of emotions, and I thank John Foster and Janet Wiles for discussion of that. This was a much bigger project than I was capable of, and it devolved into an inquiry into theories of agents that choose in terms of demons and cyborgs (cf. Mirowski, 2002). This led to the idea of the nomad, which became the prologue to a work with Kurt Dopfer (*Tractatus Economicus,* forthcoming), whom I thank for kindling this idea. This, in turn, became 'the demon, the cyborg and the nomad', and I thank the Emergent Complexity Group at UQ Economics for discussion of that hopelessly ambitious project. The final product, partial as it may be, aims simply to critically explore the meaning of evolutionary economic behaviour in the context of the evolutionary economic agent, as, indeed, is part of the purpose of this volume.

NOTES

1. 'Without names, our knowledge of things would also perish.'
2. A point that Herbert Simon had also made, and similarly been misunderstood on (Mirowski, 2002: pp. 452–72).
3. The inspiration for this thesis comes, as some may have inferred already, from the wonderful and sublime novel *The Songlines*, by Bruce Chatwin (Vintage Classics, 1987). This book explores, in relation to the Australian Aborigine, the idea that the origin of language was the songs of nomads as they socially constructed maps of the environment.
4. Although, this does depend upon whether we follow the Schumpeterian and Kirznerian concept of entrepreneurship, in which *some* agents are entrepreneurs *all* of the time, or the Shacklean and Loasbian concept, where *all* economic agents are entrepreneurs *some* of the time. The theory of universal nomadism denies the former and promotes the latter.
5. Cosmides and Tooby (2000) suggest that emotions are 'superordinate programs each of which jointly mobilizes a subset of the psychological architecture's other programs in a particular configuration...This coordinated adjustment and entrainment of mechanisms is a mode of operation for the entire psychological architecture, and serves as the basis for a precise computational and functional definition of each emotion state. Each emotion entrains various other adaptive programs – deactivating some, activating others, and adjusting the modifiable parameters of others still – so that the whole system operates in a particularly harmonious way when the individual is confronted with certain kinds of triggering conditions or situations'.

REFERENCES

Barkow, J., L. Cosmides and J. Tooby (1992). *The Adapted Mind: Evolutionary Psychology and the Generation of Culture.* New York: Oxford University Press.
Chatwin, B. (1987), *The Songlines*, New York: Vintage Classics.

Corballis, M. (2002), *From Hand to Mouth: The Origins of Language*, Princeton, N.J.: Princeton University Press.

Cosmides, L and J. Tooby (1994), 'Better than rational: evolutionary psychology and the invisible hand', *American Economic Review*, **84**, 327–32.

Cosmides, L. and J. Tooby (2000), 'Evolutionary psychology and the emotions', in M. Lewis and J. Haviland (eds), *Handbook of Emotions*, New York: Guilford.

Dennett, D. (1995), *Darwin's Dangerous Idea: Evolution and the Meanings of Life*, New York: Simon & Schuster.

Diamond, J. (1997), *Guns, Germs and Steel: The Fate of Human Societies*, New York: W.W. Norton.

Dopfer, K. and J. Potts (forthcoming), 'Evolutionary foundations of economics', *Journal of Evolutionary Economics*.

Freeman, C. and L. Soete (1997), *The Economics of Industrial Innovation*, London: Pinter.

Hirschfeld, L. and Gelman, S. (1994), *Mapping the Mind: Domain Specificity in Cognition and Culture*. New York: Cambridge University Press.

Kirman, A. (1992), 'Whom or What Does the Representative Individual Represent?', *Journal of Economic Perspectives*, **6**, 117–36.

Loasby, B. (1999), *Knowledge, Institutions and Evolution in Economics*, London: Routledge.

Marchesnay, M. (2000), 'L'entrepreneur face a ses risques', *Innovations* **12**, 9–26.

Metcalfe, J.S., M. Fonseca and R. Ramlogan (2001), 'Innovation, growth and competition: evolving complexity or complex evolution', CRIC Discussion paper, no. 41, University of Manchester.

Mirowski, P. (2002), *Machine Dreams: Economics Becomes a Cyborg Science*. New York: Cambridge University Press.

Nelson, R. and S. Winter (1982), *An Evolutionary Theory of Economic Change*. Cambridge: Cambridge University Press.

Pinker, S. (1994), *The Language Instinct*, New York: W. Morrow & Co.

Plotkin, H. (1995), *Darwin Machines and the Nature of Knowledge: Concerning Adaptation, Instinct and the Evolution of Intelligence*, London: Penguin.

Plotkin, H. (1997), *Evolution in Mind: An Introduction to Evolutionary Psychology*, New York: Penguin.

Popper, K. (1985), *A World of Propensities*, Bristol: Thoemmes.

Popper, K. (1999), *All Life is Problem Solving*, London: Routledge.

Potts, J. (2000), *The New Evolutionary Microeconomics*, Cheltenham, U.K.: Edward Elgar.

Potts, J. (2001), 'Knowledge and Markets', *Journal of Evolutionary Economics*, **11**, 413–31.

Pronk. J. (1993), 'Migration: The nomad in each of us', *Population and Development Review*, **19**, 323–7.

Sahlins, M. (1972), *Stone Age Economics*, Chicago: Aldine-Atherton.

Simon, H. (1959), 'Theories of Decision-making in Economics and Behavioral Science', *American Economic Review*, **49**, 253–83.

Velupillai, K. (1995), *Computable Economics: The Fourth Arne Ryde Lectures*, Oxford: Oxford University Press.

Vromen, J. (2001), 'Stone-age minds and group selection: what difference do they make?', Paper presented at The Nature and Evolution of Institutions, MPI Jena, January 2001.

Witt, U. (1997), 'Self-Organization and Economics—What is New', *Structural Change and Economic Dynamics*, **8**, 489–507.

Name Index